Pip + Jim
... at last!
Much love,
Mark

THE ROAD
TO KAMJI

A VERY PERSONAL JOURNEY THROUGH LIFE AND BHUTAN

MARK SWINBANK

authorHOUSE®

AuthorHouse™ UK
1663 Liberty Drive
Bloomington, IN 47403 USA
www.authorhouse.co.uk
Phone: 0800.197.4150

Published by AuthorHouse   12/08/2014

ISBN: 978-1-4969-9357-1 (sc)
ISBN: 978-1-4969-9358-8 (hc)
ISBN: 978-1-4969-9356-4 (e)

CONTENTS

PREFACE

It was after my fifth and latest visit to Bhutan that I felt compelled to express how I felt about the country in my own way. The chapters that follow are imperfect representations of my precise feelings about this special place. Such feelings are deeply seated and almost impossible to express in words.

In the expression however the emotion is bound to come to the surface, and I make no apology for that. For this is, in so many ways, a love letter; one of deeply felt thanks that I have been privileged beyond words to travel to such a unique country, to travel amongst its wonderful people, to experience their smiles, to make friends there, and to see the vistas that only the Himalayas can provide.

So yes, it is a very personal journey: a diary of sorts, a drawstring for my life as a whole, and a way of illustrating how far flung places closer to home probably spring boarded the leap to embrace the last Shangri-La.

More and more is being written about this country; it regularly appears in the travel supplements of the daily and weekend papers and, almost without exception, there is a mention of the nation's gross national happiness ('GNH'), prayer flags, smiling and well-dressed people, forestry conservation, and the Snowman Trek. I will leave the more detailed reporting of the pertinent facts about the country to those far more knowledgeable than me. These words are about how I felt the moment I passed by road through the Bhutan Gate in Phuntsoling in 2006, and why I never looked back. Yes, I definitely want to share those experiences, but perhaps more importantly I would like to spark interest in the reader's mind that might make them take this, still quite difficult journey to Bhutan, themselves.

International tourist numbers have doubled (reaching in excess of fifty thousand people in less than six years), so I fear for its uniqueness, resources and infrastructure. The Bhutanese Government is still trying to leverage the so-called high-end tourist market in an attempt (crudely put) to maintain control. I cannot help but think that things could shortly and easily get out of control, though I sincerely hope that is not the case. The simple things in life are the things worth remembering – and that is one of the mantras the Bhutanese live by. You do not have to be a high-end tourist or a wealthy person to recognise this fact. Indeed, material wealth is of little interest to many of the population there. I hope to relay such messages to my readers.

I was lucky enough to be in Bhutan at a pivotal time in its modern history, namely the coronation of their fifth king ('K5'). As would be expected, in any country at a time like this there was great excitement and high hopes for the future. In deportment and words, K5 certainly stepped up to the plate. However there was massive change afoot, and I cannot help but feel that the Bhutanese are wary, sceptical, and perhaps even a little worried. They willingly accept visitors in, and they are extremely patient with them, but it is their country, and they very much like it as it is (as evidenced by minimal net emigration).

Their last prime minister travelled the world espousing the concept of gross national happiness, which is generally a message received with open arms or, at the very least, supportive words.

Bhutan was essentially unknown to most ten years ago, but now, many knowingly say, 'I've heard about it: that place in the Himalayas where they wear funny clothes and are very happy.' Those words are trite, but pretty near the mark.

You cannot help but see, when looking at the map, that Bhutan is squashed between two of the modern world's superpowers. The Chinese, I am sure, are not that interested in Bhutan – they never have been over the centuries – but that does not stop them from claiming some Bhutanese territory as their own. So far, that has been limited to the high, inaccessible Himalayan region, but through words, such claims extend into the Paro Valley, which is the logistical hub of the country.

If Bhutan held oil reserves, I am sure that India would have been more incursive. As it is, Bhutan has the tap on hydro-electric power, which suits both countries economically. India has always seen Bhutan as something of a child who needs to be shown the ways of the world, particularly from an economic and strategic point of view. It was a case of 'mummy knows best'.

Now that democracy is afoot in Bhutan, the reluctant people are now getting used to using their franchise. During the elections of 2013, India was not happy with the direction its child was taking and turned the economic screw. Much against their natural instincts, the Bhutanese have begun looking across their northern border to China for possible friendship. They should be wary.

Much about the Bhutanese way of life comes back to their form of tantric Buddhism, which governs their lives absolutely. Apart from keeping Christians and other religions at bay, there is not a lot that can be said against their choice. It wholly guides the people in the right way, urging them to support each other and to give, not take, from their neighbours and the land.

Buddhism, however, is taking something of an unpleasant turn in some parts of Southeast Asia. A noticeably peaceful theme has been overtaken in some parts by an aggressive ethnic twist, particularly in parts of Burma and Thailand. This aggression seems to be targeted mainly at Muslims and Christians. For a religion that is famous for its pacifism and tolerance, this is a very worrying trend. Almost mediaeval in his approach, the radical Burmese Buddhist monk, Wirathu, together with his entourage, who act like henchmen, have been literally burning Muslim people out of their homes in Mandalay. How is that tolerable in terms of the karma so generally espoused by this faith? The faith's founder, Siddhartha, who sought enlightenment and nirvana (and seemingly attained it in the sixth century BC) would certainly not approve. With around half a billion followers worldwide, Buddhism is less than a quarter of the size of Christianity and about a third of the size of Islam. Somewhat surprisingly, China has around half of all Buddhist followers, closely followed by Thailand and Burma.

So many religious problems are caused by adherents to known extremists in mainstream faiths, such as Islamic militants, fundamentalist Christians, and ultra-Orthodox Jews. The world I am a part of thinks of Buddhism as a non-violent practice that advocates kindness, karma, and mutual support. Unfortunately, in Burma Wirathu is listened to. He is charismatic, and his message (that most Muslims are radicals and need to be eradicated) strikes a chord locally. Similarly unwelcome developments are happening in remote parts of Sri Lanka, and more worryingly, Thailand.

Although in a comparatively recent development, the door to all this new thinking was laid open by K4 when, in 1999, television was officially allowed in Bhutan for the first time. Access to the Internet followed shortly afterwards. Up until then, the Bhutanese knew little of how the world outside their comparatively hermetically-sealed border worked and were seemingly disinterested in it. With the new free access to knowledge, and despite deep poverty, resentment and rebellion have not arisen. I hope it stays that way.

Certainly, the newly elected government in 2013 seemed to feel that the old way may not, in fact, be the only way. Even total reliance on gross national happiness seems to be challenged. Their fifth king seems to have been silent on this matter and, ultimately, I am sure that it is he who holds the key to any major underlying change in how the people think and act. For the time being, all who have the pleasure, joy and privilege of travelling there will worry about what the future might hold for Bhutan. I am not so sure that the people there share similar concerns.

In truth, I suspect a lot of my feelings are based on a deep-seated hope that they do not change. Yes, that is probably being selfish, but I also recognise that, somehow, despite the simplicity of lifestyle and the absence of the instant-gratification culture that most western countries live by, the Bhutanese seem to understand life better than most others.

This is where we can learn and, in modest ways, which would have deep significance, we could and should adopt some of their values. High on that list is Bhutanese stretchable time (BST), which allows for less haste, more consideration, less worry, more contemplation, better decision making, happier dispositions, and an understanding and appreciation of karma which undoubtedly refreshes and invigorates the body and soul.

Bhutan is at one a special, unique, beautiful, inspiring, perplexing, uplifting, but above all a magical place. I hope these chapters, meshed with stories of my travels there and how my first visit came about, will enthral my readers as much as Bhutan has captivated me. If it does, do not thank me; rather, thank the Land of the Thunder Dragon, *Druk Yul,* and its wonderful people. Please, join me on *The Road to Kamji.*

Tashi Delek! (Good Luck, and may Karma go with you.)

Ardroil, Isle of Lewis
May 2014

Chapter 1

The trail from Lewis

'When this vague yearning for something that worldly life cannot satisfy becomes unbearable, it may be a sign that [you] are ready for this Quest.

Paul Brunton, Notebooks, Vol 1, Perspectives

I hold Joanna Lumley responsible!

Actually, I thank her, and not just because she went to school with a cousin of mine, which is a very weak claim to dubious fame, or because her comedic acting skills are a treasure to us all. Nor is it because she rightly stands shoulder to shoulder with the Nepalese Gurkhas, in whose ranks her father served as an officer. No, it is because of her 1997 BBC programme: *In the Kingdom of the Thunder Dragon* that the seed was sown.

Before we go any further, I must mention that this book is not a travel guide. That ground is more than adequately covered by Lonely Planet and Footprint, whose detailed, constantly revisited guide-books are mines of information for 'all you need to know'. However, I make no apology for the travelogue nature of some of the chapters, which I hope will give a sense of what it is like being in this special place.

No, this book is about the feelings of a traveller who was spellbound in 2006 on the road to Kamji, and who has been changed by the visits made since to this unique and exceptional country. I make no apology for the very personal and emotional nature of my travels there, because I truly and deeply believe that, as much as it has changed my life (for the better, and forever), I also sincerely believe that it has so much to offer the world in general. I am not here to speak for the Bhutanese people; they are beginning to do that very successfully for themselves. Rather, I seek to provide an insight given the fact that I went expecting nothing that first time and came back with so much. I really hope that it will inspire others to take the same journey, as I know they will not be disappointed.

Come along for that ride and what a ride that will be if you fly into Paro Airport with Drukair, the Bhutanese National Airline. Check in at their counter at Indira Gandhi International Airport in Delhi. If you are lucky enough to travel in business class, then the 'dragon carpet' will literally be rolled out for you! Alternatively, gird your loins, set aside your fears of the huge crush of humanity that is India, and take the night sleeper from Sealdah Station, Kolkata to New Jaipulguri (NJP), near Darjeeling. I promise you that you will not regret it, especially if you finish the journey to Darjeeling on the Himalayan Railway, which now has UNESCO World Heritage status.

But we will not start with any of these things, though we shall of course return to them. Instead, let us start with the question that few can answer: where is Bhutan? Those who have heard of it often believe that it is part of India. Indeed, it borders the north eastern Indian states of West Bengal and Assam, an area few would readily know is part of India when they are looking at a map. There were once three independent Himalayan kingdoms trailing along the line of that mountain range, east of the Hindu Kush, in what is now Pakistan, namely: Nepal, Sikkim, and Bhutan. Nepal has now dispensed with its monarchy, once revered in the same manner as the Thai Royal House, because it was torn apart by internecine murders and subsequent deep unpopularity. After that the current, secular government was formed, in the main, by the communists who had been fighting an insurgency campaign for years. That campaign was quite brutal at times, and those insurgents were often compared to the Shining Path guerrillas in South America. Sikkim was, at the request of its people, absorbed into India as a new and separate state which occurred in 1975, and its monarchy was also dispensed with at the same time.

To the east of Everest is Bhutan, nestled between India to its south and Tibet (China) to the north. It is approximately the same geographical size as Switzerland, and was not fully united until 1907. It has never been wholly conquered by anyone, despite the might of the neighbours mentioned. The nearest to try, and partly to succeed, were the British, who were fighting for land and tea in the wake of the success of their East India Company. The British, through a succession of skirmishes, pushed the Bhutanese back from the duars (literally: doors) of Assam to the foothills and mountains that dramatically and sharply rise up from the gangetic plain. By the terms of the Treaty of Sinchula in 1865, and in return for a paltry rent, the Bhutanese agreed to let the flatlands go, and as my Bhutanese friend Pema Drukpa pointed out, there is now nowhere for them to build a proper international airport of any practical size. (However one of the three planned new domestic ones is going to be built at Gelephu, on the Indian border which, with the requisite financing, could probably be converted into an international airport.)

The skirmishes were tough. Frankly, those British who ventured inland into mountainous and rugged Bhutan, did not fare well. The beautiful people of whom I shall speak much of later must not be crossed. They are a tough breed with a Mongol appearance, but even more striking. There are some gruesome tales of some British making it as far as Trongsa the gateway, or rather 'doorway' between east and central Bhutan, (there actually is a doorway within the huge dzong fort there through which all travellers had to pass and pay suitable dues) and found themselves literally cut to pieces by these fearsome warriors. Dark tales of the remnant limbs still being held somewhere in the deep dark recesses of Trongsa dzong are quietly, and perhaps somewhat teasingly, recounted by current day Bhutanese guides!

The country may be hidden away like secret treasure waiting to be discovered, but it has now been discovered by a small (though growing) number of discerning visitors. However, it does not offer theme parks, and there are certainly no fast-food outlets. At the other end of the holiday scale, the mountains are sacred and may not be climbed. The long-distance treks around them are some of the toughest in the world. In between these two extremes, there is little to obviously attract a common tourist. Or is there? There are superb vistas of the high Himalayas, a landscape unchanged since the middle-ages and distinctly feudal in appearance, a very friendly and beautiful population that is incredibly well dressed, polite, and eager to smile. English is a language that is largely understood, especially by the young, and particularly if spoken slowly. A lack of variety in food for western tastes can be a problem outside of the top-flight resort hotels, but you will soon get used to red rice, fresh vegetables and hot chillies with cheese produced at each meal time.

Just wait a minute, why am I sitting here, in my wonderful retreat on the Isle of Lewis in the Outer Hebrides, situated right on the northwest edge of the United Kingdom, thinking about Bhutan, The Land of the Thunder Dragon? Well, all journeys start somewhere, and we must first go to Lewis.

Lewis, commonly referred to as the Promised Land One ('PL1') by one of my dear friends, Jon, has a magnetic draw and a fearsome beauty to behold. Nearby is one of the finest beaches in the land: Uig Sands. History abounds: the world famous *Lewis Chessmen* were uncovered in the dunes nearby on what I often refer to as 'my beach', apparently by a local's cow, in 1831. That very beach could also tell some harrowing tales, despite its beauty. It has seen Viking hordes coming ashore in the Dark Ages, raping and pillaging, and stealing the land from the inhabitants. This area became, for a while, part of the Kingdom of Norway. This legacy has left the island with many Norse names such as *Uig,* and the name of my own village, *Eadar dha Fhadhail*, once rather irreverently and crudely translated by a local friend as 'white settlers sod off!' It actually rather more prosaically means 'between two tide flows'. Those two tide flows, or rather rivers, come onto the near three mile wide beach from each side, and salmon are found leaping up them in the season. The beach from where, if the world were flat, you could spy Newfoundland, which is the next landfall two and half thousand miles away directly across the mighty Atlantic.

This place has drawn me since I first came here with my walking partner, Gerard, in 1989. We had agreed that we would prise ourselves away from walking in the English Lake District, where Gerard's parents lived (and with whom he regularly argued whenever we stayed there), and cross the border into Scotland. My late parents loved Scotland, especially Wester Ross and the Torridons. For my part though, I had always had a slightly uncomfortable and wholly illogical feeling that anyone or anything north of the border should be avoided. Perhaps the prominence given to the escapades against the English by William Wallace in my early historical education was the cause of my unfounded bigotry, but fortunately we pushed on and of course those thoughts were soon completely dispelled.

Taking after my father, though not having his academic brilliance, I was a stickler for written plans and marked maps. Thus, a detailed itinerary was laid out for a two-week tour around the Scottish coast, including the Outer and Inner Hebridean Islands. It would be no more than an initial foray, and despite those ridiculous inner feelings, I felt genuinely excited about new lands and uncharted territory. My feelings were all the more ridiculous given the fact that I had already been fortunate enough to travel much further afield than that, particularly in the antipodes.

After crossing the border and subsequently the Erskine Bridge near Glasgow, we headed towards the far north and Inverness, Gateway to the Highlands. The Dunain Park (now the Loch Ness Hotel) was chosen for the first night as a little piece of luxury before we faced the less savoury hordes further north. The next morning we tore ourselves away after one of those ridiculously gargantuan breakfasts that hotels like that serve after an equally heavy feast the night before, and we headed further north for decidedly more spartan fare at our next night stop, Thurso. The weather and scenery around Thurso were bleak, and I do not think we even bothered going to the famed John O'Groats, though we had passed by the late Queen Mother's personal favourite home: the Castle of Mey, an idyll in the middle of bleakness.

On the third day, we trailed the far north coast, past Dounreay, and we went down to the small west coast fishing village and port of Ullapool. It is from there, since 1973, that the ferries have set sail to Stornoway on the Isle of Lewis, having previously plied the Minch from Portree on Skye, and then Mallaig on the mainland. Caledonian MacBrayne, known as 'Calmac' to all who sail on their vessels, is still (Scottish) government owned, and they ply all the west coast routes in Scotland. The route from Ullapool to Stornoway, the main town on Lewis, is not their longest, but it is certainly one of their more unpredictable ones. The seas rushing up and down the west coast and round the northern tip of Scotland are funnelled into the Minch, and its smaller relation, the Little Minch, causing massive and unpredictable seas.

Indeed, unpredictable was an understatement. Gerard, who had far better sea legs than I, assured me that, as islanders with long service experience in the merchant marine and navy, these folk would know how to cope. However, I was not so sure that I would.

At the time, there was a tub called *Suilven,* named after one of the Torridon peaks, plying this route. Like all roll on/roll off ferries, she was flat bottomed, and she had no keel or stabilisers – so she just loved to roll with the Minch! Those who have travelled this route will know that folk are lulled into a false sense of security as the first forty minutes or so are spent exiting the glorious calm of (the sea) Loch Broom and passing the magical (as their name implies) Summer Isles. It is a wondrous exit, but it was as I was enjoying a coffee below deck that we were hit by the said running tide, which caused quite a loud bang and shudder as she came into main swell. That swell on that day was not particularly bad I am sure but it was frightening enough for me, and it lasted for the remaining two hours or so of the crossing.

I was pretty relieved to sight Stornoway during the last, and slightly calmer, remaining half hour.

I was therefore rather glad to drive off the car deck and onto terra firma, despite the fact that Stornoway can, by no stretch of the imagination, be called visually impressive. The exception being Lews Castle set by the inner harbour and the surrounding woodlands of Lady Lever Park. Built by the Mathesons, allegedly from the proceeds of selling opium to the Chinese out of Hong Kong, it and the island had been bought by Lord and Lady Leverhulme of Lever Bros fame in the early 1920s. And it was she who fully developed the parkland woods and castle grounds. Apparently, Lewis was once covered in forests, which one would never know now given the dearth of trees remaining on the island.

We had booked rooms on Lewis for two nights at a small privately owned hotel, or perhaps more aptly described as an inn, on the west side of the island, in the village of Timsgarry, about an hour away. The photograph in the tourist brochure had shown this location and drawn us there with the by-line: 'rush hour at Baile-na-Cille!' I had never seen such a perfect spot, and that was just in a photograph! The journey took a very long hour, and the road became narrower and poorer as we drove further west. In fact, we wondered whether we were ever going to get there. Suddenly, after driving through the slightly spooky Glen Valtos, which we now know is a superb example of what is left behind by a retreating glacier, the vista opened up onto Uig Sands. It was love at first sight.

The hotel indeed had a prime location, as the brochure had shown, overlooking the whole stretch of Uig Sands. And what a rush hour it was to behold: there was not a person in sight. It was a fateful arrival, and it marked a turning point in my life. The somewhat eccentric host proffered a very welcoming gin & tonic to 'Mr Swingbin' and despite the really quite intimate communal dining, which was not to everyone's taste, the place was a marvel. We were billeted in part of the stables annex, which was set up for self-catering if needed. The Family who ran the establishment had rescued the old manse, minister's house, from near dereliction some ten years previously.

Richard had set about the task of being 'mine host' with relish, and his wife, Joanna, who had no formal cookery training, produced the most superb food. Although we returned through Skye, which had its own marvels, including the magnificent Black Cuillin mountains, something about Lewis had lodged into my soul and was to burrow deeper with each visit.

So, subsequent holidays in Scotland were always to be spent there. We got to know the family very well, becoming daytime child minders for their kids, Sarah and James, while Richard and Jo tended to the hotel. Lengthy walks on the beach and dunes in the company of kids and dogs set the seal for a lifetime friendship with James, which was subsequently affirmed during visits to the family's winter quarters in southwest Florida.

It was there, during such a visit, that Jo mentioned in passing that they were thinking of downsizing their operations on Lewis. In addition, as all chefs do (!), Jo had taken up flying and obtained her private pilot's licence and (even more significantly), her PPL(Helicopters). Not content with that, she had decided that helicopters were for her and that she also wanted to establish a flying business over there. It was a fantastically exciting prospect: haute cuisine on Lewis morphing into flying an old Hiller helicopter along the Gulf Coast of Florida.

I was not too sure what Jo had meant by downsizing in Lewis but it soon became clear that, as well as the hotel, they also possessed a number of associated self-catering cottages in the area. One, at Ungeshader, was in a dream location. With the road access petering out about a quarter mile from the house, it looked down the sea loch (Roag). Perhaps fortunately, practical common sense prevailed, and she mentioned another one in Uig, located in Ardroil, or 'Eadar dha Fhadhail' in gaelic.

Gerard and I made comments about this property every time we had passed it, observing that it was a lovely house and speculated that one day we might be able to buy it. And that is what we did. Set in its own small feu (plot) with another smaller property on the same site, which we acquired later, it was just perfect. It had easy access to the beach and was in reasonable condition, so it was ideal for us to put down roots and have our own base in the area. The only blot on the landscape was that our front-facing view of the immediate scenery was blocked by a recently erected bungalow, built by the local estate to house the factor and his family. Still, it provided us with nearby neighbours in this small village of only fourteen houses, which were rather distant from each other

It had been a good decision, made for life reasons rather than investment, and we set about carrying out improvements. In the year 2000, we opened for business, providing self-catering accommodation when neither of us was in residence ourselves. Eleven years later, and after Gerard had long since moved to settle and marry in the United States, I now owned both properties. And through my own time there, and in company of family and friends, the 'Promised Land One' came into being. Many, many times I have returned from visits there to be greeted by friends and colleagues 'down south' who said that the change in my demeanour was palpable. The rugged and dramatic grandeur of Lewis, and Uig in particular with its deep history, spirited self-reliant community, and the forever changable weather – all caused the spirit of Lewis to make a deep and lasting impression upon me. There is a plaque in a forlorn and exposed spot near my house there, called Mealista, which was the site of a nunnery in the middle ages and a substantial military camp during the Second World War. That plaque, inter alia, reads:

> This beautiful and tranquil area was once home to people who lived and thrived here for three thousand years or more. The landscape has evidence of powerful forces and stories tell of mystery and misery[…].

> The rocks of the hills and the shore were once part of a very ancient mountain range as high as the Himalayas[…].

> Two thousand years ago dwindling land resources, squabbles over land ownership and raids of pirates meant a more precarious existence. Later fierce raiders from the north, the Vikings, came

and carried off slaves. Later some of those Norsemen returned to settle [...] their genes still persist in the local population and all the local place names are Norse.

Mealastadh [is] once again a place of tranquillity, with just memories and traces of the people of the past [...] respect those memories and reflect on the sadness of the people who unwillingly left their stone and turf blackhouses (during the Clearances) and all of the others who lived and loved this place. It was once their treasured home and that is why it is such a powerful place.

It was the 'promised land' for me indeed. I found myself talking about it at every opportunity. Far from being bored by a southerner talking with such love, affection, and respect for Lewis, folk actually started to listen, rather than just hear, and converts were born. It was not that I wanted to become an amateur ambassador for those parts, but rather, I felt that I just had to tell people about this secret place and what it meant to me. I had always loved the open countryside and being amongst uplifting and inspiring environments, but this place definitely ticked all those boxes and more. Could there be anywhere else that was so special I quietly wondered.

Chapter 2

The road to Kamji

'There is something crazy in this idea that we were put into this world to separate ourselves from it.'

Paul Brunton, Notebooks, Vol 1 Perspectives

It was by now early 2006. I was not necessarily searching for deeper inspiration during my travels because I was lucky enough to have a foothold on Lewis. However, one day, a chance conversation with Ryan, a friend at work, triggered a new journey. I hope he will not mind me saying that, at one time in his life, he had a close association with India and its people. He knew that I had been there and knew the pull that the country and its people had on me. His exhortation that I had to go back rekindled a sleeping ambition to return. Now that was where Joanna Lumley came in. My first visit to India, in 1986, had included a short trip to Nepal. The latter country had recently had some nasty flare-ups due to the longstanding, communist-driven insurgency. I wanted to visit somewhere else in the Himalayan range as well as India. Joanna's BBC production, *The Kingdom of the Thunder Dragon,* following her grandfather's footsteps into a hidden land, had enthralled me. I knew nothing about Bhutan, nor how to get there, so I hunted about for those who did. Out of the ether came

Jonny Bealby's Wild Frontiers Travel Adventure Company. They seemed to have just the tour: *East India and Bhutan.* They would fix the visas and provide a week's insight into each of those locations. The only problem was that it was a group tour, something of an anathema to me. However, I noted that the group maximum was twelve, so I decided to swallow my reticence and go, which was a fateful and life-affirming decision.

We arrived very early in the morning at what was once Kolkata's wonderfully named and still anachronistic Dum Dum airport. Why ever did they change that original name? It reminded me of the old airport at Paya Lebar in Singapore before it was moved to Changi. It also reminded me of the renaming of Calcutta to *Kolkata* at the start of the new millennium. The city is still Calcutta to most both outside and inside India.

It had been twenty years since I had left Indian soil, and it was indeed a joy to return to the as-yet-unvisited City of Joy. A bumpy and lengthy journey from the airport to the Tollygunge Club, or 'Tolly' to her friend's, was like going back to the days of the Raj. Going back? 'They still live on my dear!' Old fashioned values of golf ('goaf'), 'g&t' and squeaky old-fashioned ceiling fans in down at heel and slightly musty rooms. 'Run the hot for at least five minutes if you want a shower' we were told and, oh yes, there were some very dodgy electrical fittings.

For the first time, I had the opportunity to meet my fellow Wild Frontier travellers: vivacious tour leader, Sue; experienced Wild Frontiers hand, Jenny from Sawbridgeworth, Jane Darling (really that name was true and so appropriate!) from Hong Kong; Fiona and Edna respectively from 'Battersia' and Tel Aviv, Janine from Arbroath in Scotland, and Sandy from 'somewhere in Kent'. There was to be a late joiner, Soody, the following night at the railway station.

So after a very hot and humid afternoon of sightseeing – the Victoria Monument, which was particularly ugly, the Botanical Gardens with the world's largest banyan tree, teetering old trams, some of the three and a half thousand yellow Ambassador taxis, the ubiquitous Tata buses, always packed and bashed, together with many a glimpse of the old capital city of the Raj – all in all I began to like Calcutta very much. I recall I was up for what sounded like an even more exciting down-to-earth experience than I had ever imagined. So I bought the ladies some home-made ice cream at the Tolly, always an easy way to their hearts!

Our Kolkata guide, Asif, and his wonderfully named driver, Mitoo, took us to the food, and afterwards to the flower markets, for walkabouts. We were definitely the only foreign tourists about, and the colourful sights and pungent smells were just exquisite. The people, too, were beautiful, calm, and usually smiling. For those who had not seen the real India before, it was a revelation. Kolkata also sported a single-route metro, so given my mad-for-it railway enthusiasm, we took that route back to the Tolly. I had begun to relax and recall the real India and we were all to get an actual dose of that in the evening at Sealdah Station, where we were to join the overnight Darjeeling Mail to New Jalpaiguri Junction (NJP).

As I saw it Sealdah Station, Calcutta, especially at night, was all a station should be. It was noisy, frenetic, and ever so slightly disconcerting, but it was worth just every second of being there. Massive baggage being forced into the baggage car of the overnight Varanasi Express, all sorts of platform sales, and then 'our train'. It was eight to a sleeping compartment, including two three-tier bunks. I was on one of the top ones. Mixed sexes and parties, of course; fellow traveller, Edna, was not amused though. However I was being rocked to sleep by the train's motion and my iPod on shuffle. It was a wonderful, surreal sensation. On-board food sellers came along and took bespoke orders for curries and all sorts of delights which were rapidly fulfilled on small stoves in the end vestibules, there was no room for 'health & safety' rules here. It was so far from my comfort zone that it hurt, but I was enjoying every second.

Arriving at NJP an hour and a half late, we transferred straightaway to the narrow gauge platform. I was sent to the director's carriage for the first part of the journey to Kuersong, no more needed to be said, though I suspect my constant commentary about railway matters had been noticed by tour leader Sue. We were to travel to Darjeeling, which was over 60 miles away and 7,000 higher feet up, all in eight hours or so. It was to be an incredible journey with just wonderful people and scenery en route.

I wondered 'just how did they build tracks up here' as in places it was mind bogglingly steep. I was disappointed that the train was hauled by a diesel rather than a steam engine, particularly as those were British built, but I took what I could get. The views as we climbed, and particularly as we broke through the mist, more than compensated for the fact that minor disappointment. There were school kids who used it to get to school and back. Others, usually youths, just 'surfed' it seemingly for fun. Everyone was very friendly and polite, and they offered very good conversation in very competent English.

Two daughters from Chennai (formerly Madras) travelling with their mother were rather taken by me. They wanted group photos with me (these were pre-selfie days), which were duly taken, causing broad grins all round. The remaining three from our group who saw the whole journey through were: Fiona, Sandy and I all clapped heartily when we finally arrived in Darjeeling. We all recalled seeing tiny shops, which were virtually sitting on the track, at every village we passed through. All seemed to be selling the same things especially for those folk with the 'sweet tooth'. There were smartly dressed school kids who had walked for miles when they were not jumping onto and off the train. I remember seeing villages clinging to the hillsides and the stifling heat from the gangetic plain causing a fog that dissipated as we ascended. It was a journey to be savoured and never forgotten. It had indeed been a privilege as Sue so rightly observed.

We travelled through a surprisingly busy Darjeeling to the Mayfair Hotel where we were treated to colonial elegance in a simply stunning location. 'Let's go to the Library Bar, ladies!' I proposed, which was a suggestion that was swiftly and eagerly accepted.

Somewhat disconcertingly we were awoken at 3:00 a.m. for an early departure to Tiger Top in order to hopefully witness the sunrise over the high Himalaya. Even at that early hour there were already masses of people there, and we were herded into the 'posh lounge' at the viewing point. It was a really weird place and very frustratingly the early morning mist would not dissipate. The postcards for sale showed what it would have been like had it had been clear, but it was not to be. At one point the crowd outside cheered loudly as a small hole appeared in the mist, but it was short-lived. I felt a little deflated because I had been really looking forward to my first real sighting of the world's highest mountain range. However I hoped that the next day might provide the view I craved.

Darjeeling is situated in a simply magnificent setting immediately below the permanently snow-covered Kanchenjunga range, with beautiful wooded foothills all around. Jenny and I wandered into the main town square where there was an active Bollywood film set. I was not feeling too well but was rightly distracted from my self-pity by Jenny's own tales of her recent redundancy and a seemingly disastrous marriage, just ended.

In the afternoon, we went to the Tibetan refugee self-help centre. We saw more fantastic faces there. We also visited the Himalayan Mountaineering Institute, where Sherpa Tenzing, who was the first to successfully conquer Everest together with Sir Edmund Hillary, was buried. After passing the zoo, we were brought to a halt by a huge funeral parade that completely snarled up the traffic.

The Darjeeling taxis were an experience to witness, their style of driving appeared to verge on extreme madness. Later, we went back downtown to have the mass of photos we all had taken so far printed out (this was the pre-digital camera age) at a tiny shop whose owner was understandably most appreciative. Joining Jane at a local café I tried a sweet lassi in an attempt to counteract my symptoms. I was further tickled by Jane's ribald conversation which soon had me laughing uncontrollably. I reflected that all of our group were becoming such good company, including our guide and drivers, which definitely enhanced the many fantastic experiences we were having. The smiling faces of the locals just kept appearing at every turn, and I did not feel insecure for our safety in any way even though there was a strong separatist mood in this region.

Departing early again the next morning, very sadly leaving behind the marvellous Mayfair hotel, we headed towards another former British Raj hill-station at Kalimpong, but not before seeing the Darjeeling mountain railway for the last time, but from the road this time. It was the last time we were to see it properly and it was like saying goodbye to a newly-made friend. The first part of the journey (to a spot marked by a mass of vertical prayer flags, which was my first encounter with these very special sights) was misty but it cleared quickly, and the journey began in earnest. This was the first time I had spent so much time in a jeep, and I really enjoyed half hanging out of the front in army style, and was able to deal with the many bumps in the road more easily. I really enjoyed the view from the open door, especially when the sun emerged and bathed the area in light and we could see how startling the scenery was.

At one point we stopped and walked down through the beautiful tea plantations until we reached what turned out to be a real highlight of the journey so far: the Peshok Tea Estate Primary School. The kids were out playing during their break, and we soon made friends and went photo crazy. It was such a precious moment, and as Janine said: 'we are all in danger of an emotional overload, and it is so early in our adventure.'

Back at the school, Jane was playing the part of the 'supply teacher' by drawing Bugs Bunny on one of the classroom blackboards. A few classic school group photos were taken, but we are all too soon on our way. There was an unusual pit stop at Johnny Gurkha's cafe, near the border with Sikkim which was set high above the Teesta River. We were not too sure if Johnny was a Gurkha or not but we enjoyed good chai. The journey continued down and alongside the river, rather too close at one point where the bridge had been washed away in the previous year's monsoon and we had to navigate a rough section very close to the river's edge.

We eventually arrived in Kalimpong. This area was, at one time, actually part of Bhutan, but I was not aware of that on this, my first visit there. Though misty again, we could see more of the surroundings. In the days of the Raj, it was a favoured spot to escape the heat of the cities on the gangetic plain, and it came complete with a parish church that looked like it was plucked straight from England.

Our first visit was to a monastery at Zang Dhok Palri Phodrang. We all felt something in the presence of the monks there. They were from the Red Hat sect of Tibetan Buddhism. There was an aura about the place, and we felt filled with the feeling of peace that pervaded everything. As the monks were of various ages there was also a lot of fun and joy.

We attended prayers in the temple, and Jane and I sat down to listen and take it all in. Much to our surprise, we were invited to participate and asked to circle the holy shrine three times in prayer. We knew to go round three times because one of the novice monks held up three fingers very pointedly. Afterwards, we were told by our guide, Uday, that the prayers were being uttered for world peace and health. Jane and I were overwhelmed with spiritual emotion. It was a treasured moment.

That evening we went downtown to shop and got caught in our first Himalayan thunderstorm. Lightning was flashing and there were flickering electric lights everywhere. I was thinking that in its heyday this must have been a wonderful place. Anyway the locals were happy because they were beating England at international cricket, a national obsession everywhere in India. In fact, street cricket and board games played alongside the road seem to be the national pastimes; 'perhaps healthier than the English tradition of visiting pubs' I mused.

We were up very early the next day to try to catch those elusive views of the high Himalayan peaks, especially Kanchenjunga. Uday first took us back to the monastery and we were recognised immediately. Although we caught only glimpses of the mountains, they were a sight for sore eyes (even if they did look like clouds). Sadly, we had to leave Kalimpong after an all-too-brief visit and be on our way again.

The next part of the journey turned out to be very much up hill and down dale. We travelled over the George V Coronation Bridge (built in 1937) and onto the tea plantation plains of northeast India and, in particular, Assam. It is an area that many people forget is actually part of India. We then drove on for a further five hours, passing no fewer than thirty-two tea plantations of, as Uday described it, 'curl, twist, cut' tea. (This description reflects the tea picking process carried out by armies of women and girls all beautifully dressed in very colourful clothes, and as with everywhere else on our journey so far, displaying the most beautiful smiles, despite the hard work they were engaged in).

As we continued our journey, the barrier hills of Bhutan began to become more obvious, before we eventually checked into Jaldapara Game Lodge. Our English guide, Sue, had been warning us about this place for some time, and now we could see why. Used mainly by the local tourists, and not usually foreigners, it was certainly of a different standard. Sue was right, though: it just had to be seen. The ladies loved it in the end, especially the trips to see the one-horned rhino while riding on elephants. After my experience about twenty years previously of riding on the back of an elephant at Amber Fort, India, I gave that particular trip a miss.

It was all very basic but survivable, though we were in the heart of mosquito country. Therefore, creams, sprays, and smoking coils were a must. Kingfisher and Cobra beers in the poorly lit bar enlivened the situation, but it all seemed a little bit blurred to me as I was beginning to feel a little unwell again, the result of my normal western diet being subjected to the sub-continents food, and more particularly, the local water. (Although receiving a surprise call on my mobile from friend, David, in the UK, was both surreal and uplifting.) Sandy was also not feeling too well, and Fiona said she was exhausted after the long days' travel. To top it off – and this comment was expressed in a firm Arbroath accent – Janine did not like any of the *fud!*

The style of driving, too, was very different to what I was used to. The drivers just seemed to slam down on the accelerator and lean on the horn whilst careering around sharp hairpin bends. We saw some with very salutary poster boards with dire warnings on them about speed and death. A typical one read: 'let heaven wait, see out today'.

Finally, we met our Bhutan guide, Pema, for the first time, together with his aide in India, Panchuk, who actually came from Kalimpong. We left Jaldapara at a civilised hour the next morning for the short journey to the border and onwards to the Bhutanese capital, Thimphu. As it turned out after thirteen and a half very long hours later, we finally completed the 180 km journey.

What a journey it was to be though. We had all been looking forward to crossing into Bhutan, and somewhat surprisingly we passed through the very grubby joint border towns of Jaigaon (India) and Phuntsoling (Bhutan) really quite quickly. The Indian border crossing looked like it was straight out of a film about the Indian North West Frontier with Afghanistan. It was comprised of a single khaki tent, presumably left behind by the departing troops of the Raj, masquerading as the border Office. We never did see the Bhutanese one but we did see and go through the 'Bhutan Gate', which was simply magical. Its very design somehow conjured up mystery and secrecy which added to the general air of excitement. Once across, we had to wait for a couple of hours for Pema to sort out the formalities. During the delay we took the opportunity to say goodbye to our northeast India drivers and our wonderful guide, Uday. The ladies shed a few tears.

And then our long drive to Thimphu started in earnest, and we found that we were heading almost immediately uphill on roads that were very steep and narrow despite having to cope with large lorries and buses as well as the smaller traffic. The roads, arguably, even worse than the narrow ones I was used to on the Isle of Lewis. The general rule was that, from here-on in, everything was up. It was very different from the beautiful, flat plains of Assam, with their ubiquitous tea plantations. Although I could not readily identify the signs, this particular area was once rich in lime deposits, which had been exploited by the Nepalese settlers in the first half of the twentieth century.

The views were simply incredible, but the sheer scale could never be caught on camera; certainly not with mine, anyway. We passed ridge after ridge and valley after valley, up through the clouds; we even caught sight of some snow. Before long, we stopped to have our lunch at Kamji, and it was with some surprise we realised that we had driven right into a community secondary school yard where morning classes had just finished and the kids were engaged in post-school entertainment.

Unbeknownst to us, the minibus (we had that and a jeep for our transport in Bhutan) had suffered a breakage on one of the suspension leaves. Pema, and the driver Sunnam, were soon hard at work trying to fix it. In the meantime, we tourists self-consciously ate our sandwiches while the kids looked on with interested curiosity.

Something happened there at Kamji Community School that will remain with me forever. It was probably my first exposure to what I have since tried to encapsulate in the phrase: 'beautiful people, beautiful country, beautiful culture'. It sounds trite but that says it all and, for me, it all started at Kamji.

I have since thought that I would love to go back to Kamji (in fact I did briefly, on a subsequent visit in 2008) and although the people, especially the kids, would be unlikely to remember me, I met some there on that day who, in the short few hours, came to mean a great deal to me. In particular Sonam Tobgyel (and his merry gang of followers) and Som Bdr Rai left an especially strong impression.

It started when, after lunch, I mentioned to Sue that I was going to walk across the road to the nearby temple. Almost immediately, I was engaged in conversation by one of the students and a growing crowd encircled me. He asked about me, asking in very passable English where I, and the rest of the tour group, came from. It is unfortunate that I did not obtain his name because he was the first person, other than my local guide and driver, who I had spoken to in Bhutan. What I did find out was that he was a distance runner (3000m), and he was going to participate in the Bhutanese inter-schools championships soon, though quite some way away at a place called Wangdue (which

22

I was to subsequently visit and became to know very well) although at the time though it was just a place name and meant little to me.

Nearby in the village recreation area some men were throwing the *kuru* (large darts) over a huge distance between two marker posts. Archery and *kuru* are the national sports in Bhutan. One of the kids in the temple area, Sonam, appeared along with his excitable group of friends and stayed around for the next two hours. Jenny observed: 'you have already become the pied piper of Kamji, you clearly should have been a teacher!' And rather more directly from Janine in her punchy Arbroath accent: 'stuff work in London and come here'. Thoughts echoed by Sue, and perhaps even more poignantly from one of the school teachers as we were leaving later: 'you are really good with the kids'. Those comments still strongly resonate with me now many years later. I have tried to describe the feelings I experienced at that time as my Damascene moment. What I knew immediately, though, was that Bhutan had found a place in my soul which would always stay. Perhaps it was the parting comments of a pretty young girl who said: 'you are such a handsome man' that finally won me over. No, it was much deeper and more meaningful than those kind words. I had suddenly and totally unexpectedly found myself feeling absolutely 'at home' in an environment so far from my own. It was exciting, disconcerting and mesmerising: emotions I simply had not anticipated. Was there something in the air, the altitude perhaps? No I think it was, rather bluntly expressed in hindsight, the early stages of falling in love with the country and its people.

I had previously read in my travel books that all schools in Bhutan now taught lessons in English, and that the kids especially just loved to practise their language skills with English speaking travellers. Certainly my early conversations at that time underscored what a successful and forward thinking policy that was. Anyway, this most wondrous experience there at Kamji seemingly went on and on, but inevitably it was eventually time to leave. The minibus was apparently fixed – God and My Lord Buddha only knew how – but I was pleased for Sunnam! We were all rather sad as we said our goodbyes, but we smiled and waved vigorously at the assembled students but then we were all too quickly through the school gate and on our way. It was the first of many departures that resulted in tears in my eyes. I had a particularly heavy heart, not because I was leaving, but because part of me had been left there and I desperately wanted to return. I could already sense that this land, so far away from my own, was already very close to my heart.

We went onward and upwards as before, but there was a sudden stop when we ran into a traffic jam caused by attempts to retrieve a lorry that had driven over a precipice a few days before. We were told that fortunately the driver was all right. The scenery just kept getting better and better as we travelled higher and higher, it opened up giving us fantastic views of the grand mountain vistas. However given the environment and the poor state of the roads, we soon realised that progress on our so-called 'short journey' was going to be very slow. Sunnam was, very wisely, being very careful whilst driving with that suspect suspension spring.

Twilight came, and we all wondered whether we would even reach our destination that day! A quick pit stop at a friendly roadside café for some very welcome chai was followed by mile after long mile of extended road works. These repairs, or rather significant upgrades, were being carried out by the Indian government on behalf of the Bhutanese in a certain style. The Indian strategy was to dig up the existing road, pile up the excavations alongside, and and let traffic figure out for themselves how to navigate the mess. This was particularly hair-raising at times because there were many totally unprotected precipitous drops to avoid, and it was beginning to become quite dark.

At last the lights emanating from the centre of Thimphu appeared. I immediately thought: 'thank God, and my Lord Buddha'. Eventually we found ourselves on proper roads again, though not for long, as there were huge road-works and bridge construction projects here as well. Soon, after negotiating our way through two more police checkpoints, and on one occasion with our guide having to do some fast talking with the traffic cops who alleged we were taking the wrong route, the world famous police post in the town centre came into view, as did the Hotel Pedling, our accommodation for the night.

Everyone was absolutely worn out, and after a brief meal, sleep beckoned us all. For my part I was looking forward to reflecting on the fantastic day. I had those immensely strong and happy memories of Kamji to recall. Thimphu was yet to be seen, but we were all very pleased to be there at last. Before heading for bed, we had all been warned of the night dogs, and they certainly howled quite a bit all through the night, though sleep finally overtook my reflective thoughts and those barking dogs. The next morning the scent of spices wafted through the air, and although it was a Sunday, noisy work had begun on the adjacent construction site at first light.

I was thinking: 'yes, we are all here in the capital of Bhutan at last, but I can hardly believe it.' Unsurprisingly the more permanent repairs to the minibus were taking longer than expected so we took advantage of the extra time by taking a short walk around the town and heading to the Thimphu dzong (opposite the Royal Palace). No photographs of the Palace were allowed, but we did sneak a look at the Crown Prince ('CP1') who was having a lunch party on the lawns in front of the Palace. He and his group appeared to be listening to some rather loud western style pop music. His father, King Jigme Singwe Wangchuk ('K4'), was very popular despite his autocratic authority. However he was planning to hand over the monarchy to CP1 in 2008 and to introduce a democratic parliamentary, process. I had the feeling that the people would rather have him stay on, ruling in the same style.

Thimphu dzong gave us our first close look at the Bhutanese style of architecture. All buildings are very loosely based on the design of the typical Bhutan farmhouse, and indeed, all buildings must be built like that as part of the King's decree that seeks to preserve their culture. As part of this decree the Bhutanese must wear their national dress in all dzongs (which serve both as monasteries and the local area's administrative offices), schools and government buildings.

Television and access to the Internet had only been introduced into Bhutan as recently as 1999, at which time tourist numbers were restricted to around 3,500 per year, and foreign travellers were still quite a rare sight. At the time of this visit, which was only seven years later, international tourist numbers were increasing (they stood at around twenty thousand per annum) but the infrastructure, particularly accommodation, was still very stretched. As part of the king's cultural decree, all international tourists were charged a daily rate of USD200. This provided for modest accommodation, food, transport and a local guide. Despite the common assumption that tourist numbers were still capped, this was now a misconception, the only proviso now being the payment of the daily rate. Whilst this approach blatantly attracted the 'high-end' tourist market, and decidedly deterred individual travellers, it had the effect of controlling usage of the fragile infrastructure and provided direct employment in this sector. Access to specific areas of the country was not, in the main, a problem but the provision of a local guide gave the country the opportunity to explain their culture to visitors on their own terms.

The Bhutanese people are very proud of their nation, religion, and culture, but they are also very aware of what is happening in the world. They are seemingly obsessed with sex, but not as overtly as many western cultures appear to be. However somewhat shocking to the western eye are the houses that carry hand painted murals, many depicting the image of a large, ejaculating penis. Apparently such paintings were very effective in warding off evil deities. Our local guide Pema was regularly subjected by the ladies on our tour crying out: 'Pema, Pema, take us to the willy house!'

We eventually arrived at the main market in Thimphu which, like Calcutta, was very clean (save for the simply awful toilets). We saw wonderfully fresh and truly organic food, including fiery red hot chillies, which appeared to be consumed with everything. We all observed that we all would no compunction about buying any of the food on offer.

Afterwards we left Thimphu and drove over the spectacular Dochu La Pass. This was really one of the 'must see' places to visit in Bhutan, particularly on a clear day, as there was then, as it gives a spectacular view of the majestic Himalayas on the near horizon. We were overwhelmed by the huge mass of prayer flags blowing in the stiff breeze at the summit. The Bhutanese believe that the messages of peace and karma on these flags are borne on the winds to the heavens and to the rest of the world. Thus, if they are not blown away the flags are burnt, perpetuating this process. Prayer flags were to become an integral part of my spiritual life, and as far as I am able, I always have some blowing in the wind at my home in the UK.

After descending down the other side of the pass we arrived in Old Wangdue's town centre, where I recalled that student I had spoken to at Kamji, and who was to come to an athletics event here. There were some 'off-duty' young monks, looking impressive in their very colourful red robes, just hanging out in the main square. Needless to say as they were so photogenic we took lots of pictures, and they seemed to love the attention. It was a very picturesque place, but I was saddened to hear that it was to be relocated and brought into the modern world with completely new shops and housing. I felt glad that I was able to see it in its original state. Driving on, we made it to our night stop: the spectacularly located Kichu Resort, which, like the Mayfair in Darjeeling, was of a much higher standard than we were used to. Set beside a glacial river, we all thought that we were in heaven. Numerous beers were consumed, and we nattered on the terrace with American guests who had just been trekking in central Bhutan and who had clearly enjoyed a thrilling experience.

We all felt at peace when, the next morning, we wandered by the river in glorious clear Himalayan sunshine, crystal clear and clean and quite unlike anything we were used to, we felt suitably enlivened and certainly did not feel like leaving. However, leave we did, and our next stop was Wangdue Phodrang dzong (set on a dramatically precipitous location, this beautiful building that was very sadly totally destroyed by a fire in 2012). It was home to those town square monks we had met the previous evening. The dzongs, though ostensibly similar, are actually quite different and each had its own distinct feel and ambience. Here, some of the ladies – Sue, Jenny, and Jane – were taken upstairs by a group of monks for a personal blessing by the lama. Sadly, I missed out.

And then it was off to our next dzong at Punakha, the old capital of Bhutan before it was established in Thimphu, and it still remains as the summer residence for the monk body based there. This was Sue's favourite place, and I have since come to see why. In her case, she loved it largely because it was home to the 'smiling monk' she had informally adopted. She regaled us with tales of his love of red socks, so before going there, she had frantically looked for some suitable socks to give him. In fact we all contributed, in my case delving into my travel bag and finding a suitable new pair I had bought in London before my departure. I felt sure he would approve of those even though they were not red!

Inside, the enormous gold-leaved prayer hall in the inner temple was wondrous, but I could not help mentally wincing when Pema told us that young monks were flogged there in the olden days when failing to learn the Buddhist mantras properly. Further up the valley and were treated to an even clearer view of the high Himalayas. It was particularly inspiring for me, with my love (tinged with fear) of mountains and I wanted to get closer. Walking quite steeply uphill, across a swaying suspension bridge, we arrived at the Queen Mother's gift for peace she had built for CP1, the Kasum Yuly Namgyal chorten. There was a particularly peaceful karma in the atmosphere prevailing here, and we discovered the routine of walking slowly, clockwise, at least three times around it in order to garner peaceful thoughts. Jane performed the prayer ritual with a gaggle of three splendid old crones who were great characters, giggling loudly at anything Jane said, though I doubted they understood her. The local monk novices were polishing the wooden floors in advance of the King's imminent visit. We had walked up the hill with one of them, and Soody joined in with his ablutions at an outside tap, both smiling broadly and enjoying the refreshing moment. Soody was our late-joiner at Sealadh station on our departure from Calcutta. He lived in Harrow and was endeavouring to become a professional photographer, so he saw the trip to India and Bhutan as an ideal hunting ground for unusual photo opportunities. After the visit I zipped down the hill with a surprisingly sprightly Sandy, who had struggled quite a bit on the ascent. We were joined for part of the trek by Pema, who cleverly spotted, hidden deep in the foliage, a beautiful long-tailed cuckoo.

Whilst en route to our lunch break we were much delayed by a lorry that had collided with a narrow bridge. The ingenuity of the locals operating in remote areas with little equipment to rescue the situation was very impressive. Eventually, the lorry was freed, but certainly not in compliance with UK Health and Safety rules!

The three hour journey back to Thimphu on very twisty roads meant another quite tiring day, mainly due to the heat, which affected two of the ladies quite severely. Along the way, we spotted an eagle soaring over the pass just as darkness was falling. By the time we got back to the hotel, there was little in doing anything other than getting some rest. Some in my party seemed to be completely out of it, which perhaps was not surprising as it had been our fullest day so far.

Waking the next morning I felt really tired, despite having slept well, which was probably due to sunstroke from the day before, and I think that the rest of the group were suffering in the same way. There was no time to feel sorry for ourselves as we were off to the Paro Valley, which we knew was getting ready for its famous festival. This had featured prominently in Michael Palin's BBC TV series 'Himalaya', which in turn had done wonders for the Bhutanese tourist industry, raising high profile awareness of this little known country. Before we left we visited the General Post Office in Thimphu in order to buy some special edition stamps. I had heard that Bhutanese stamps were particularly beautiful and were so popular with tourists and collectors that they were a welcome boost to the local economy. The Post Office was the nearest building I had seen thus far that resembled a building in the UK. In fact inside the counter layout and polite queues appeared to be very similar. The beautiful stamps were somewhat surreptitiously being sold from a 'room at the back'. The counter staff there were both very helpful and knowledgeable, though understandably very keen to sell us as many stamps as they could, but all conducted with a disarming smile of course. It was also the Danish Film Festival week, and I hoped that fellow film lovers Fiona and Soody could have attended at least part of it. That would have been a unique experience and I could have claimed to have visited the only cinema in Thimphu, and possibly the whole of Bhutan.

Departing the capital, and whilst en route to a farmhouse museum and town zoo, we experienced Pema in full tour guide mode. It was not for me so I let these visits pass whilst I chatted with our driver, the clever mechanic Sunnam, about his home far away in the east in village called Lhuntsi, which I gathered was quite remote. Sunnam's conversation in English was not as competent as Pema's but it was more than passable, and I experienced feelings of guilt that I could not reciprocate in his own language.

After the zoo we stopped at a spot where there were an abundance of prayer flags flying above Thimphu. It was an idyllic location and suitably photogenic, so needless to say Soody was hard at work with his camera, in fact we all were. I was very glad we had stopped there before we started heading for our next main destination at Paro. Our driver for this section, Namgorgi, aka *Lama*, was young and appeared to be quite shy and he spoke very little English, but he simply loved music. So the drive was made very pleasant by him putting lots of local music on the creaky cassette player, including the simply marvellous soundtrack for the made-in-Bhutan film, *The Perfect Girl*. This was to become a real favourite, conjuring all the memories and even smells of Bhutan, every time I played it back home.

The journey was again lengthened by those badly managed Indian contractor's road-works, which seemed to be made much worse by the absence of any form of traffic control. However, the trip was shortened when we were surprisingly waved through the army checkpoint at the wonderfully named junction, 'Confluence'. These checkpoints could sometimes delay our journeys quite a lot as all the necessary paperwork was submitted by our drivers and suitably scrutinised, often with furtive looks in our direction by the army staff manning them. It was not disconcerting, rather more amusing, though frustrating on our long travel days. All inconveniences were forgotten however when we drove into the beautiful and impressive Paro Valley. After driving through adjacent narrower valleys leading to it, the main one suddenly opened and took our breath away. Somehow Lama's music made it even more unforgettable. We suddenly had our first sighting of the airport situated in a difficult and tight location with high mountains all around, and we could immediately see that flying in or out of there was going to be exhilarating. We finally left the 'main' road and drove up to an old farmhouse further up on one side of the valley. We had been told that accommodation at festival time was in very short supply and that we would have to put up with what was available, but this did not appear to be too bad, at least at first blush. The farmer had built a bunk-house block with modest facilities and we found ourselves billeted in there.

That evening there was a local singing and traditional dancing show put on for the benefit of the farmhouse guests, which was simply magical. We were all invited to join in during the last dance but tiredness and the strong local beer prevented me from participating properly. Before retiring, Pema gave us a really interesting talk about what to expect at the festival ('tsechu') on the following day. Though it had been a really interesting and varied day I think I was both very tired and pretty drunk by the end of it!

The following morning I watched the sun stretch into the clear blue skies as I walked the short distance down to the Paro riverside with Fiona whilst having a lovely chat about our respective lives. I thought: 'what good fortune to be travelling with such nice people and with very similar interests'. Though Fiona had really surprised me on the long drive back over the Dochu La pass the day before by expressing her interest in the heavy rock band 'The Cult'. I would never have put her down as a fan! After breakfast, we drove down to the tsechu ground which was located near to Paro dzong, but unsurprisingly up quite a steep path which we accessed after crossing a really mediaeval looking bridge. There were simply masses of people around, all clearly excited about the prospect of the tsechu, which was what most of us had anticipated being the major highlight of the trip. Soody hoped to write an article about it and to include some stunning and unusual photographs with which to springboard his career. The whole experience was not to be a disappointment for any of us.

On the way to the tsechu ground we had seen stalls selling a wide variety of goods, mainly of a religious theme, and of course food and drink. Everyone was very friendly and welcoming, even if respective language skills were not the best. Smiles and the general air of excitement was all that was needed. It was clearly a very special occasion for the Bhutanese, who we learnt had come from far and wide in very large numbers. They were usually in family groups and were all immaculately dressed in the most beautiful colourful clothes. You could sense their pride at being there and it rubbed off on us. The colours were simply stunning, so much so that it was almost an assault on the senses, but one none of us would have wanted to miss witnessing those events. The formal singing and dancing were also colourful and impressive in equal measure, but although we had all read the short written spiel about what the convoluted dancing moves signified, it seemed a little remote. I quickly learned that watching and mingling with the locals was the key. Simply smiling, as they did in abundance, would elicit a positive response. Whilst the younger folk would ask questions in English the older ones used sign language and facial expressions. Sue repeated her earlier summation about Bhutan which was so pertinent: 'this was indeed the most beautiful country, with the most beautiful people, and the most beautiful peaceful culture.' She was right, and it had really got under my skin. I felt immensely happy and I was enjoying every moment.

C J Morris, an English officer who had served with the Gurkhas, seen service on the Somme during World War 1, and latterly the dangerous north-west frontier on the border of India and Afghanistan, visited Bhutan in the 1930s, described the scene thus:

'The big dance of the year at Paro is held in early spring and usually lasts three whole days. It is carried out entirely by parties of monks who live in the monastery attached to the Dzong and must, I imagine, necessitate many months of arduous practice throughout the year, for there did not seem to be the slightest hesitation or mistake throughout the entire performance. Very early in the morning people started to arrive from all the surrounding villages. Most were dressed in their gala clothes in which brilliant reds and yellows dominated, many, with a view to staying throughout the three days, carried supplies of food and drink with them.

Punctually at ten there was a crash of cymbals […] then entered
a slow procession of various officials […] and all the elders from
the monastery. All were dressed in magnificent robes of brocade
and silk and many […] carried large drums which they beat
rhythmically as the procession moved around the court.

One would imagine the[se] dances to be extremely exhausting, but
in actual fact none of the performers appeared to be in the least
tired after dancing in the hot sun for two hours without a rest.'

(C.J. Morris, 'A Journey in Bhutan', *The Geographical Journal*,
Vol 86, No.3 1935)

The scene was exactly thus in 2006 as well. A very early start was
called for the following day as this was to be the real highlight of
the whole tsechu, the unveiling of the great Paro thangka. This is a
simply huge religious mural that is kept secreted in the dark vaults
of the dzong, and only brought out on this one occasion each year
to be unfurled for the benefit of the adoring pilgrims. Although we
were all tired, we immediately forgot about the lack of sleep when the
procession started. It was so exciting for both the locals and tourists
alike.

The lead carrier seemed to really struggle on the steps that led up from
the dzong to the tsechu ground. The load looked really heavy and
it took quite a few men to carry it on their shoulders. We joined the
locals and ran alongside, rushing to actually touch it. The unveiling
itself, which was quite a slow process as obviously great care was
being exercised, was a very impressive and special moment. I sensed
great peace and karma in the midst of all the excitement, and for a
while, it seemed like the tourists outnumbered the locals – though not
for long. The darkness added to the atmosphere of reverence. It was
only to be left unveiled until around dawn so as to avoid the sunlight
damaging it. After the unveiling there was a sudden rush to give
offerings and to touch it again. Fortunately we somehow managed to
get to the front of the queue and offered our own respects. After doing
so, we found that the queue had suddenly become really enormous.
We all were felt very privileged to have been there to witness that

very special event and to have participated as well, so much so that a wave of inner gratitude appeared to consume us all.

After the unveiling a long procession of dignitaries, including the dzong's lama and monks, came along soon afterwards. Last in line were the very young novice monks who were kept in line with the presence of a vicious-looking cat-o'-nine-tails, being suitably swished by the monk's master. Fortunately these days this is only for display purposes and not for actually punishing the boys. We did not stay long because it was still very cold, but the chanting and sentiments were mesmerising. After all the anticipation it had not been an anti-climax, which was probably just as well as this was obviously the highlight not only of the tsechu but our journey to Bhutan as well. I continued to feel really privileged to be among such wonderfully disarming people and I already knew that I would miss them very much when we came to leave.

We headed back to the farmhouse for our, by now rather late, breakfast and found ourselves laughing a lot over quite trivial things throughout the meal. At times like that it was clear that the whole group really gelled, though apparently I was to be reported by Sue to Jonny Bealby (Wild Frontier's managing director back at their London HQ) because my sense of humour was allegedly leading the party astray! One of the trivial matters that set off gales of giggling was recalling the deep, and clearly religious, sound of the Tibetan horns being blown as a background for the reciting of the mantras, accompanied by jangling cymbals and the deep intonation of the lama himself. Only to be rather rudely interrupted by the announcer obliviously shouting over the PA system: 'will the owner of vehicle registration BP1–10725 please move their car'! It seemed to be a priceless moment, well for the English sense of humour anyway.

If all that was not enough, there was to be yet another adventure that day: a trek up to the Tiger's Nest, the place where (tradition states) the Guru Rinpoche landed after flying in from India on the back of a tigress and thus bringing Tibetan Buddhism to Bhutan. The three hour trek consisted of two sections of walking paths with a cafe just beyond the halfway point. There was some consternation at the start because Pema had previously ordered some donkeys to make the trek easier for the ladies, but the animals had been seemingly hijacked by others, presumably folk from the festival who had apparently got there first.

We all made it to the lookout point towards the end of the second section which offered a spectacular view overlooking the Tiger's Nest. A senior monk was resting there, and he seemed bemused by our enthusiasm. As I lay on the rock nearby, which gave the effect of lying on a precipice, I uttered aloud that I felt that I was experiencing sheer bliss in that spot. The monk smiled knowingly.

Janine had witnessed all this and got onto the rock after I had vacated it and she was as awestruck as I had been, and the monk continued to look on in a bemused fashion. When we arrived back in town, Soody, Jane, and I went for one final visit to Paro dzong. I wanted to get some *sunki* (neck cords), which I could use as a lucky charm round my wrist. The sunki had been blessed by the lama in the dzong's temple. Soody had spotted some earlier though, and he had kindly bought me a couple. It seemed to be the perfect postscript to our visit to the Paro Valley.

Soody was on top form as he practised his martial arts techniques for the general amusement of a group of exhausted tsechu dancers, who all seemed incredibly young, and the usual gaggle of novice monks. As ever they were all extremely friendly and one of boys, who was dressed in mock military fatigues somewhat touchingly said: 'see you same time next year'. Those were to be prophetic words as it turned out.

Later Pema and Sunnam showed us all how they put on the 'gho' the national dress for men. It was a very convoluted procedure but they both looked very smart, and according to the ladies, very dashing as well! Shortly thereafter, the electricity failed yet again and remained off for the rest of the night, doubtless due to the pressure caused by the sheer number of extra visitors in the area.

The next morning we made our way with heavy hearts to Paro airport for what turned out to be some pretty detailed security checks. Somewhat surprisingly at the end of the procedure we ended up having to identify our own baggage actually on the tarmac by the aircraft. That gave us all an opportunity to view from airside the simply spectacular, if somewhat daunting, location that this airport occupies. There are mountains all around, and I could see immediately why it would difficult for aircraft make an approach from any direction. It was visually stunning though and we took advantage of the unusual situation of being able to take photographs. The airport buildings are also built in Bhutanese style given a very unique feeling to this place, rendering it somehow quite unlike an airport.

Apparently, only a dozen or so pilots with the national airline, Drukair, are licensed to fly to and from this airport. Indeed, Drukair was the only airline operating here at that time with flights to and from either, Delhi and Calcutta in India and Bangkok in Thailand. Suddenly, two Airbus A319s, comprising Drukair's entire fleet, landed in quick succession from opposite directions. It was all very exciting!

Saying goodbye to Pema, Sunnam, and Lama was as emotional as I knew it would be. I certainly did not really want to leave the country or its people, but we did have Himalayan view seats on the plane to compensate for our sadness.

So, it was to be 'lazimbe jon' (goodbye) and 'tashi delek' (good luck) to all our new friends for the time being, or at least until the next time, which I sincerely hoped would be very soon.

Future Film Star in Kolkata Fish Market

to the Hotel Bar Ladies!

Top bunk on the night train to NJP

Sue and the Mahandi Boys

Surfing the DHMRly

Peshok Tea School

sandwiches at Kamji!

Kamji....first contact

Sonam's gang

Sue weaves her magic!

that World famous police post!

Town Square Thimphu

Thimphu Market   *novice monks in Old Wangdue market*

Prayer Flags over Thimphu

Magical Punakha Dzong

Paro Tsechu

happiness at the Tiger's Nest!   *see you next year!*

East India & Bhutan gang at the Paro Valley Farm

CHAPTER 3

LET'S HEAR IT FOR THIS TINY COUNTRY

Happiness is not a place but a direction.

Buddhist tract

It is all in the guide books, but here is my take on it. I am transported back there every time I put on the soundtrack of that Bhutanese-made film *The Perfect Girl,* which I first heard when played by our driver, Namgorgi, on the 'East India and Bhutan' tour. I am not sure whether the film was ever released outside Bhutan, and I sadly do not own a copy. However, the music and songs always spurs that special feeling of actually being there, to come flooding back into my mind. I shall forever be grateful to our guide, Sue, for buying us all a copy of the soundtrack. Listening to the music makes me feel as if I am being carried back there on the back of a tigress!

John Earle, mountaineer, featured in an article by the *Daily Telegraph* observed that he had been to every Himalayan country. He commented after his first visit to Bhutan, that it would be impossible to find anywhere more memorable. He noted: 'walking down the main

street in Thimphu everyone I passed made eye contact and smiled.'
I have been lucky enough to see the self-same thing, and whilst it
might seem a simple observation not worthy of further comment,
the fact is it does leave an immediate and lasting impression quite
unlike anywhere else. With his vast experience of other places in the
Himalayas, and indeed elsewhere, John Earle certainly thought it
worthy of comment, and I can fully relate to that feeling.

The American travellers, Russ and Blyth Carpenter, who have fallen
in love with Bhutan, made similar comments in their book, *Blessings
of Bhutan:*

On the country: 'Life changing terrain' [...] inner selves stirred [...]
and after their first visit [they had a] 'nagging feeling that they were
on the edge of learning something important, something primary [...]
and they felt their anchors beginning to drag'.

On the culture: 'Good morning Sir, good morning Madam [...] we
all fall in love with Bhutanese children!'

On the people: 'Handsome People [...] smiles that would win awards
anywhere on Earth!'

Upon their return to a very rural and remote part of the United States,
they put up prayer flags in the forests nearby. They wrote: '[We're]
not sure we are responding to them in the right way, but they whisper
things to us: let go of attachments, live compassionately, search for
the next life, even in this one.'

But let me start from the beginning: I joined this world in July 1949,
when times in post-war England were tough. My parents had married
a year earlier, and I am sure the extra ration books my arrival afforded
my family helped them survive on my father's meagre teacher's
salary. Coincidentally in that very year, Bhutan was recognised as
an independent country; in truth, though, it was more akin to a
mediaeval fiefdom, albeit with a benign dynasty at its helm. Nearly
ten years later, in 1958, Prime Minister Nehru of India rode, together
with his daughter and small entourage, along the Haa Valley and up

over the Chela La Pass into Bhutan and the Paro Valley. There, he addressed the people with words of peace and friendship. The small dais erected for this auspicious occasion is still standing outside Paro dzong.

Bhutan, at that time, must have seemed a world away from post-Raj India, which, after kicking out the imperialists, brought Queen Victoria's 'jewel in the crown' into a whole new world. The wretched caste system prevailed, as it does today, but the new-found wealth picked the country up by its bootstraps. Again, the legacy of those momentous changes continues today – India has one of the world's few 'tiger' economies. But Bhutan was still in the Dark Ages, despite the strenuous efforts of the Wangchuck Dynasty to bring it into the modern world. It was, as it is now, rich in spirituality but otherwise desperately poor. In the following year, neighbouring China, forcibly annexed Tibet, and brought it under the care and control of the motherland. It was a terrible time for Tibet, and that region has still not recovered. Although viewing Bhutan in much the same way it has largely left it alone apart from disputing the actual line of its border along the top of the Himalayas. Admittedly, though, the life's work of the magnificent fourteenth Dalai Lama has helped Tibet along. The Dalai Lama regularly gets under the skin of the Chinese authorities with his outbursts and support groups are now formed throughout the world, particularly in the United Kingdom.

China has always seen Tibet as part of its original territory, but it easily could have eyed Bhutan in the same way. China may have had the desire to conquer Bhutan, but the Bhutanese people have one key defence against intruders: the Himalayas. Bhutan has never been ruled by any outside country, despite the fact that, until 1907, it was only a collection of small, independent principalities and fiefdoms. Even the great Shabdrung was not been able to unify everyone completely. The British claim that Bhutan was once a British protectorate, but that was more as a result of threat, not conquest. In any event, its affiliation with England was short-lived. The British needed (and they received) Bhutan's help in dealing with Tibet, and then the British were on their way.

The honorary British consul in Bhutan, Michael Rutland, shares his time between Thimphu, the capital of Bhutan, and Surrey in the UK. The majority of his time, though, is spent in Bhutan. He first went to Bhutan in the early seventies to tutor the royal family's children, including the soon-to-be K4. Although male, his story can be likened to that of the British governess in the film *The King and I*, set in Siam (Thailand), which told the true-life story of the king being taught by an English governess. Michael has commented that, when he first went to Bhutan, there were few roads, no tourists, and no electricity. It was effectively cut off from the world. I do not know for sure, but he may have come in via the same route Nehru took (albeit then it was a much less established road). Rather more likely was that he travelled in by the same route I took to enter Bhutan in 2006. Reluctant the tutor-to-be may have been, but Michael Rutland is still there and totally committed to the country. He is now the UK ambassador there in all but name.

K3 started a road-building plan, including a north–south route and an east–west highway (NH1). The engineering of these routes was exceptionally difficult. Although I am sure that, to some extent, the routes were surveyed, it was more a case of where the route could, rather than should, go. The result was a roller coaster that still requires nerves of steel to negotiate. It is best not to look down! If you travel by road from either of the two main access points from India, there is no avoiding some particularly perpendicular sections, especially above Samdrupjongkhar. Even the original and main route from Phuntsoling is not immune to similar frightening drops. (appendix 3)

C J Morris, addressing The Royal Geographical Society in May of 1935, forty years earlier had declared:

'Bhutan is probably the most closed country in the world at the present day, and beyond occasional ceremonial visits [...] very few Europeans have been allowed to enter the country.'

(C.J. Morris, 'A Journey in Bhutan', *The Geographical Journal*, Vol 86, No.3, 1935).

Apart from access and visa permissions, not a lot has changed!

The airstrip (later, the airport) in the Paro Valley (IATA code PBH) did not get built until 1984, by which time the skeletal east–west road, National Highway 1 (NH1), was in place. However, do not imagine that either of these constructions were sophisticated affairs. The airstrip was served by a hair-raising ride in a small Dornier prop aircraft that approached the very difficult strip with virtually no landing aides. The roads were very narrow and precipitous, and they are still prone to avalanche and mudslide damage when snow blockages or monsoons crop up. Around 1990, the airstrip was expanded to become an airport, and Drukair acquired jet aircraft, initially a pair of second-hand BAe 146's. These have since been replaced by new Airbus A319's, which are fitted with uprated power plants to cope with the very tough flying conditions.

Things have improved in terms of air travel due to the introduction of these modern jets, which are manned by a very experienced flight crew who use landing aides (installed by the Australians) making the approach, through omni-present cloud, viable if not still a little hair raising. The roads, even today, are being improved by both the Indian government firm Dantak, which maintains the border roads and Bhutan's own Department of Roads (DoR), which maintains the rest. There is no way to avoid the weather hazards, and perhaps as importantly, the topography. Standing atop Chela La on a clear day will show you the problem: valley after valley, high ridge after high ridge – and they all have to be navigated. It was not an easy task to engineer or maintain these routes, and travel is always a time-consuming process. The quickest one can travel from the extreme west to the extreme east of Bhutan is three to four days. The present government is trying to establish airstrips in central and eastern Bhutan, but this is proving very problematic. (As of 2013, these airstrips have been established, and aircraft have begun serving the airstrip in the Bumthang Valley, in central Bhutan.)

It was to be a further fifteen years after the airstrip was built in the Paro Valley before television, and subsequently the Internet, were introduced by K4 in 1999. That construction certainly opened the world to the Bhutanese. Many people I talk to believe that there is a maximum quota set on the number of tourists who can visit, and that there are bureaucratic difficulties one must surmount in order to get into the country. Only following the gradual increase in tourist numbers after the coronation of K4 in 1974, and the opening of the airstrip in 1984, was a maximum ceiling was placed on the tourist numbers for a while. This was done to protect the fragile infrastructure, and on the practical front, to avoid situations in which tourists could not find accommodation, especially outside Thimphu and Paro. By the end of the nineties, the quota limit, which by then had risen to around seven thousand people per annum, was finally dispensed with. 2011 saw upwards of forty thousand tourists, a very rapid increase in a country that still struggles to provide for its own population, let alone tourists, particularly during festivals. There is no disputing the fact that hotel accommodation, and infrastructure generally, is still very stretched, especially in the east.

The bureaucratic problem of tourist access is something of a myth, and is far from insurmountable, though what is certain is that a fair amount of forward planning is required. Individual travel is discouraged and group tours, including bespoke tours, are the norm. At least one leg of your travel in or out of the country is now 'encouraged' to be with Drukair, which used to be compulsory, though in reality it is in fact the most convenient and time-friendly method anyway. The fact is that land entry from India via West Bengal and Phuntsoling or Assam and Samdrupjongkha can be very slow, tedious and decidedly uncomfortable. Although improved, clearing a border post can be a very time-consuming task that is mired in bureaucracy. Modern technology generally does not prevail at these posts, one almost half-expects to see a quill pen and ledger. I got a taste of the Indian border post experience at Phuntsoling, during my first trip in 2006.

But to obtain a ticket on Drukair, you must have a Bhutanese visa, which you do not actually receive until your passport is stamped at Paro Airport, upon arrival. Without a visa, you cannot technically buy a ticket! So to manoeuvre your way round this jigsaw a local travel agent will liaise with your home country travel agent. Included in these arrangements is the need to identify an agreed itinerary in Bhutan, again a task for the local agent. There are no prohibited areas as such, though the National Parks in the south, particularly Manas, are not easy to get into. Indian separatist insurgency is still a risk in the south, and the Bhutanese are very sensitive about that issue. Another reason for the itinerary is that the daily rate includes the services of a local guide and driver. This provides employment, and it allows the locals to explain the culture of the country. It is effectively part of the concept of gross national happiness, if you will!

The presence of two great nations, India and China, causes tension in the area especially because those two countries are involved in various border disputes. Indeed, Bhutan has seen China redraw the map along the line of the Himalayas and lost territory, including one or two mighty peaks, in the process. Bhutan enjoys strong economic ties with India. The countries' currencies are matched, and the Bhutanese government receives in excess of 50 per cent of its annual income through and from India. The Indians do not walk away empty-handed, though. They have access to considerable hydro power resources from Bhutan. Yes, they helped build the infrastructure, but Bhutan's needs are quite small, so the export of electrical power is big business. Indeed, the title of this chapter refers to an article in a 2012 edition of *Newsweek*. The article reported on a huge power outage in India, which affected nearly half the population. Who came to the rescue - Bhutan, and as Newsweek subsequently somewhat pithily, yet appropriately, commented: 'now let's hear it for that tiny country'.

India also uses Bhutan strategically in order to keep China within its own borders. This is particularly true in the Haa Valley, in the north-west. That valley is effectively a joint Bhutanese and Indian army camp. Ostensibly, it has been created for Bhutan, but it is clear who is in charge. In all this, it should not be forgotten that the country sports a great natural defence: the Himalayas themselves. That said, people still cross the border for trade purposes, mainly using yaks or mules. It must be a tough, tough journey.

In addition to the India problem, China has a huge distraction in the region: Tibet. In China's eyes, the area is an integral part of

China (despite its rather pompous and wholly inappropriate name: 'Tibet Autonomous Region'). Recently, young people, mainly novice monks and nuns, have conducted the practice of self-immolation in an attempt to draw world attention to what they see as their plight. The Chinese have systematically repressed Buddhism in Tibet, and most of the monasteries were destroyed in the early days of annexation. In addition, many thousands of Han Chinese people have been encouraged to move to Tibet – thus, the culture, language, and religion of a once proud and independent country are being diluted and effectively extinguished. The world's reaction has been slow and poor; though perhaps that is not surprising in view of the military might and economic power of China. In response to the self-immolators, the Chinese have attempted to lock down Tibet to outside tourists. Those who do manage to get in are carefully monitored and their movement is highly restricted. There is, of course, a public denial of these actions on the part of the Chinese authorities.

Back on the Bhutanese side of the border, another key date was the year they joined the International Postal Union in 1969. (That was the year after I left school to start work.) In 1971, Bhutan joined the United Nations. A current quirky fact is that, in order to secure UN financial support, the country's population had to exceed one million. Bhutan's population has never been anywhere close to that number. In view of its poverty and lack of proper records, though, population numbers are difficult to ascertain, particularly when allowing for the large numbers of migrant workers from Bengal, Nepal, Bangladesh, and other countries in the region. Despite those uncertainties, the population is thought to be around eight hundred thousand people, but the UN allows the country to conveniently claim it has one million.

Going further back in time, the Shabdrung built the majority of the twenty dzong fortresses in the country during the seventeenth century. Most have survived to form both the centre of the local monastic operations and also the seat of the local government. Very sadly, one of the oldest and most beautiful, at Wangdiphodrong, was destroyed by a suspected electrical fire in 2012. The prime minister announced, almost immediately, that it would be rebuilt in the original style. They are going to need help and lots of it, both financially and technically, but I am sure they will be successful in the end.

The dzongs were built originally for the same purpose as the castles that were erected throughout England, Wales, Scotland, and Ireland: military suppression. In view of their dual function today, these are places where the government requires respect to be demonstrated, and no Bhutanese can enter them without wearing national dress (and in the case of the temple within the dzong, they must additionally wear a white 'kabney' or shawl).

Church and state have always been close in this country, certainly since the days of the Shabdrung. This closeness is reflected in the two-colour flag: yellow for monarchy and state, orange for the Monk Body. And the flag has a ferocious rampant dragon at its centre. Next to the king, the most powerful man in the country is the Je Kempo, the most senior religious figure. His powers are virtually equal to those of the king, and he is respected in comparable fashion.

The Tibetan form of tantric Buddhism practised in Bhutan places a lot of stock in the belief in and respect for deities and superstition. This means, in practice, that the king and state government will always listen to religious astrologers before making decisions or scheduling events. As an outsider, this seems to be an integral part of the karma that palpably prevails in and supports the backbone of this unique country.

It is often said, including by the natives, that the Bhutanese are lazy, and that nothing ever gets done. There is, I suppose, an element of truth to both of those statements, but the 'laziness' is probably more attributable to the severe poverty in the country than anything else. That is somewhat ironic considering the excellent education that is available to the Bhutanese people throughout the country even in its remotest parts. Although there is a general and increasingly large migration from more rural parts to bigger towns, especially Thimphu, this is still a country of farmers and poor people eking out a living off the land and bartering with nearby villages. Recent government measures have recognised the need to bring the country to the people rather than vice versa. Everywhere you go in rural Bhutan, you will see 'farm roads' diverging from the sealed roads, often going up impossibly steep inclines. These roads were built to provide access to remote communities and individual homes which make accessibility to markets and medical care more practical, and they make it easier for the children to attend school.

Running alongside the ever-evolving programme is the government target to bring electricity to all Bhutanese people anticipated to be completed by the end of 2014. As has been seen, the country has a surplus of hydro-electric power, but not all Bhutanese people have access to it. Things *are* changing, though. On my recent trip to the remote east, mobile phones and kids logging into Facebook were not unusual sights. But seeing such things seemed a little incongruous, and perhaps even a little strange, when paired with people wearing traditional dress. Perhaps it seems strange because I am a 'chilip' (foreigner)! Things might move slowly in this land, but they do nevertheless continue to change. As I have previously observed, the Bhutanese are fully aware of what is happening in the wider world, and that knowledge motivates them to bring about change from within.

The government certainly sees the development of tourism as a key part of this change, and there are very ambitious plans to increase the number of visitors to one hundred thousand within the next five years. Most people I have spoken to – including those connected with the tourist sector – deemed this an unattainable target simply because the infrastructure is not developed enough. It looks like ambition has made some blind to reality. However, this nation can achieve high tourist numbers and other equally ambitious targets if it sets its mind to it. You will read in the sixth chapter of this book an account of my visit during the 2008 coronation. The display, which was put on for the benefit of the country, rather than to impress the rest of the world, was indeed really very impressive, and visually was a feat that any country would have been justifiably proud about.

Bhutan was afforded two wildcard entries at the London Olympics in 2012, which were made available to smaller countries. Two female entrants participated, one in archery and one, somewhat surprisingly, in rifle shooting. Neither got through the first round, but one met the Queen in the Olympic Village during an unannounced walkabout, which very understandably made the trip for her. Perhaps the Queen had been briefed by her enigmatic, esoteric eldest son Charles, who had in fact been to Bhutan and by all reports rather enjoyed his time there. Looking at his other interests and causes, this should come as no surprise.

Speaking of getting things done, I commented elsewhere that the Bhutanese are not to be messed with. Although this statement is largely historical, there have been recent and dramatic events that support such a statement notably in two situations: one heroic, another rather less so. The north-eastern Indian states of West Bengal, Assam, and the even more remote Manipur have persistently been in conflict with Delhi. They feel left out, forgotten, underfunded, and disrespected when it comes to central government help. It is not surprising to see why when one looks at a map of India. The aforementioned areas are indeed remote, and there is only one narrow access point to reach the rest of India, near Darjeeling. And Darjeeling has its own independence aspirations, caused by the Bangladesh land squeeze. Indeed, many outside folk looking at the map of India would be surprised to see that those areas are part of India at all.

In recent times, insurgency has been rife, particularly in Assam. Random terrorist attacks have taken place throughout the state and its populous capital, Guwarhati. The news of such matters tends to be suppressed by the Indian government (and greatly restricts the ability of foreigners to travel to these remoter states). The Assamese insurgents set up bases outside India, in the subtropical rainforests of southern Bhutan in the early years of this century. Rightly or wrongly, the Bhutanese took great offence to this incursion on their territory. In truth, it may have been pointed out to them by their mighty neighbour and financial buttress (India) that the presence of these insurgents in their territory was not a good idea, though somehow I doubt that.

As I have recorded elsewhere, the Bhutanese are a proud nation, and they have never been ruled or invaded by another nation, apart from a short, disputed, and ineffective spell by the British. So literally led from the front by K4, they set about doing something about these incursions, and very effectively too. In 2003, the king led his Bhutanese forces (numbering a little under seven thousand) on a short campaign to root out the insurgents from the dense, tropical forests in the south. Eleven Bhutanese and countless insurgents lost their lives. All the dead are remembered by the one hundred and eight stupas of the Druk Wangyal chortens, set at the summit of the Dochu La Pass. Earlier, during two fateful days in December of 2000, insurgents had killed fifteen Bhutanese people and injured nineteen more, mostly women and children. As mentioned previously, as gentle as they are, the Bhutanese are not to be crossed, and doubtless this earlier provocation set the tone for their tough action in 2003. As preparations were made for what became known to the Bhutanese as the 'Two-Day Low-Intensity Conflict' in 2003, K4 addressed his nation in a somewhat Shakespearean style in his call to arms:

'If volunteers are reluctant and hesitant, they will demoralise the other volunteers and regular soldiers. However, if they are genuine in their patriotism and love for their country, and are truly ready to sacrifice their lives for their country, they will be a motivating force for all security troops. Such men are needed today by their country.'

The people responded, and this elegant poem was penned by one:

> I can hear the distant thunder
> And I rise up to its call
> I can feel a stirring in my soul
> A voice so soft yet clear
> Whispers of truth and of love
> Freedom, courage to stand tall
> Love for my King, my country
> To them I will give my all

From Henry V's battle cry on St Crispin's Day to Lord Kitchener's 'pointing finger' on the recruiting poster in the First World War, these sorts of sentiments, right or wrong, will be recognised by many for years to come.

The campaign was swift and successful, but there was no dancing in the streets. Death is not a friend of the Bhutanese, and they expressed regret and empathy with the very insurgents they had been fighting and as K4 remarked afterwards: 'there is no pride in war.'

The other situation was not so savoury, and the legacy of this particular problem lives on (though it is largely suppressed by the Bhutanese government and ignored by the majority of the citizens.) Again, it involves the south, where a large number of Nepali people had settled in the country. They were seen, perhaps a little unfairly, by the Bhutanese authorities as a burden on the country. They were deemed incapable and unwilling to integrate into Bhutanese culture, and they failed to learn the language or respect the Buddhist traditions of Bhutan. Some violence accompanied this conflict and, in 1988, Bhutan evicted some Nepali-speaking residents from southern Bhutan. International refugee authorities say that upwards of a hundred thousand people were displaced as a result and sent to camps in Nepal and northern India. The camps became full and unsanitary, and the conditions created resentment among those being held there. After years of negotiations, some Nepali-speaking Bhutanese people were allowed to return. However the problem was still far from resolved. If all legitimate folk had been allowed to return to Bhutan, their presence would greatly upset the demographics and economics of the country. Despite the good karma I have often referred to, this was a seemingly intractable problem that most Bhutanese, and indeed the Bhutanese government, would rather ignore but it must be addressed.

During a later trip it was suggested to me that gross national happiness was estimated to be running at eighty per cent. I am sure that statistic does not apply to the Nepali people in Bhutan. The problem has not gone away and certainly has not been properly dealt with by the Bhutanese. It is still seen as a running sore, and rightly so.The Bhutanese strategy which effectively entails ignoring the problem does the nation no favours and cannot go on forever. I am a little surprised that the UN has not taken a tougher line on the issue. My driver on my trip in 2008 (Wangchen) was married to a Nepali girl, and I gained a little insight into this seemingly insoluble problem. Yet, this was a far cry from the situation in 1935, when British traveller C J Morris reported the following to the Royal Geographical Society:

'The Bhutan Government does not in any way interfere with its Nepalese settlers, and provided they pay their taxes they are entirely free to live as they wish.' (C.J.Morris, 'A Journey in Bhutan', *The Geographical Journal*, Vol 86, No.3, 1935.)

There is one more story that will bring this section to a close on a more positive note for the Bhutanese people. Although both Tibet and Bhutan practise tantric Buddhism (which began in Tibet), the two countries have never got along. There have been military skirmishes, which the Bhutanese have managed to walk away from mostly unscathed. The battle 'Victory over Tibet' saw the Bhutanese accomplish exactly that in 1647, and the event is recognised by the dzong bearing that name ('Drukgyel') which is at the head of the Paro Valley. Sadly, that grand edifice, set in a very striking position, was destroyed by fire in the early 1950s, but its substantial carcass remains. It is a magnificent site, and it is the starting-point for many a trek into the high Himalayas. It stands guard to the passes leading to Gasa, Jhomolhari, and the Snowman trek. It is a suitable gateway to protect all these treasures for the country.

Tiny country or not, where do the Bhutanese go from here in the rapidly changing twenty-first century? They are not going to stop folk from visiting their country in search of the last Shangri-La. This host of people includes the Hollywood faithful who always seem to seek out such places. Notable among those are Leonardo DiCaprio, and his mother, (as supporters of the World Wildlife Fund) and Keira Knightly. After he lost the American presidential election to Obama, the defeated Republican candidate, John McCain, went to Bhutan for some peace and solitude. There was no better place!

However, famous people visiting the country will not solve its problems. This was probably the thinking of K4, when he announced in March, 2005 that he would be establishing a democratic process in 2008. The new style of government would replace the benign, autocratic mode of ruling championed by the Wangchuck Dynasty. In addition, he said he would step down from the throne in 2006 and hand over the crown to his son. His son, who had been partly educated in the West, including a spell at Oxford, was only twenty-six years old at the time. K4's main reasoning for his unpopular set of decisions was that his son had youth on his side and the skill-set to take the country into the twenty-first century. K4 embarked on a nationwide tour, mainly on foot, to address the people directly and persuade them that it was the right thing to do. K5 was crowned in November, 2008.

K5 certainly did have youth on his side, which complemented by his good looks and the easy charm that he had with folk of all generations, garnered him widespread popularity. Although perhaps not directly relevant to Bhutan, he gathered a vast female fan base in Asia. They must have been sad when he married his childhood sweetheart, Jetsun Pema, an airline pilot's daughter. It was a very colourful ceremony, shown throughout the world in 2011. Time will tell whether K4's forward-thinking plan was correct, but whatever happens, I believe that these structural changes had to happen. The creation of an elected government was an un-ticked box, and now that it has been created, it seems to be working quite well. Their previous Prime Minister (the 'Lyonchoen') Jigme y Thinley, had begun to gain a worldwide profile. He had travelled extensively and spoken a great deal about the concept of gross national happiness, which has now been formally adopted by the UN. Many countries, including the United Kingdom, have embraced these ideals. 'Let's hear it again for this tiny country'!

The K5 has travelled officially to India and Japan, and unofficially elsewhere, including the United Kingdom. The unofficial nature of such visits does not reflect a lack of respect on either side; rather, because Bhutan cannot afford to reciprocate such lavish welcoming parties, even if they wanted to. India and Japan are strong financial supporters of Bhutan, so the situation with them is different. But even so thus far, only India has been afforded the equivalent of a state visit.

Indeed, the Indian president was received formally at the time of the coronation of K5. These celebrations included throngs of children waving flags along the cavalcade route, just as one might see in the United Kingdom.

Perhaps K5's more important visits, like his father before him, were to his people. He has made it clear that he wants to visit all parts of the kingdom and meet as many of his people as he can during his reign. That will mean long, arduous, and time-consuming journeys, many of them on foot. He has already shown that he is good at such acts. He is a good listener, and his charm works on young and old alike. Though not held in god-like reverence by his people, he is very much respected and loved. With all these attributes, I think that K4's decision was right, and that his son was indeed the right man to take Bhutan through the door into the 21st century. As I see it, the key is currently in the lock, but it has yet to be turned. I am confident, however, that it will be turned successfully.

This country has much going for it, as indicated by K4's espousing of GNH. The country wrestles with extreme poverty on the one hand and a deep richness of character and culture on the other. In his own words, he encapsulated these thoughts in this one simple sentence: 'we are a poor country and have nothing to offer to the world but our spirit and culture, but we do this freely for the benefit of the world as well as ourselves.' These sincere thoughts were deeply held by both himself and his subjects. One only needs to travel to any high mountain pass in any Himalayan country – particularly Tibet, Nepal, or Bhutan – to see the ubiquitous prayer flags blowing in the wind, sending their prayers for peace and karma into the world. The rest of us are gifted indeed by these selfless actions, and we should learn from them.

Thus although it is a tiny, poor country seemingly in the throes of irresolvable ethnic problems, many countries are plagued by similar difficulties. At around position one hundred and fifty five on the world's Gross Domestic Product listing, the country certainly is impoverished but no less positive or forward thinking for it. In 2013, the country announced that its agriculture would become wholly organic, a unique and landmark development that neatly fits in one of the key tenets of GNH. Despite the apparent poverty, travellers do not usually pay much attention to it after journeying through the social maelstrom that is India in order to get there. Bhutanese folk are polite, well dressed, and always ready to show a winning smile. Surprisingly there is virtually no begging or complaining. Most of the country has access to clean water, and, very shortly all will have access to electricity. Additionally, a reasonable level of healthcare and education is provided to all citizens.

It has built a nascent legal system based on Western culture from scratch. Until comparatively recently, power, wisdom, and autocratic justice was meted out by the king, chiefs, and dignitaries throughout the land based on the tenets of GNH. It was really quite feudal in concept. It was similar in neighbouring Tibet when the Chinese invaded in 1950: although the Tibetan people were treated cruelly, the Chinese insisted that their action was needed to rid the country of feudalism, epitomised in their view, by the Dalai Lama. Although never conquered by outside forces, Bhutan remained totally isolated. By the late 1950s, it was the last state in the modern world with a political entity that was almost totally unknown and ignored by the rest of the world. When K3 came to the throne in 1953, Tibet had already been invaded by China; and thus he felt it was due time for Bhutan to 'come out' as a nation, and he nailed the colours of improvement to the transport infrastructure and education to his mast.

Although the Shabdrung had established the law in a text carved into slate at the entrance to Punakha dzong, a more developed and sophisticated system was clearly needed. K3 created a National Assembly for the first time in 1953, which included elected representatives, members of the monastic body, and other high civil servants. Over the next five years, those people created the Supreme Laws, which was the codification of civil and criminal law. In the 1960s, a two-tier court system was established with twenty district courts and a high court of last resort, and a Chief Justice was appointed. Initially, however, local judges lacked any formal education and learned the ropes and the law as clerks of the courts, before being promoted to dispense the law in their own right.

Fast forward forty years found the *Civil and Criminal Procedure Code* enacted in 2001. Although clearly Anglo-American in context, the chief justice espoused that it mirrored the national soul by enshrining the principles of their culture and religion. There are, thus far, no western-trained lawyers in private practice in Bhutan. The exercise of law still tends to be left in the hands of elders, especially in rural areas. Until as recently as 1996, these local people had no formal legal training but since then there are now national courses available.

The past decade has seen increased professionalism on the part of those exercising the law, particularly in the capital and in southern Bhutan. Western experts have been invited to advise and provide educational assistance. In particular, mediation is being extensively used, pushed along by the faith placed in GNH. The concept of mediation in a non-legal sense has a strong foundation in Bhutan, even if, over the centuries, it was not known by that name. There were social pressures to settle differences in this way, which was considered a virtuous deed. Mediation certainly comes before any referral to the court process, something very much encouraged in western legal culture. What Bhutanese jurisprudence lacks in sophistication, it more than compensates in to its effectiveness, which is very Bhutanese I would say!

The capitalist model would not recognise that inner happiness and well-being cannot be bought with a high enough annual income. Truly however, money cannot buy love and happiness. Although they were reluctant at first, the people now have political freedom and full access to the World Wide Web. But it is their inner spirit and resilience that is the key. It is a difference visitors immediately feel upon entering this very special country. Surely, we can all learn something from the people who live in this tiny and beautiful place. After all, we do not have to be rich to be right or happy!

CHAPTER 4

DRUK YUL,
THE KINGDOM OF THE
THUNDER DRAGON

'The stages of the quest are fairly well defined. First the aspiration
toward spiritual growth manifests itself in a man's heart.'

Paul Brunton, Notebooks Vol 1 Perspectives

It was by now April 2007, and Dum Dum Airport at Kolkata seemed
like an old friend. Asif greeted me straightaway in the, still decrepit,
arrivals hall: 'it is an honour that you visit us again.' I was thinking:
'no, surely it is the other way around'.

The new group assembled: tour guide Carol from Oxfordshire; Edgar
and Mary, friendly folk from the West Midlands (he immediately
loaned me a dollar so I could tip my porter); Karen from Portsmouth,
a lady whose mail for this trip had somewhat mystifyingly been
sent to my home; Ian from Blackheath London, who came without
his partner since she was pregnant; Polly and Sophie, sisters, also
from London; Maria, from Lisbon; together with Amanda, Jackie,
and Jill, who were all ready and raring to go on this adventure; and

finally Katrina, readying for a holiday herself, as her husband and daughter were separately on their way to Kanchenjunga base camp, via Darjeeling.

After the familiar drive to the Tolley Club, it felt good to be back (though the mosquitoes thought so too.). As with last year's Wild Frontiers tour, the party was an eclectic mix: the nice, the straightforward, and the esoteric. There were coincidences too: Katrina and her husband, Peter, had once lived in my former home village in Buckinghamshire. Peter's brother, Mike, who was also on the base camp trip, was interested in railways, as was I, and so apparently was the sisters' father. There seemed to be a lot of 'us' about.

Carol was completely different from Sue, and far less authoritarian. In fact, she appeared at first glance to be a little scatty, but she turned out to be a great and knowledgeable tour leader. Her specialist subject was Tibet, and we soon had a nice chat about the Buddhist 'Red Hats' and their base in Kalimpong, India. Everyone, except me, went off into Calcutta for the classic tour of the sight-seeing sites, I had done all that in the previous year, so I stayed in and rested.

The Tolley did not look quite as it did last year, partly because the favourite golfer's bar was being refurbished, or was it perhaps that return visits are never quite the same. Maria observed, in her inimitable Portuguese style, that it was nothing at all like the place displayed on their website. Still, the grounds remained as I recalled them, peaceful and full of exotic birds, beautiful trees and shrubs. I was so inspired that I bought the book detailing all the fifty bird species on site. Apparently, there were an equal number of tree specimens.

The early trek to the airport was pushed back for a while because an extra flight had been laid on for the Paro Festival in Bhutan. I hoped that we could still get in before the noon landing curfew (in fact that had long since been dispensed with, but I was unaware of that at the time) and that we would be on one of the new aircraft recently acquired by the Bhutanese national airline, Drukair, (namely the Airbus A319).

We all met up again for dinner that evening at the Belvedere, and I had a lovely, long chat with Carol about Salim, my sponsored child in Kolkata. I had been so fortunate to have actually met him at the end of my last trip to India. It had been a salutary visit to the slums and to meet both Salim and his mother, siblings and friends, who were living in tents on the pavement on a very busy street. They had all been taken under the care of the Calcutta Samaritans, who were doing a wonderful job caring for their health, education and general well-being. Carol explained that she supported a Bhutanese school, with the aid of Pema, the guide we had met on our last trip. I said that I would love to help as well and, as we talked more, Carol made the suggestion that we visit a monastery near Thimphu, where she had seen young monks shivering in the cold there during the previous November. She had since raised money to buy fleeces for them all, and everyone on the current tour group had donated new pairs of long socks.

I had travelled into Bhutan over land the previous year and as we were to fly into Paro this year I began to feel a little trepidation about the flight, as I had heard that it has one of the most difficult civil landing approaches in the world. (A visit to YouTube would prove my point.) We arrived at Kolkata Airport (CCU) and suitably positioned ourselves in the queue with the hope of securing the world-famous left-hand seats, which provide superb views of the Himalayas on a clear day. We had successfully fought off the European hordes just as a frenetic party of Japanese tourists arrived, further adding to the chaos.

Our scheduled departure time came and went, adding to my tension. While waiting, though, I met the Japanese party tour leader, Daishi. Eventually, flight KB211 (indeed an A319) arrived, and we grabbed those coveted seats. And then we were off on the fifty-minute flight across the gangetic plain to Bhutan. Everest, I swear it was, and Kanchenjunga, appeared on cue, stage left, and what wonders they were to behold. There was a palpable sense of excitement in the aircraft and, sadly, the photos taken did not do the spectacle justice. It was a surreal, magical, albeit brief, moment, and I felt blessed simply to have been there seeing those incredible and exhilarating sights. Suddenly, after a warning from the cockpit about 'slight to moderate turbulence' because of the clouds and wind, we descended into Bhutanese airspace and headed down towards Paro airport. We descended through cloud and threaded our way through the valleys, seemingly skipping across the ridges. It was a spectacular experience, and as we flew into the valley I immediately recognised it from my last visit. The pilot executed a sharp 180-degree turn within the valley itself, and as we flew past the dzong it felt as if we could almost touch it. Banking sharply again to finally align with the runway we finally touched down. What an exhilarating entrance into Bhutan and an unforgettable start to our journey it had been. As we disembarked most of us just stood still on the tarmac, somewhat shell-shocked by it all, but we all agreed that it had the best way to arrive, though I would not have wanted to miss the wonderful road journey through Kamji in the previous year.

Eventually, after we had negotiated our way through passport control, I immediately saw Pema, who was waiting for us. He greeted me like a long-lost friend, and it really felt simply great to be back. Soon we went off to that same farmhouse further up the valley. We had a new assistant guide, Dawa, a nephew of Pema, and a different driver, Sonam. I found myself in a single room in the main farmhouse, rather than in last year's bunkhouse block. Carol and Pema told us that the festival was making accommodation difficult to come by, so having a single room was a definite bonus. However all this passed me by as I simply felt sheer joy and everything just seemed that it was meant to be.

After lunch, we went to the National Museum, situated above the airport in an old watchtower and located in a very impressive location. I had not visited this before, so this was exciting for me. I bumped into Daishi again; he was leading his own group around the museum too. We talked about the early morning unveiling of the 'Great Paro Thangka' and agreed that we might cross paths again there. Heading back to the farmhouse we had a raucous dinner and great conversation about our trip experiences thus far, and life generally. The group was beginning to gel nicely, and I felt it was going to be a good trip, though we still had a very long way to travel together.

I was up before the rest and wandered down to the Paro riverside for a glorious, early morning walk. On my return I was walking back up the rough road that led to our farmhouse lodging when I saw a prayer flag bedecked stupa, a Buddhist shrine containing reverent artefacts, and often used as a place to offer up prayers. The early morning mist was swirling, and the smoke from pine cones and branches being offered up as an act of faith by a local, was drifting into the still air. The scent was intoxicating and I immediately felt spiritually uplifted, as I often had in this very special country. Two young kids were playing nearby, one on his bicycle, and they stopped at the sight of a tourist clearly slightly overcome with emotion. We exchanged a few words of greeting, in Bhutanese, and then happy smiles lit their faces. Afterwards our whole group drove further up the valley to the ruined dzong at Drukgyel, (which commemorated Bhutan's victory over an earlier attempted invasion by Tibet). From there we saw the magnificent snow-capped mountain Jhomolhari, standing at over 24,000 feet, it the second highest peak in Bhutan. It seemed to stand alone and thus made for a very striking view, even though it was quite some way off, in fact it takes a three-day trek from this spot to reach base camp. We actually saw some of the trekking horses and mules near the ruined dzong, and I could only think the simple, obvious but nevertheless awe-inspiring thought: 'this really is the Himalayas!'

On the walk back from the dzong, we witnessed a local archery match. Contested with vigour over a 150-metre range, the shooting of the arrows was accompanied by much yelping from the participants, spectators, and animals in the vicinity. After witnessing these sporting skills, we were off to the tsechu (festival) ground, which was as impressive as ever. It seemed somehow different though, perhaps because the shop stalls had been removed from the approaches in order to keep the religious ambience intact. The somewhat less frenetic atmosphere that resulted was a shame, but I was a visitor and this was their festival.

I joined the seemingly mad long queue in to obtain one of the sunki cords that were being blessed by the lama. It was a chaotic scene, but it was a great place to photograph the dancers. I met a local boy in the line and we chatted about Liverpool FC, whom he supported, as indeed I did, some coincidence I thought. Bumped into Daishi again, and we chatted again about Bhutan and his home in Tokyo, and he made the nice suggestion that I should perhaps visit there someday.

I met with some very pleasant Americans and we agreed that we all loved Bhutan and its people. Most other tourists we bumped into displayed similar permanent smiles and felt pretty much the same way: very happy, privileged and blessed to be there. Our group then adjourned to the market back in town, where we all tried to spend some of our local currency (the 'ngultrum', which was issued on simply beautiful bank notes). This was especially so in Jill's case – apparently her apartment in Hong Kong was going to be 'Bhutanised!' We had another good evening at the farmhouse before turning in for an early night in anticipation of the very early departure for the ceremony of unveiling the thangka; it had been quite a day.

We all got up early, as planned, however the short journey to the ceremony was abruptly blocked by an early morning road accident, which was quite unusual in Bhutan despite the seemingly wild driving habits. As we had been slightly delayed, there was a rush to make it up the steps opposite the dzong to see the thangka being brought out. We passed a particular group of tourists that seemed to be rather over-zealously guarding their seating territory, which I thought was not in keeping with the ambient karma of the occasion. Daishi was sitting on some nearby steps with his group, a coincidence again, though I was thinking: 'good timing and good positioning Pema'. The ceremony took place and most of our ladies seemed to enjoy it, though Maria appeared singularly unimpressed, and although I had seen it all last year it remained a very moving and impressive spectacle nevertheless. I spent most of the ceremony behind the lama's dais and thus saw and heard his deep intonations. Seemingly not as deep as his intonations of last year, though perhaps that was due to the poor positioning of his microphone, but I nevertheless had a reasonable view of the proceedings. I then joined the queue to actually touch the unfurled thangka. This appeared to be even more frenetic than last time, though I found it to be similarly worthwhile, moving and exhilarating.

Afterwards we departed for the ever spectacular trek up to the Tiger's Nest. It was a particularly warm day and heavier clothing dispensed with as we pounded up the steeply graded path. Polly, Sophie, Jackie and Ian actually reached the Nest itself, which comprises a small temple overseen by a small group of monks, together with Pema and Dawa, whilst the rest, including me, rather lazily retreated to the café for some refreshments. Needless to say, Daishi was there too together with his group. As we picked up on our previous conversations he commented, somewhat amusingly, that he thought that I was the tour leader for our group! As we retreated back to the farmhouse in order to pack up our things for the drive to the capital the next day, a sudden, unusually strong squall swept through the area. We found that the upgrade works on the road to Thimphu were still not complete, and the journey still quite slow; in fact, it appeared to be pretty much as I recalled it was the last year, though made worse by the additional works being carried out on the road south, to India. All these road works were scheduled to be completed by November 2008, so as to be in time for the coronation though this seemed like a very ambitious goal.

Once again, we were to stay at the Hotel Pedling, however this time I was to share a room, with Ian, which turned out to be an interesting experience. 'I have not shared a room since I was in the barracks twenty-five years ago, old boy!' he observed. We had a very interesting discussion, though I did not find out what he did for a living. 'I cannot tell you that, old boy,' he remarked. Still, I did hear all about his various lovers and children!

Actually, it was not a bad night's sleep despite the room-share, though I wondered whether I had kept Ian awake with my snoring – which apparently he had heard through the farmhouse wall on the nights spent there. We had arrived late the night before, and as we were not staying a second night, I found that, yet again, I was not able to visit the cinema. Whilst disappointed I resolved that I must come back yet again so that I could hopefully do so. I saw the cinema building from the outside though. It appeared quite ordinary, slightly scruffy, though covered with colourful, and somewhat gaudy, film posters. I felt even more intrigued to look inside.

Our destination that morning was the Dechen Phodrang monastery, situated high above the Royal Palace, which was where Carol had mentioned she had seen the 'shivering monks'. One of the taxis carrying members of the group went to the wrong place, so were quite delayed, but fortunately many of us were able to see Carol monks, together with their warm red fleeces, and were able to personally give our donation of socks to them. Carol's contact there was a Bhutanese business woman, apparently connected with steel industry. This lady seemed to take a shine to me and said that I must indeed return to Bhutan and that if I did, she would personally introduce me to the recently retired king (K4), whom she knew well. We saw some of the five hundred, or so, poor (and in many cases, orphaned) novice monks, who were aged four to fifteen years. They were all receiving a disciplined primary education here, and appeared to be well fed and cared for. They also looked very striking in their bright red robes. We were allowed to visit some of their classrooms in which a variety of skills were being taught, often using the rote method, seemingly threatened with the cat-o'-nine tails, though very fortunately we did not see that being inflicted. They slept, worked, learnt, and played in those rooms, keeping what few personal possessions they had with in small trunks, which were piled in corners in each of the classrooms, which in turn also doubled as their dormitories. These sights were all too much for Jill, in particular, who spontaneously broke down in tears; it was all very emotional.

Apparently, K4 supported these monks as well and spent some of his time tending to the gardens there. He had always lived life frugally, choosing to live in a small house in the palace grounds when he was king, rather than in the palace itself. So his work here, in a location very close to his own home, complimented his own lifestyle very well. We began to understand why he was so popular with his people. Afterwards, we adjourned back to Thimphu and went to the GPO, for the stamp buying tradition, before departing for Wangdue, via the Dochu La Pass. On the way up to the top of the pass, we stopped at the Huntscho Community School, which Carol also supported through her charitable work. As with our time spent at the Peshok Tea Estate School in Assam during the previous year's tour, we were freely invited into the classrooms to mingle with the kids. It was a simply amazing experience which, for political correctness reasons, would never have been allowed in the United Kingdom. The photographs we took during that time spoke for themselves. Each time any of us took a photograph we were mobbed by the kids whilst striving to see themselves on the camera screen. It was a very sad moment when it was time to leave. Driving down the other side of the pass we arrived at Wangdue, and this time went to the Hotel Tashling near the market square. Sadly, we were not going to be staying in the marvellous Kichu Resort by the glacial river that I fondly recalled from last year. There was certainly no emphasis on luxury here, as had been promised in the trip brochure. However I had my own room, though I feared I would be back to sharing again before the journey was over.

After nearly a week with my new friends, it was now nearly time for the tour to strike out into new and unexplored territory for me, so I privately relaxed in the hotel bar and surveyed the different personalities. Carol, the tour leader, was always full of good stories and indeed, good causes. She was totally non-interventionist, perhaps too much so at times. She had travelled extensively, especially to the Mount Kailash area in Tibet, a particularly favourite spot for her, and in fact she was pretty much an expert in all matters pertaining to Tibet. She was also very keen to give something back to each of those places she felt privileged to have visited, which was a sentiment with which I totally empathised.

Amanda, whilst holding a senior position in the education world, was still really a hands-on teacher at heart. She had a superb sense of humour, often reducing us to fits of uncontrolled laughter. She lived in Pembrokeshire, a part of Wales familiar to me, as my own family had holidayed many times there in my youth.

Edgar and Mary were from the West Midlands, and he loved his bacchanalian comforts just as much as I did. In fact they had come along armed with a keg of wine for the journey, which seemed to be a wise move. He had recently been diagnosed with diabetes. They were very well-travelled and just lovely people. We seemed to hit it off immediately, and later on in the tour very kindly said that they would like to travel with me again in the future.

Jill was from Hong Kong, where I understood she lived the expat life with some high-powered job in marketing. She was a self-admitted 'shopaholic', but she had a wonderfully generous heart.

The sisters, Polly and Sophie were similarly easy going likeable characters too. Polly lived near my brother, Robin, in Tooting, London. They seemed to act just like my dear friends, the Shrimpton sisters, and seemed similarly very close and empathetic.

Jackie, from Buxton, was married, but she travelled on her own because her husband did not like overseas travel. She was a dance teacher, classically blond, who acted the dumb part rather too well, even though she most certainly was not. She was great fun, thoughtful, and considerate.

Karen, from Portsmouth, was a senior nursing sister. Coincidentally, she often did hospital theatre work at Southampton General Hospital, supporting the senior registrar there, Keith, who had been to the same secondary school as me. She had also worked abroad, particularly in Saudi Arabia, where she had personally tended to the late king. She was an excellent photographer and a particularly well-organised person, and was always interesting company during the trip.

Katrina, from Chester, looked and spoke uncannily just like, my boss's wife. She and her husband had three children, the youngest, Tom, was nineteen and apparently quite a handful. 'Simply no interests' she once observed, and it was clear that he frustrated her no end. I once rather cruelly suggested to her that he needed a spell of discipline at the dzong might be an option!

Maria hailed from Lisbon. How could one describe Maria? Well for a start, she was eccentric and very single-minded. Her time living in the grandest Portuguese social circles had left her with plenty of fascinating tales to tell about that, so she was great to have around – though she was definitely the group's outsider.

Ian, from Blackheath, was currently with his third partner, and she was expecting his third child but her first, I think. His other kids were Laura and Harry, each by different mothers. Emma wanted to come to Bhutan, but she could not as she was pregnant. He did not want to come, but did! Definitely not a group traveller though, he was complicated and slightly odd, but underneath the facade, he was pleasant enough, though difficult to get to know, possibly a result of his schooling at Fetties, though I never really found out.

After all that reflection on my fellow travellers, with whom I felt blessed to be taking this journey with me, I retired to bed. My last thought was of the cold shower that awaited me the next morning as there was no hot water in my room, just like it was in the monastery we had visited earlier perhaps.

Cold shower it indeed was, but I recovered over a good breakfast before heading off to Wangdue Phodrang dzong, which I particularly liked. Although most meals in Bhutan followed a similar format, breakfasts could almost be classed as near western as you could get here. I liked the healthy simplicity of Bhutanese food, though perhaps not the omni-present hot chillies, but to have some eggs and bread was very welcome. The dzong was just as I had remembered: old and unkempt, but well-positioned and somehow a little secretive. It seemed that it belonged more in mediaeval times. I wandered about and got cornered for a 'photo-op' by a novice monk. Actually I think he wanted one dollar and cried out: 'I have nothing!' After duly handing it over, he said he wanted 'five hundred dollars'. 'No can do' I said, 'but you will go far!' Top marks for cheek and entrepreneurialism, I thought, though if the dzong master had learned of his actions, I am sure he would have received a painful punishment.

We later visited the crown prince's temple, though this time we were able to go out onto the balcony near the top for a great view. After lunch in New Punakha, at the Pungthang Dechen restaurant, I posted a batch of postcards, from myself and others in the tour group. I suspect it was an unsuccessful outing for the local 'Postman Pat' as over a dozen of my cards never made it through. The post boxes in Bhutan are painted red in the style that I was familiar with, but the boxes themselves looked like recycled tin cans, somewhat precariously and randomly poised on the sides of buildings. I am not too sure what caused the postal hiatus that day, save to say that the infrastructure, and all that goes with it in Bhutan is stretched, and I am sure that the operation of the postal service in rural parts is not seen as a priority.

From there, we travelled to Punakha dzong, set in that simply splendid location I had seen previously, below the mountains and at the confluence of two rivers. I immediately thought that the coronation here next year was going to be simply spectacular. Whilst driving back, we stopped at a typical farmhouse to witness how local families lived and to take tea and the local hooch (ara).

I sat this particular visit out last year, which was a mistake, as it turned out to be similar to the privilege of visiting the novice monks near Thimphu, and the community school at Dochu La, and was an equally humbling experience. There were plenty of memorable moments, including playing games with the kids, one of whom I had nicknamed 'Marbles' as it appeared to be his favourite game. Tea and hooch were accompanied, much to the family's chagrin, by a very drunken granny who had been unwittingly let out of her room. Much giggling and shrieking ensued, particularly with Maria and Edgar. She definitely took a shine to Edgar, much to Mary's bemusement. It was one of many 'Bhutan moments' during which we all felt uneasy and at home in equal measure.

Back at the hotel, I chatted with Pema and Jill about the single accommodation drought, which we resolved, with Jill praising my diplomacy. Almost immediately, the 'fire men' from the dzong invaded the hotel. Not firefighters, but rather monks dressed in garish garbs waving fire-brands. They made a lot of noise and used the fire-brands to exorcise the evil spirits from the building. There was great commotion, whistling, and shouting with the full support of the large crowd following them, all overseen by the lama. Apparently it was an annual tradition here and was obviously much enjoyed by locals and tourists alike, some of whom were unexpectedly disturbed in their bedrooms during the proceedings!

We had another rowdy evening, this time in a local restaurant where great fun was had by all. 'What a wonderful couple Edgar and Mary are', I thought, but I was secretly hoping that they would break out their keg of Chilean merlot soon, as a long day's drive loomed ahead. As it turned out it took eleven hours for the seemingly short distance of one hundred and forty miles. There were twists, turns, hairpins, and very steep gradients on the route – all expertly navigated by our driver, Dorje. The spectacular scenery, which was difficult to photograph, included mountain passes, virgin forests, (allegedly home to the legendary Bengal Tigers), misty passes, and beautiful valleys. It was just a brilliant journey. On the way, we passed Chokhor Rabtentse (Trongsa dzong), the longest and most spectacularly positioned in the country, but sadly it turned out to be our shortest such visit. We did not stay long, which was a pity because the tantric chanting by the monks in the cavernous depths there was the best we had heard. Maria and I found it especially exhilarating and she was particularly annoyed to be dragged away by Pema, and the two seemed to subsequently fall out quite badly over this incident, which brought an unpleasant atmosphere to the group for a while.

It is an incredible place, and forms the effective border between central and east Bhutan. All journeys between these two areas had to go through the dzong itself, which clearly profited from this process. Sometime in the past, a group of British suffered unspeakable cruelty when captured in this area, and Pema explained, with some relish, that severed body parts were still kept somewhere deep inside the building!

We then drove into beautiful central Bhutan area and the Bumthang Valley system, and briefly stopped at a local crafts shop where I conversed with a young football mad boy called Thinley. The Bhutanese never ask for anything, but he asked me for some pens. Unfortunately, I did not have any, but he was mortified that he had asked me. He was so heartbreakingly respectful, though with a sense of fun too, so the situation did not become too awkward. As with so many young Bhutanese kids he spoke excellent English, and he was quite worldly, given his tender age and the fact that he had hardly travelled outside Chumey valley in Bumthang.

Arriving at the Rinchenling Lodge near Chamkar bazaar, we found ourselves at a Swiss-style lodge that had great rooms, which each featured a log-burning stove. Over a delicious supper of red rice, noodles and vegetables there was lots of amusing gossip, and fired along by shots of the lethal local gin, the earlier tensions of the day thankfully disappeared. It was a charge valiantly led by Carol, who was definitely 'on a roll'.

The next morning I was awoken really quite early by somebody coming into my room light the log-burning stove. I was somewhat surprised, but then gratified, as the room was soon warm after their ministrations, and it was clearly cold outside. We all took an early morning walk, first visiting the now-derelict first king's palace: Wangdicholing Phodrang, which ceased being used by the royal family in 1952. It was a simply wondrous place dominated by beautiful and colourful hues, mainly in various shades of blue. I thought that it must have been simply spectacular in its heyday. As we had a nurse in our group we dropped by the nearby regional hospital, which, like every other building, looks like a dzong. We were allowed to view parts of it, and it seemed like a clean and well-equipped facility.

We then walked across the nearby rice fields to 'Kurje Lhakhang', which is a very significant place for the Bhutanese people. Just like the Tiger's Nest, tradition had it that the Guru Rinpoche stopped here on his journey from India in order to conquer a local evil deity and, in doing so, introduced Buddhism into Bhutan. This is also the revered burial place of all the kings of the Wangchuck dynasty, and was also the farthest east Joanna Lumley had travelled on her journey retracing her grandfather's steps into this country. He had brought the Star of India medal to present to the then king (K2) as a gift of gratitude from the British government in India and as a reward for the help given to them by the Bhutanese in dealing with Tibetan skirmishes. This location was deemed by the king to be the right one for such an important occasion.

Continuing our walk, we came across the very old monastery, Thangi Lhakhang, which was founded in 1470. We saw Pema Lingpa's chain mail there, apparently a particularly significant national treasure. It was here that we all first took the 'holy water', dispensed from what appeared to be a pewter tea pot, which was a particularly inspiring and emotional moment. These feelings were to be replicated on all subsequent such occasions, and I found myself looking forward to receiving that special opportunity whenever it was proffered.

That afternoon we visited the nearby dzong at Jakar, which turned out to be yet another impressive location. From a distance across the nearby valley the design of the building looked like a large white bird with its wings spread wide. We climbed the difficult and very steep wooden steps up the central tower, but we were not allowed to go to the very top, which was a pity, as I am sure the view would have been spectacular. However we did reach small chapel, though only men were allowed inside, but we did not venture in because it was guarded by some fearsome wall hangings, whose origin I did not enquire about.

We wandered round the local market in Chamkhar bazaar and I watched three schoolboys liberate free condoms from a nearby store, which they promptly blew up like balloons for my bemusement! Back to the lodge Pema foreshadowed another early start for the drive to Mongar, one hundred and forty miles away. He explained that we would find it was rather like a frontier town, and indeed it did border on east Bhutan, which in turn was the remotest part of the country.

Our group was beginning to tire, and I thought that a break from travel and sightseeing was warranted. Here, in the Bumthang valley, was the real heart of Bhutan – and not just physically. It had an ethereal feel and was a beautiful and peaceful place, more open somehow than I imagined it would be, and quite different from the Paro and Thimphu valleys. Surprisingly, even our twenty-two-year-old guide Dawa, said he could see himself living here. We were getting into remoter territory and in fact this area had been pretty inaccessible until the east/west road was built across the country in the 1970s. Even when the king travels this way, he has to stay in modest local guest houses. The only university in Bhutan is located in the east, so the king, bureaucrats and politicians, who are just emerging into Bhutanese life, have no alternative when travelling in these parts. There was talk of opening an airport in this area but, at that time, no further steps had been taken with this project. This was a place that I felt we should tarry for a while, but our schedule demanded that we press on.

What a day the next one turned out to be; it was the best and most dramatic part of our journey so far. It was to take ten hours of tiring journeying to travel from Jakar to Mongar. We arrived to the sound of thunder during a Himalayan shower, 'how appropriate' I thought, given the fact that we were actually in the 'Kingdom of the Thunder Dragon'. We started our journey at the bazaar, passing some school marathon runners, and headed up into the remote Tang valley, stopping by a firebreak in the forest. We got off the bus there and walked downhill for a couple of miles into the village of Ura. It really was a major relief to simply get out of that bus, convinced, as I was, that it was built by the Japanese for distinctly smaller people, as it was very cramped. Anyway, Ura was lovely, made more so by a group of local children who treated us to some spontaneous singing. The village was ramshackle and clearly very poor. However it had an unmistakeable charm and the people, especially the kids, were very friendly. The kids clothes belied the poverty and were care-worn unlike we those we had witnessed our journey thus far.

We then drove over our first pass, since crossing Dochu La, at Shertang La (3590 m). Unfortunately, mist there similarly obscured the views, as it was usually possible to see Bhutan's highest peak from here, Gangkar Puensum (7541 m), but we could not see any mountains, which was a great pity. We then proceeded to the pass at Thrumshing La (3750 m), the highest on our whole trip, which actually is set in its own National Park. We hung out our own individual prayer flags there, and offered prayers, as is the tradition, in this moving place, which we still felt was very special despite the clouds. I had accidentally trodden on an obscured nail during our visit, and subsequently received plenty of attention from the ladies on the tour! We moved on again, and the scenery kept changing. We came out of the higher mountain passes and stopped at a picturesque field for a picnic, it looked just like a Swiss meadow. A small fire was lit by our drivers, and fiery noodles were served. There was also some western-style food available as well, which I really appreciated.

Nothing can quite describe the dramatic scenery or the precarious roads. There are high mountain passes, ravines, and valleys everywhere, but the sights are hard to photograph due to the ever present mist and clouds. During this section of our tour, we had passed through dense, virgin forest, allegedly home to the red panda. And then the landscape changed to deep valleys that were almost arid. Finally, we descended into a subtropical region on the final approach to Mongar. Alongside the roads, which were invariably very narrow and steep, we saw workers maintaining them, who lived where they worked, which often seemed to be many miles from any habitation.

On these high mountain passes, there were many signs of serious landslips and repairs were seemingly still ongoing from the impact of the previous year's monsoon season. One particular section appeared to be actively slipping down the very steep mountainside, though the workers seemed oblivious to the danger, despite signs indicating 'shooting rocks'. The road workers were apparently from India, Nepal and Bangladesh, as well as Bhutan. Most workers appeared to be women or boys, and worked all the time regardless of the weather. Living in rough-shod tents or hovels at the roadside, they invariably returned our smiles and waves, which we all deeply felt was a lesson in humanity for all of us, and I shed a tear at the sight of these folk on more than one occasion.

On the final approach to Mongar we were treated to what appeared to be a dress rehearsal for the new king's journey through this region, scheduled for the following day. Kids along the side of the road put on quite a show, and instead of simply waving, they offered supplicant arms to us, bent at their waists, and then stuck their tongues out. We were told that this was a great honour, but I was not so sure, and suspected it was a joke at our expense. I was assured by Pema that I was mistaken, and further explained that they would have been taught the routine at school that day.

The Druk Zhongar hotel in Mongar was a welcome pit stop, though not great, but it would certainly suffice for the night. A new hotel was being built nearby on a high spot at the entrance to the town, but was not yet open, though the positioning looked just superb. 'Perhaps next time?' I mused. We were all tired, though elated, after having seen so much variety on the journey that day. We had all particularly enjoyed the forest walk, the picnic, and the spectacular waterfall at Namling.

A short walk around Mongar the following morning proved that it was perhaps not such a bad place. A huge new hospital, serving central and eastern Bhutan, had been built here recently, and was clear that the town was an important crossroads in that region. Our journey that day was to take us via the Kori La Pass to Trashigang which was only sixty miles, and an anticipated four-hour drive, away. The scenery continued to impress, and in the somewhat amusing descriptive words of Pema, 'the pushed-up mountains' never ceased to amaze. We reached Trashigang – (what a great name!) – just in time for an al fresco lunch before wandering to the superbly positioned dzong.

Unlike me, I thought the group had become somewhat tired of visiting dzongs, which was a shame because each one was different, made especially so by the differing locations and people who lived and worked in them. Here, in the east, the monks, usually very friendly elsewhere, were very shy and introverted, and were deeply fascinated by us. Pema observing that the people here are generally more reticent anyway.

We had now seen six of the country's twenty dzongs: Paro, Wangdue, Punakha, Trongsa, Jakar, and now here in Trashigang, I felt that I liked this one the most. Before long however were off again, this time to our accommodation at Rangjung in the nearby Radi valley. We were to stay in the somewhat Spartan, yet comfortable guest house, run by the local monks which was spectacularly perched high above their monastery. I had no hot running water in my room but hot water appeared, in a bucket, after a polite request to a monk, who was helpfully hovering nearby. I immediately thought: 'this really is the hidden Shangri-La that Bhutan always threatened to be'. It was a unique place, and we spent the first evening sitting outside around a campfire, soaking up the atmosphere of this remote area, where very few tourists venture.

Amanda was just on great form, perhaps as us all, fired up by more local hooch. She led the raucous evening of truly great fun, much of it spoken by her in her own version of the Nepali language, where she had travelled recently. The hysterical banter included talk of 'rungy pungy' and 'wak wak', whatever that meant. I thought that young Dawa, and driver Dorje, both looking on in more than just detached bemusement, looked as though they were going to die laughing. I did not recall having laughed so uncontrollably for a long while. It was all topped off by trained chorister Edgar, singing wonderfully. In the meantime, Mary had finally broken open that keg of merlot. It was quite an evening!

So came to our last full day in Bhutan, and yet more tears were shed when I realised it would soon be all over; I did not want to leave. Before departing though we drove six miles or so up a nearby farm road. We had seen many of such roads on our trip, but we had never before taken one. We had heard a lot about them from Pema: a government initiative, recently taken over by one of the nascent political parties, the aim was to bring access for the high hill farmers with their nearby communities and markets, and indeed the rest of the country. After a short walk in the rain, we arrived at Sonam's parents' house. (He was the manager at the monk's guest house where we had been staying, an unsubtle coincidence!).

Soon, the local bush telegraph began working, and many country folk came laden with wares to sell to us, setting out their produce on bamboo blankets. How could we have refused? So after enjoying splendid hospitality of food and chai, and after making our purchases we walked back to our lodgings in glorious sunshine. Although at the end of our journey, this had undoubtedly been a major highlight of the trip for us all. We were miles away from anywhere, and indeed our own home comforts, but we all would rather have been there, at that moment, than anywhere else. (Most of the purchases made that day are now in my house on Lewis, which seems particularly fitting.)

There was not much time left, so upon our return, Jackie, Maria, and I wandered down to the nearby monastery. Before finally joining them I wandered around and found the school-bus, or rather army truck fulfilling that role, dropping some kids off after school. They were very photogenic, and indeed very keen to be photographed, and it was certainly a very unusual 'we are home from school' shot! We of course exchanged pleasantries, with the kids as ever wanting to practise their English language skills, especially with an Englishman! It was all great fun and indeed very funny. It was very wet after a heavy Himalayan shower, and after re-joining my group we found that the temple was locked. Eventually, though, I found a monk, who found a monk, who opened it up for us. At that point we were joined by Polly and Sophie, and soon found that it was time for evening prayers. Not only were we readily invited into the temple to witness the proceedings, but we were also allowed to take some photographs, a rare privilege, and we felt particularly blessed.

Our informal guide there, Ugyen Llendrup, rather amusingly observed that he would like have had Jackie as his mother, and Polly and Sophie as his sisters! Despite this rather brazen approach, he was actually very charming, helpful, and informative. He of course spoke English very well and gave us an insight into the Nyingmapa form of Buddhism practised there. He discussed their belief that karma led to enlightenment, and we all listened intently and were very moved by his words. Afterwards we processed the obligatory three circuits around the outside the monastery, in pouring rain, before going to a small temple and lighting our own butter lamps. Ugyen suggested that we thought about what we would like to feel within ourselves before lighting our own lamps, and although a simple sentiment, it was such a magical, mystical, and spiritual moment for all of us, that most had tears of spiritual joy in their eyes afterwards.

Feeling that we had hopefully reinvigorated our souls, it was to be three circuits round the stupas outside, whilst the sound of the thunder dragon rumbled around the valley and the skies darkened dramatically. The view we spied up one of the nearby valleys, looking towards the snow-capped peaks, and ever-changing cloud formations, was simply unforgettable, and we all walked back up the hill to the guest house feeling on top of the world.

The final evening at Rangjung was filled with celebration and traditional dancing, with dance teacher Jackie coming into her own and bravely joining in with Dawa; what stars they were. Amanda had compiled a quiz about the tour, which became very competitive, but I found myself on Mary's team, and she was certainly ready for the challenge. It was all very special, and emphasised just how much I shall truly, truly miss this country and my travelling companions.

We had another early start for our final day and went in search of the future fifth king. He was scheduled to arrive shortly after we arrived at the university town of Kanglung (if Pema had his timing right). The crown prince was due to preside over the annual convocation and graduation ceremony, which would be a particular honour for the students. We got there about half an hour ahead of the anticipated arrival time and secured a great location just by the main gate. Unfortunately, we were moved on by security almost immediately. The new king, like the last one, was a man of the people, but the modern world has its dangers even out here in the remote east of the country, and the rebels in Assam were not far away, so his personal security was an absolute priority. An additional problem was that the Assamese looked very similar in appearance to the Bhutanese in the east, so no chances were being taken.

It was a shame and disappointment, but we all appreciated that these were the risks of the modern world now. Thus, we continued our journey, south to the border with Assam. The mountains seemed to close in again, perhaps even more spectacularly than ever. They showed off their verdant, steep slopes as before and soon the clouds appeared to be below us. The many warning signs put up by the Indian contractors, who maintained the roads, exhorted our drivers not to 'rally in my valley', there was no chance of that, and perhaps the more relevant exhortation was to, 'be gentle on my curves.'

We saw again the results of many landslides and washouts, and as the road became steeper and even more obscured by mist, I became, for the first time, quite anxious. This became even more exaggerated when the main descent started, suddenly and very steeply. I later discovered that this particular road was notorious for its very frightening steep drops and very sharp curves, and unsurprisingly numerous accidents occur here. It was some journey though! We arrived at a small roadside café, and sitting at the tables outside, Pema served us the food he had brought along, including some very delicious Swiss-style cheese from the Bumthang valley, which was a welcome treat. Pema did do the decent thing though and purchased drinks and chocolate for us all from the cafe's owner.

We went ever onwards and downwards until, after ten hours, we reached the border with India at Samdrupjongkha. (Go on, say it; it is easy!) It was not a pretty place at all, the least Bhutanese-looking one we visited, and in truth, it was much more akin to India. There were not enough rooms at the hotel, so I found myself billeted at another one nearby. The room there was not bad, but the nearby locality was a nightmare, and for the first time in Bhutan I felt disconcerted and perhaps even a little frightened. The area was very run down, the buildings did not look at all Bhutanese in the style with which I was familiar, and the locals seemed furtive and suspicious, in sum it did not 'feel like' Bhutan. 'I will live though, and good karma would see me through' I thought.

Dinner back at the hotel was to be our last one together with Pema, Dorje, and Dawa, so I was asked to say a few words on behalf of the group when passing over our gifts of heartfelt thanks for the hard work they had all done in making our journey across the whole country so memorable. It had been another long day's drive, and we had to be at the border early the next morning in order to go through the respective country's immigration checks, which was anticipated to be a lengthy process. We would then be driven in jeeps through India, for a further seven hours, to Kaziranga National Park. 'What was that all about?' I had asked Carol. We had all loved Bhutan, and the two days or so to be spent in India could have been better used to ease our journey through Bhutan.

It was quite late when Dawa accompanied me back to my hotel, and unbeknownst to me, there was a curfew in force at that time. We were soon accosted by some soldiers, though luckily, Dawa dealt with them deftly and I was able to reach my hotel safely. Saying goodbye to Dawa was very sad, and I knew he felt the same too as there were tears in his eyes. I would miss him: 'Good luck, Dawa!'

It was nearly time to finally say goodbye to the Kingdom of the Thunder Dragon, which had given us that dramatic display of thunder and lightning during a storm in the Radi valley the previous day, thus giving us a strong reminder of its Kingdom! 'So until next time', I thought, 'and there certainly will be a next time!'

Dzong and tape!

Happy Landing!

concentration lapse!

Paro Thangkha

Ian misses the sartorial point!

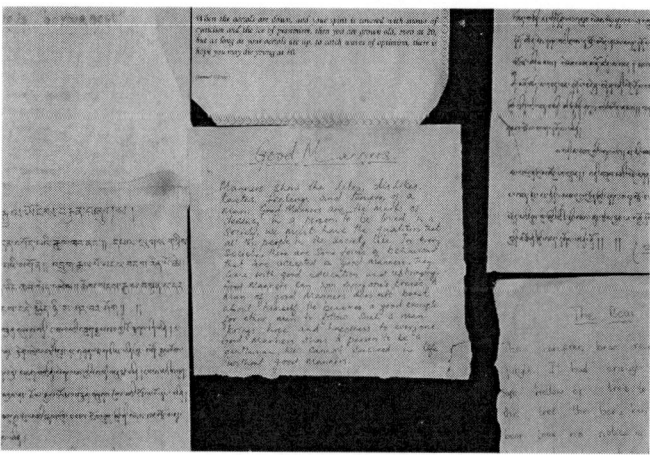

but they have manners

Huntscho school class riot!

Sophie & Polly   *simple but spot on*

the temporary bridge at Punakha Dzong

Ura choir

Firestarter!   *Jakar Boys will be boys!*

LotTD tour group

monsoon repairs on NH1   *Thinley Wangchuck*

close to heaven

Rangjung school's out

Amanda makes Carol die with rungypungy!

on the road DOWN to Samdrupjonghar

CHAPTER 5

MOTHER AND FATHER
STAYED AT HOME

'We get more and more in terms of quantity but less and less in terms of quality.'

The fourteenth Dalai Lama

I lost both my parents some time ago. Mum, born in Devon, the daughter of a solicitor, had never left the shores of the United Kingdom. In fact, it took the Second World War to take her out of Devon and onto the Royal Brompton Hospital in London, for some rather testing nursing duties. Thereafter, she moved to Cothill School in Berkshire, to take up nursing duties at the prep school there. She cared for the health of the young boys who boarded for the full length of the school terms and who, in many cases, were far from their own homes and families. Her nature and skill-set were ideally suited to this task. She was a very sociable person with a good sense of humour and her innate loyalty was typical of her generation.

Dad was of Yorkshire stock, though he was brought up in Cheshire and Surrey. His Father was a stern but very successful businessman who rose to great heights within the old Imperial Chemical Industries Company. Dad was called up just before the War and joined the Royal Artillery Regiment. He left the shores of the United Kingdom to go to war. He had travelled to Germany once prior to that and was mightily shocked to witness first-hand the rise and insidious power of the Brown Shirts. Whilst attending one of their rallies with a German friend, he felt obliged to carry out the *Sieg Heil* salute. He vowed never to return, but that was not to be. His regiment landed on Juno beach in Normandy on D-Day +5, and he and his company hot-footed along 'Hell's Highway' through Belgium to Nijmegen Bridge, which spanned the Rhine river in Holland, on the border with Germany. There, his unit valiantly defended that bridge against the many Luftwaffe attacks, some of those involving a new and fearsome jet fighter: the ME262. As a result, he received the military MBE (by letter from King George VI) for his services. Afterwards, when the war was over, his German language skills were put to use debriefing suspected SS officers in the post-war mop-up operation.

Dad was by nature a shy and insular man, highly academic and an excellent all-round sportsman. After the war, he demobbed, and tried a business career with Unilever, which he simply loathed, despite, though perhaps because of, his own father's successful career in business. Instead, he decided to teach at Cothill School. (Somewhat coincidentally, the co-founder of Unilever, Lord Leverhulme, had for a while in the early 1920s actually owned the Isle of Lewis.) Soon after joining the staff at Cothill and casting aside post-Edwardian mores, Dad made advances on a certain young nursing sister, who had recently arrived from the Royal Brompton hospital. Their relationship blossomed, and they were married in 1948. I was born the following year, 1949, the very year that Bhutan was recognised as an independent country.

Mum and Dad never left the United Kingdom again. I do not think that Dad's family had travelled much, but interestingly, Mum's had. Her father and eldest sister had emigrated to Southern Rhodesia (now Zimbabwe). Her younger brother had also emigrated, together with his family, to Melbourne, Australia. Her other brother was lost during the war while serving in Malta with the RAF. He had been helping hunt down German shipping supplying Rommel's forces in North Africa. Given that background, it is perhaps unsurprising that all three of their sons travelled abroad extensively.

After leaving university and working briefly for Sainsbury's, my middle brother, Bill, had emigrated to Sydney, Australia. He married a local girl, though they were not together long. After fifteen years there, he travelled to Thailand where he explored the country before settling down and working in Bangkok. During his time in Thailand, he met Mam and they married upon their return to the United Kingdom. They have a son, Luke. They are presently living in the United Kingdom though for some reason I have always imagined that they might go back to Thailand or Australia one day.

My youngest brother, Robin, travelled extensively in the United States in his late teens. He was chasing life and probably a girl or two! He flew in on the late, and lamented, Freddie Laker's *Skytrain* armed with a bunch of free add-on internal flights, but he soon had to resort to using Greyhound buses. This proved to be quite an experience, especially when he stopped in towns and cities en route. As Robin explained, the America of the sixties – with all its social iniquities – was an interesting place. The buses often stopped in the less salubrious parts of town, where life was lived dangerously. Arriving virtually penniless in New York City, he was befriended by a family living in Greenwich Village, and was subsequently shown the best, and, I suspected, the worst of NYC life! He is now happily married with three wonderful grown up daughters.

I can only imagine what my parents thought of all this, especially our mother, who never travelled abroad. For my part, I had no wish at that stage to live abroad, but as well as holidays in Europe, made more accessible by the nascent charter flight holiday market, I had also been fortunate enough to travel to the Far East, Australasia and America. It all started shortly after I had moved jobs, transferring from an insurance company office in the provinces to the City of London. After a brief spell with my second-choice job, a further transfer took me into the exciting, bewildering, and somewhat unknown world of the Lloyds of London insurance market. I previously discovered that most folk in the insurance business had simply fallen into it rather than viewing it as their ideal first career choice. That was certainly true in my case, and my route in had been no different to most. I had failed to achieve university grades at 'A' level and, after leaving school aged nineteen, I found that I had to quickly join the 'university of life'.

After leaving school I found that I had no really clear ideas about what I wanted to do, but one day, Dad mentioned that one of my uncles held shares in Royal Insurance, which had provided him with a solid return and he had told Dad that it seemed like a good company, and so it proved to be. After an interview in their City headquarters in Lombard Street, I started work in November 1968 in their Oxford branch in Cornmarket Street. Their office building there had once housed a gentleman's outfitters and still felt like it. It was overseen by a Branch Superintendent who, for all intents and purposes, looked and acted rather like the senior butler, Carson, in the television series 'Downton Abbey'. I had an ordered mind, and I quickly discovered that office life suited me well. I soon got used to wearing a suit (despite the fact that I sported ridiculously long hair; the style at the time).

I was bounced around the various departments within the office and had a five-week spell at the company's residential training facility in the Wirral, near Liverpool where the company was now head-quartered. Although I had been a school boarder since the age of ten, I found the experience of being away from home challenging on the social skills front. Also during that time, I gained an unfortunate love for the demon drink. I could not hold it then, and I still cannot!

At an early stage, I found myself handling claims matters rather than taking the rather more career savvy route of underwriting (taking on the business) or better still, winning new business as an inspector. These guys were given a company car, together with a bonus incentivised income and usually got all the girls. I did not do too well in that latter department, though I was very fortunate to meet Lynne and we were married in July 1973. She also worked at the Oxford office, and shortly afterwards we were both moved around on the company staff department's 'drafts board' and transferred to Watford. We were told it would be a great career move, but we both rather suspected that it was an expeditious move that suited the company rather more than us.

Finding myself in a busier environment, I found myself going out on investigation calls, largely in the north London area, two or three times per week. During that time, I had the use of a company pool car, and that certainly appealed to my sense of independence. Mum had told me that this trait had started at a very young age when she had often found me playing contentedly on my own, despite eventually having two siblings.

During that period we found that our marriage was failing so we both agreed that, if I were to move to a job in London, we might ease the stress of working together. I thus found myself working for that Lloyd's syndicate. At the time I knew little about this niche part of the insurance industry, and I soon became aware that the syndicate had in fact only been established just five years earlier. I also found that I was part of a business venture that was young, vibrant, and quite unlike anything I was used to. All this was inspired by the mercurial founder of the business: the late, great Michael Payne.

It was an auspicious start and, within a year of my joining the syndicate, I was on my way to Australia and New Zealand for a month-long business trip. I travelled in business class with Qantas to Sydney, which seemed unreal and as far from the somewhat mundane handling of routine claims in Oxford and Watford as anything I could have imagined. Needless to say, it was all tremendously exciting and was further fired by an exciting social life in the City. There was a lot of face-to-face interaction in my new business life, and as a consequence, I made many new friends. At the time, Bill had just moved to Sydney, and so I was able to meet him there during those business trips to Australia, and life felt terrific.

I recall landing in Sydney for the first time, it was very early in the morning, and after the then two required stop-overs in Bahrain and Singapore. Prior to leaving London, my well-travelled boss had urged me to stay up all day after that early morning arrival, which he said would help me adjust to the time change. I recall doing exactly that, aided by taking the magical trip around Sydney Harbour on the James Cook cruise. However, jet lag soon took hold, and whilst out to dinner in the revolving restaurant atop the Sheraton Tower, I found myself falling asleep next to my new found Australian hosts! Despite the great view, tiredness and alcohol were taking their toll. I do not recall falling asleep into my soup, but I suspect that scenario was not far off.

This was my first business trip of any note, and certainly my first overseas. By then I was in my early thirties, and I felt the weight of responsibility upon my comparatively inexperienced shoulders. I found myself jetting off here, there, and everywhere in a style I could only have imagined whilst I was sitting at my desk in Watford. I visited all the key cities in Australia, apart from Darwin (that came later), and the three major cities in New Zealand. It all seemed quite unreal and whilst business trips are correctly praised for their opportunity to see the world, I soon found that most of my time was spent in airport lounges, hotels, and offices, rather than seeing the local sights. However, needless to say, there were great places to see and new people to meet. As a visitor from London, there was much 'wining and dining' required, both at lunch and dinner and quite often at breakfast too. In truth, it was hard to keep going at times. That said I did heed my boss's advice from, a very experienced traveller to the Antipodes, who had wisely observed: 'they may speak the same language, but they are a different country, and should be treated with respect as such.' That advice seemed to work as I quickly made personal friends through my business contacts, some of whom, thankfully, continued with those friendships in the following years and indeed into my semi-retirement. I have not travelled for business reasons to the region for quite some time now, but I still do visit from time to time to nurture those friendships. Sitting on high rocks with the Joyce's, needless to say with a glass in hand, overlooking the remote Kakadu National Park in the Northern Territory, driving along the spectacular Great Ocean Road in southern Victoria with the Simondsons, the pleasure of sharing a proverbial Aussie beer with friend Luke in the Rocks area in Sydney Harbour, or just hanging with the Hunt family on the northern beaches, were all irreplaceable moments. Indeed, I was determined that some of this book would find its genesis in Australia – and it did, especially on the very special Kangaroo Island, South Australia, in 2012.

Aside from these personal visits, there were some journeys to places of interest outside of the cities. In no particular order of merit, I recall the Blue Mountains and Blackheath outside Sydney; the Puffing Billy Railway in the Dandenong Hills outside Melbourne; the vast and somewhat lairy Jupiter's Casino in Brisbane; the Surfer's Paradise beaches to the south of that city; the wineries in the hills and valleys outside Adelaide, especially McLaren Vale; and the incredible Cradle Mountain Lodge in Tasmania.

That first business trip was followed by many others, usually made in alternate years, and New Zealand, the Far East, and the United States were regularly added to my itineraries. Subsequently, those trips became rather more personal, made in order to keep up with those friends and to visit those places, many of which were off the beaten track, which I had missed during my business trips. I particularly fondly remember my rail journeys to Adelaide and Alice Springs, before crossing the vast emptiness that is the Nullabor desert, whilst en route to Perth. The reverse of that journey was just as thrilling, and I was later able to travel south from Darwin when the 'missing (rail) link' to Alice Springs was completed. It was during that journey that I had also taken in the Kakadu, but of course being Australia, there were many other truly unique places, all with their own special vibe. Chief amongst those was Uluru (or Ayers Rock to the rest of the world), in the so-called 'Red Centre' of Australia. I was lucky enough to stay with my dear friends Lindsey and Susie at a resort (Longtitude 131) located directly opposite Uluru, which gave amazing us views of the sunrise and sunsets over 'The Rock' and the desert. It never ceased to amaze me how the desert constantly displayed a plethora of ever varying colours, which constantly changed throughout the course of the day. The sights and sounds of that place remain indelibly etched in my memory, perhaps enhanced by recalling the rather decadent cocktails taken on the terrace, whilst looking out over the bush in the evening light, in the company of fellow travellers, who had been similarly led astray by us. ('Longtitude' was subsequently substantially destroyed by a bushfire before arising from the ashes again.)

The country had sort of got under my skin. It was good to catch up with Bill whilst he had lived in Sydney, and I also had relatives in Melbourne. My coterie of friends had grown right across the vast country, and distant as it was, it became very close to my heart. Visiting there, especially Sydney, always felt like 'going home'. I had come to realise that, although I knew deep down I was a homeboy, the lure of travel, uncomfortable as it was at times, was very appealing to me. I loved home, but I also loved seeing new places and making new friends in distant lands. During this time I recalled the holiday I took to India in 1986, where I had travelled by rail around Rajasthan on the exotically named 'Palace on Wheels', and subsequently on to Nepal for a few days. As mentioned in chapter two, I had been encouraged to go back. An interest in railways has always been part of my life; I recall being given a clockwork train set ('O' gauge for those interested) by Mum and Dad as a sop after a rather unpleasant tooth extraction, under sedation with gas, at a very scary antiquated local dentist's surgery. Despite that trauma, the train-set got me through and I was hooked!

My early teens had found us holidaying in North Wales, and one day, while passing under a familiar railway-style bridge, we came across the driveway that led to the Festiniog Railway's Tan y Bwlch Station. I was signed up immediately, and I have been a member and (lifetime supporter) of that railway, and its sister, the Welsh Highland Railway, ever since. In truth, despite the understandable ribbing on the part of my friends and colleagues, my interest has not been of the Ian Allan (well- known railway publishers) 'trainspotting' variety. Sure, I am beguiled by the sight, sound, and motion of steam, but it has always been the travel *on* them that had particularly appealed to me. So when a girlfriend had suggested that we go to India and travel on that legendary train, I did not need much persuading.

Despite my many and varied prior travels, the idea of India was something wholly different, and seemingly very shortly after agreeing to go, we found ourselves landing at the then named, Palaam

Airport, New Delhi. It was chaotic and smelly in the way that only travellers who have been there will know. Overpowering, yes, but somehow it was beguiling and not at all disconcerting. The people were very friendly, though you could not select which parts of India to see, or more pertinently, would prefer not to have seen. Thus, we were immediately and often pestered by beggars or handicapped and injured people, particularly children, and those sights became like a cross for us to bear. Subsequently we were, to some extent, isolated from such scenes whilst on the 'Palace on Wheels'. You could still smell and become beguiled by India though, and that was intoxicating.

At that time, the train was still the old, narrow-gauge stock, mostly dating from the days of the British Raj, and as the name implied, was used by the maharajas in their day. Movement between vehicles, particularly the dining carriages, could only be conducted when the train stopped and by actually getting off and walking alongside the train to the relevant carriage. This was a marvellous experience, especially when, at night, we often stopped in the middle of nowhere. We had an amazing ten-day journey through this mesmerising part of India, had great fun, and made a lot of new friends. Our holiday was capped-off by a short but awe-inspiring trip to Nepal. There was no time to trek, but there was plenty of time to sightsee, particularly the mountains. Unfortunately, our sightseeing flight planned to actually fly over Everest was stymied by a technical fault on our aircraft, very fortunately whilst it was on the ground! Apparently, there was some issue with the quality of the goat which, we were told, was a tradition to sacrifice in front of each aircraft of the Royal Nepal Airlines fleet, every year, in order to bring safe travels for both passengers and crew. It was a nice thought, but it seemed somewhat grotesque to my western mind.

The might and power of the Himalayas had got under my skin, but stayed dormant in my mind until 2006, when I took my first adventure to the Land of the Thunder Dragon. What was certain after that first trip was that, travelling with unknown companions was not the uncomfortable experience that I had anticipated. I think the key was having a small group of like-minded people. And lest it be forgotten, the excellent arrangements made by 'Wild Frontiers', led by the exuberant Jonny Bealby, and Johnny Paterson in particular, did not hurt either. I just loved seeing India again, the colour, the vibrancy, and the addition of rail travel on the night sleeper, together with the journey on the exquisite Darjeeling Himalayan Mountain Railway, was just like a dream come true.

However, it was Bhutan that had affected me most, and that is why the subsequent year's 'Land of the Thunder Dragon' tour just had to be undertaken. Unfortunately India would be largely bypassed except for entry and exit purposes. The tour was an opportunity to go across the whole of Bhutan from the comparatively well-visited west to the rarely seen east. There would also be another group of like-minded travellers to meet.

There was much talk during that tour of the prior decision of K4 to step down from his throne, after creating a democratic process, and revising the status of the monarchy, which he had designated his Oxford-educated eldest son to assume. So the coronation of K5 was to be in November 2008, when a living king would crown his son, a particularly rare event anywhere in the world. It was going to take place in a magical kingdom high up and hidden away in the Himalayas; I just simply had to go. By that time, I felt confident enough to go on my own. Of course, my journey was facilitated by Wild Frontiers, and I would have a Bhutanese guide, Pema, to look after me there. I knew it was going to be an adventure, but nevertheless a trip that flew in the face of my natural need to be fully in control.

The following year, I had scheduled to celebrate my sixtieth birthday in many ways, planning a suitably diverse mixture of events throughout the year, including attending the South by Southwest (SxSW) film and music festival in Austin, Texas. My actual birthday was spent on Lewis, but getting there was to be via Barra and the Uists, in the Outer Hebrides, which entailed landing and taking off from the beach on Barra (BRR). Those are flights I wish everyone could take, not least so that they could hold the unusual boast of flying on the only scheduled air service to land on a beach anywhere in the world.

Thereafter a rather decadent, four-day 'soixantieme annee' party in the Loire Valley, was to be the highlight, or was it? I thought: 'what better way to properly finish off my special year than going back to Bhutan for my fourth visit there'. After all, some folk had already asked to come along with me next time I went, so it was, to my mind, a thoroughly fitting end to a very special year. I was – I am – very fortunate indeed.

One of the fellow travellers in 2009 was Jon, and he readily agreed upon our return that another trip was necessary so he could show his wife and two young kids that beautiful country. I felt very gratified and honoured that he had made this suggestion, and thus the fifth trip (scheduled for 2011) was conceived. Yes there was no denying Bhutan had become an obsession for me. I just did not feel the need to travel anywhere else, apart from Lewis (PL1), of course. I felt so comfortable, so calm, so spiritually happy, amongst those beautiful people in their beautiful country.

However, after the fifth trip, I knew that a gap was necessary before my next return. The next visit was planned for my sixty-fifth year in 2014. However, realising that there would be that long gap, it caused many tears to be shed on the flight departing Paro for Delhi in November 2011 and indeed on the onward leg to London. However, a return to Australia beckoned, and there were other projects to nurture.

So what was it that set all these hares running? I think I have always had a deep-seated sense of spirituality, though I have only recently come to fully appreciate and understand those feelings in the fullest sense. Mum and Dad were both brought up in the Church of England Christian faith, and that is what they wanted their sons to do as well. However it was generally only Dad who had plodded to the local church on Sundays with his boys. For myself, I suspect it all started during my secondary education in the sixties at the small, and really quite minor at the time, public school at Bloxham. By the time I left there in 1968, England was already 'swinging', and we schoolboys had been breaking the strictured mores of post-Edwardian times, which were really quite repressive in school establishments such as that.

The school had a strong Christian background; founded by the Reverend John Egerton in 1860, it was by now part of the Woodard group of Christian schools, which included Lancing College in Sussex. It was run along high Anglican lines and, apocryphal or not, I was led to believe that they were still swinging holy incense in the chapel during Sunday Eucharist services shortly before I joined the school in 1962. By the time I left, I had become the 'Chapel Prefect', a role I felt very honoured to hold and really meant something to me. It must be said, though, that I was utterly hopeless when it came to my bell-ringing duties! Sometime afterwards, one of the closest friends I had there, Nigel, very kindly made this observation to his wife about my contribution during that time: 'I explained some details of Egerton House to Tina and explained how much had changed during our time at Bloxham, and how the fagging regime had changed to a pastoral caring role which you had led almost single-handedly.'

There was certainly some family history to all this. There were men of the cloth aplenty on Dad's side of the family, where a visit to the parish church in Horton in Ribblesdale, Yorkshire would reveal a string of vicars with our family name, a name derived it was said, from the swineherds tending to pigs on the river-banks. In fact, two of Dad's brothers had been in the church. Whilst there was no similar family history on Mum's side, her eldest sister had emigrated to Southern Rhodesia armed with a good deal of missionary zeal.

Later, at another time, the magic and mystery of the 'Great Southern Land' that is Australia touched my own soul, how could it not? It was such an ancient land, rooted in mysticism, and featured such spiritual places as Uluru and the Kakadu. Given that background, it was not entirely surprising that Bhutan's spirituality had got under my skin, and pretty much from the start. But after two visits there, and latterly taking friends from home along with me, I knew I was not alone in feeling that way. Landing in Paro after the exhilarating flight, you feel immediately that you are somewhere very special and quite different from anywhere else. In fact in 2011 that airport was voted (along with Singapore's Changi) as the 'best international airport'. Unsurprisingly, to me at least, the citation made the very pertinent point, that in almost all airports you feel that you could be almost anywhere in the world, whilst at Paro you immediately felt the uniqueness of the location; a very well-judged observation in my view.

In so-called 'western-civilised' countries we appear to live in a somewhat cynical and insular mind-set and not everyone is attuned to these same feelings, I am sure, and, it has to be said, why should they. However, after witnessing new arrivals there at first hand, I was certain that there was 'something in the air' which you immediately felt upon arrival. I have often described it as the good karma of the country, epitomised by the ubiquitous prayer flags that flutter everywhere, particularly and especially on the high passes. They encapsulate the spirit of this mountain kingdom, which is similarly shared in neighbouring Tibet and Nepal. The prayers printed on these flags are carried on the wind around the world bringing peace, tranquillity, and good karma to all. The Bhutanese call them 'lungpar' (wind horses; see appendix 6). Whichever religion, if any, we may be aligned to, the world at large is blessed by this selfless act. The mountain air here appears to be clearer and cleaner, and as soon as you come out of the valleys, the skies seem bigger and brighter than we are used to in more industrialised societies. But it is the sight of a country and people somehow left behind in time that is the most immediately striking feature. An unusual, yet smart and colourful, national dress makes for a striking impact, especially when seeing the gaggles of school children walking to and from their studies, inevitably smiling and waving in the most genuine and heart-warming manner. The buildings appear to be straight from the set of a mediaeval film, and quite unlike anything we are used to. There is often a pungent, though not unpleasant, smell in the air of pine cones burnt as a religious offering, or more mundanely, hot spicy chillies being prepared for the next meal. It seems strange to say, but it all this conspires to make one feel extremely happy; it is definitely karma, and it works on the soul.

The genesis of GNH, conceived by K4, was borne out of similar sentiments. He recognised early in his reign (during the late seventies) that his country was so poor and remote that it would be a hard sell to a fast-changing, modern world. Additionally, the country had little to offer materially. Thus, he wisely and perceptively advocated the richness of their culture and spirituality. He imagined that such values and good karma could be offered to, and shared with, the rest of the world. He espoused that 'gross national happiness' was more important to them than gross domestic product. It was certainly a somewhat difficult concept to fully grasp, but it was a priceless, cost nothing to promote, and became the touchstone and by-word for the nation.

Cynical western-thinking minds would not waste much time trying to grasp, yet alone tolerate it, for long. But as they say, small 'seeds are sown' and the concept of GNH had recently been heralded around the world, in no small measure by the Bhutanese government itself, and it has now been adopted by the United Nations. The last prime minister regularly travelled abroad to speak on the subject to international audiences. Truly, materialism does not mean a lot to most Bhutanese – but that may be changing, particularly and unsurprisingly amongst the younger generations. But even if GNH is not running at one hundred percent, it has been adopted by the vast majority of Bhutan's citizens, and is still the key to the very fibre of their country. The belief in GNH is also why, in general, folk do not leave this country permanently. If they do leave – and this is usually for educational purposes – they invariably return. When asked what happened to the young when they left Bhutan to go to university in India or elsewhere, our guide, Pema, observed: 'they almost invariably return because they miss the culture, family values, and the mountains.' I cannot think of many countries that has that particular draw. There is no tradition of emigration in Bhutan, and for those who do travel abroad homesickness is a significant problem, and almost all seem to find that true happiness cannot be found in other, perhaps richer, countries. They are only too keen to return to the land of gross national happiness, and make that decision after being exposed to the materialism of the outside world. I certainly do not believe their way of thinking is the only way to live life, but it is an undeniably precious option.

Much strife has been caused to mankind in the name of religion, but Buddhism has little that is provocative about it. Of course, some so-called Buddhists have displayed aggressive tendencies, especially across ethnic divides. Such self-proclaimed Buddhists do not show the 'right path' to take, but rather provide strict instructions to their followers on their own particular aspirations, and rebut any contradiction. In my experience, when one shows, rather than tells, others which is the correct path to take the support of family, friends and others usually follows as a natural consequence. Amongst Buddhists families it is tradition that one or more sons go into monastic education at an early age. There, they abandon possessions, and rely on others for day-to-day necessities. As well as being housed, educated and fed, the Buddhists maintain significant seats of power and influence in the monastic body and, as a consequence, in the state as well. Certainly it seems to be one of the best places to be to get on in life. Prosperity is achieved not through begging, but via the community and people doing what they do best: naturally and instinctively supporting and helping each other.

The closest we have come to this model in the United Kingdom was conscription to the armed forces, which some still believe was the saviour of disaffected and dissolute youth at the time it was in force, and certainly could be now, if reintroduced. What it did undoubtedly achieve, aside from logistical military support for the nation's armed forces, was an increase in self-discipline and the ability to be able to support oneself in alien environments where natural support seemed scarce. It quickly became apparent to the vast majority of conscripts that, in order to survive, one had to get along with others. Thus, friendships were created that made life possible and bearable and eventually I am told, enjoyable. Over time, this process simply became second nature.

It is that spirit, that form of karma that has, over the centuries, become so ingrained and intrinsic to the Bhutanese way of life. I love them for that; I respect them for that. I strongly feel that, if we tried to understand that model for life, we could learn a great deal from them. However, I cannot help but feel that the Dalai Lama was so right when he espoused that: 'life is about quality not quantity', though whether the Bhutanese would similarly thank me for championing their lifestyle is quite another matter!

Love is something that cannot be bought, but rather it must be nurtured through a process that does not involve simply 'telling'. Whether it is love for people or love for places, it does not matter as much as some might think. What both can give is a deep inner feeling of comfort and contentment. Perhaps places have the slight edge because they are always there, unlike the evanescent nature of people. Both people and places can exercise a pull, a hold, or a connection that forces us to submit. Life is short and precious, and when we have the chance to love, we would do well to recognise the opportunity and nurture and protect it. The lure from Bhutan for me is unrelenting and extremely precious in my life. It is not rose-tinted nor is it a blinkered idealistic love rather it is realistic and, for me, is utterly irreplaceable.

I believe that Bhutan is facing imminent change. No man is an island, and that phrase is also true of countries when it comes to support, especially economic support. Probably because of (rather than in spite of) its location, Bhutan has ploughed its own path for centuries seeing little need for outside assistance. That situation is understandably changing; indeed, the window to the outside world was opened wide in 1999. At that time, K4 allowed the use of television and the Internet for the first time. Notwithstanding the torrent of previously unknown information was that was made available to them then, I truly believe that the Bhutanese will see their way through this present time of change, whilst still maintaining their unique culture in their spectacular physical environment.

I feel exceptionally privileged to have seen so much of the world. My parents would have been overawed and doubtless rather bemused by the extent of my travels and those of my brothers, but it is truly a smaller world now due to the comparative ease of travel. During my father's lifetime, aviation transitioned from the Wright Brothers to

Mr Boeing's Jumbo Jet. In my lifetime, people have stood on Earth's moon and made steps towards travelling to the next planet. Who knows what the next century will bring.

Mankind will never be completely satisfied by exploration and travel alone. Inner peace and happiness are central to human satisfaction. Some people may be reincarnated and find their way in their next lives, but I am fortunate to have found a key part on that road during this life.

Kadrinche la Druk Yul

Thank you, Bhutan!

CHAPTER 6

TO SEE A KING CROWNED!

Gross National Happiness is more important to our nation's well-being than our gross domestic product.

King Jigme Singye Wangchuck, K4

It was November 2008, and I was in Delhi for the first time since 1986 when I had come to travel on the railways in Rajasthan for the first time. I was staying at the Radisson Hotel, which is on National Highway 8, near the airport. Still, I was close enough to see, smell, and be reminded of the real India. 'God it's good to be back!' I thought.

I was billeted in the business section of the hotel, and I was looking forward to enjoying the luxury features after the flight, though jet-lag and an early wake-up call beckoned a good night's sleep. After all the fuss and critical disappointment surrounding *Quantum of Solace*, I ordered *Casino Royale* for the room and realised, before falling asleep, what a good film it was.

After a smart getaway from the hotel, I went straight to the Drukair check-in desk at IGI airport well before 6:30 a.m. but, frustratingly, an English lady was already at the front of the queue and had taken the last left-hand window seat. After an interminable wait in the business lounge, it was off to a chaotic gate number one. We all boarded a bus for the ride across a busy ramp to one of Drukair's very smart A319s for flight KB205. I was surprised and relieved to hear that it was to be a direct flight to Paro, rather than via Kathmandu in Nepal. Soon after take-off the mighty Himalayas hoved into view and were to stay there for the rest of the journey.

We were soon flying over Bagdogra airport (for Darjeeling), and began the steep descent into the Bhutan valleys shortly thereafter. We were approaching from the south this time, which seemed even more exhilarating than the approach from the north over Paro dzong. Weaving and tilting, it felt like being in a computer game with absolutely *no* room for mistakes. It was brilliant, of course and luckily the flight through the hills was as smooth as the rest of the flight. We landed and I was immediately dragged by a Bhutanese official straight to the front of the residents' line. 'You don't look very Bhutanese to me, Old Boy' said a somewhat frazzled Brit. Pema, and new driver, Wangchen (pronounced *Wanchin*) Tobgyel, were there to greet me and we set off for Thimphu. The sun was shining brightly, and the completed road-works were now running all the way to the capital and were a wonder to behold, particularly after recalling what they were like last year. In the capital I wandered around near the main stadium where the Friday post-Coronation celebrations were to take place. The fifth king had already been formally crowned, in secret, at the old capital Punakha, on November 1st.

The event had been scheduled to be on the day I arrived, and I had hoped that I might have been able to see newly crowned king exit the dzong there, or during his subsequent walkabout on the journey back to Thimphu, meeting as many of his people as he could. I was later to meet a British couple, who had been trekking, and they had managed to do just that, and I was just a little jealous There was a very relaxed air of anticipation in Thimphu with flags and other bunting everywhere, and the weather was suitably bright as well. The army was rehearsing in the stadium (which was the site of the historic battle which saw in the first king of the Wangchuck dynasty enthroned in 1907.) During the coronation celebrations for the fifth king, Bhutan was also celebrating one hundred years of the Wangchuck dynasty. Pema had made it clear to me that the king and government had declared that they would not be profligate during these events as the country could simply not afford it. That said November 2008 was the culmination of years of infrastructure improvements, including roads and hotels, which had just come to fruition. The previously rather scruffy capital had been titivated to tremendous effect and was proceeding even as I arrived, with some last minute things, such as white-lining of the roads, being carried out seemingly at the very last minute.

Although the king was by now already crowned I had previously arranged to stay overnight in Punakha, but I would not be witnessing any of the events there now. On the drive there Pema had arranged for a brief stop on the Dochu La Pass at the Huntscho Community School where the head teacher there could thank me in person for the small contribution I had made towards the cost of providing them with a computer, and all-important printer. I was somewhat annoyed to find the equipment residing in his study, rather than in a classroom, I was not even sure that it was working, and there was much bemoaning about the cost of printer ink. However I made a note in his diary so that the school could see that I had dropped by. Driving over the pass itself we found the visibility clear, a first for me. Although there were some clouds I witnessed the spectacular view of the distant Himalayas I had heard so much about. The vista somewhat took my breath away and the scene was magnified by the spiritual karma caused by the myriad festoons of multi-coloured prayer flags blowing in the breeze. Driving down the longer section on the other side we arrived at New Punakha town where I was to be billeted in the Damchen resort. I found myself in a tiny single room on the ground floor, near the bar area, which was full with a group of very loud Americans 'on tour'. It was Election Day in the USA and I wondered what would happen. ('Go, Obama, go!' I shouted to myself.)

At dawn the next day it was quite cloudy and I wondered where the sun had gone. Pema said it was likely caused by the final effects of

115

the monsoon and late cyclonic activity in the Bay of Bengal. Anyway we departed and took the road towards the Trongsa but detoured to Gantey, a new destination for me. The damp and mistiness had closed in, and it made the long drive seem somewhat longer and, dare I say, a little disappointing. However, when the Pobjika Valley appeared, which is where the Gantey goemba (monastery) is located, it all opened up. The goemba itself was a really impressive building, constructed in the fifteenth century, and thus older than the many dzongs I had seen, it had recently been restored to very good effect. I really regretted missing the photo opportunity presented by two novice monks leaning out of their first floor dormitory window – it would have been a real gem of a picture, capturing the 'old and the new'!

We went in search of the very rare black-necked cranes, which migrate from Tibet into this remote valley at this time of year. The valley proves to be a great landing ground. We found them, though I have to confess that I accidentally frightened them and they took to the wing, although seeing them fly was just wondrous. Afterwards, at a nearby farmhouse, which had a great atmosphere, very friendly though for some reason Pema did not seem to like it much, we enjoyed a meal including some simply delicious baked potatoes. Closer to the western cuisine I had been used to in Bhutan, the valley is famous for this crop and I could see why. (On the journey into the valley I had seen many lorries which were laden down with their sacks of potatoes being taken to market in the capital, and indeed further afield, to India.) I met Sharon and Mary from upstate New York and who were clearly true 'Obama girls'. They declared, in between mouthfuls of potatoes and chai: 'we are not going back if that other man is elected!' I simply could not believe that they were not going to be in Thimphu for the coronation.

It was a long drive back, and the clouds and mist were really closing in by now, and I thus resorted to my trusty iPod again. When we arrived into Old Wangdue it very much looked the part for the coronation celebrations with flags everywhere. 'It really will be a pity that this old village is to be relocated to the new Wangdue' I thought. Whilst on the precipitous road back to the hotel we spotted the very unusual sight of a sightseeing helicopter, grounded in a paddy field, whilst en route to Thimphu. 'It would be a long walk back to the road for the pilot and the passengers' I thought.

Back at the Dechen resort I think the management had taken pity on me as I was given a room upgrade, which was on the first floor, away from the noise, and having a window with a view. It was still cloudy though, and I wished the clouds and rain would disappear, as I wanted to be able to see Punakha dzong, with its rebuilt bridge, in all its glory the next day. Finally, at the end of the long day, I was to have a meeting over dinner with Samdrup, my Bhutanese charities advisor, whom Carol had put me in touch with. What could I say, there was so much to do, but it was a very special and helpful meeting. Samdrup was a college professor, and a deeply religious man, who felt that he must do all he could to help destitute monks in particular. He was courteous, sincere and I liked and trusted him immediately.

When I woke up I was pleased and relieved to see blue sky through the window. We prepared to leave Damchen, but not before saying goodbye to the manager and his staff. A few well-chosen and frankly startling words came from one of them: 'here is your bar bill, sir. It was a pleasure to have you staying here. You smile, you do not complain, and you are clearly very happy to be in our country, thank you.' Although it was early there was definitely a tear in my eye, which was compounded by comments from the manager himself: 'see you next year, otherwise, we will come and find you!'

Before we left for the dzong we learned that Obama had won, and I was thrilled. The original plan had been to see the newly crowned king exit the dzong, but that was not to be. However, it was always a magical place to visit – the king being there or not. K5 had in fact been crowned by his father, the fourth king (K4), in the inner sanctum. It was a truly historic and unique event, and not just for the Bhutanese people; a living king, relinquishing the throne of his own free will, crowning his son. K5 received the 'Raven Crown' and ancient royal dhar (shawl) that had been handed down through the entire dynasty, now a hundred years old. The environs had been duly refreshed, tidied and were looking lovelier than ever. The traditional mediaeval-style cantilever bridge giving access to the dzong across the nearby river, had been painstakingly rebuilt with the help of the Swiss, and was, as I had expected, a wonder to behold. As in Thimphu, finishing touches were still being applied but it was nevertheless a spine-tingling experience.

Afterwards I went to visit Samdrup at the nearby 'College of Natural Resources', where he worked as a professor. He had personally invited me, as he was keen for me to see where he worked, and for me to interact with the staff and pupils there. Although I was very concerned about my lack of understanding of the local language ('dzongkha', which had literally derived from the dzongs) I nevertheless considered this to be a rare privilege. One stand-out moment comes to mind: I was led into one of the classrooms where I saw about thirty or so mixed students, mostly in their late teens. All exhibited the usual Bhutanese politeness when I entered the room and immediately stood up and clearly expected me to say something. 'Kuzuzangbo La' ('hello') was all the dzongkha I could muster. Although educated in a polite and respectful environment, there was clearly fun to be had as well. As was the case throughout the country the buildings were built in the traditional style, with a large preponderance of beautifully painted wood and, to my mind, it seemed a perfect place to be educated. Samdrup seemed very pleased that I had visited him there.

Driving back over the Dochu La Pass we passed a line of cattle trailing up in line and also saw that helicopter, finally making its way back to Thimphu at last. My accommodation there, at the Yeedsin guest house, was a bit of a shock after Damchen. It was a little dark and the room did not appear to match the, albeit modest, standards I had become accustomed to. As ever though, I knew that I would get used to it, and whilst out shopping, and visiting a money changer, I was offered 'home comforts' at her home in Phuntsoling, which brought on a better mood, although I was never going to make that lengthy journey even for that temptation! I went in search of some prayer flags to take home, and a 'gho' (the traditional Bhutanese garment for men, which looks somewhat similar to a Japanese kimono). Sadly there were no coronation stamps available yet though. Returning to the Yeedsin Pema and Wangchen helped me don my gho, which was quite a convoluted procedure, and was very uncomfortable in view of the very tight belt that was worn underneath. I looked the part though, with Pema commenting that I could now attend the coronation celebrations in some style. Afterwards, I took an evening walk through the somewhat frenetic main street, where folk were clearly ready for the coronation as there was much noise and a general air of expectation. Sadly, I felt the need to shake off a stomach complaint, so I returned to my lodgings and watched Obama's acceptance speech from Chicago on the Bhutan Broadcasting Service (BBS). Listening to that great acceptance speech with the sounds of simply beautiful singing, wafting across from the nearby main square, was simply surreal. I was thinking: 'it is the public coronation at Thimphu dzong tomorrow, and although I had bought the gho, I felt I should attend in a western style suit and tie' as Pema thought this would be the most appropriate way for me to go, as it was my 'national dress'.

The next morning dawned clear, bright, and cloudless, as if divined by some local deity. Certainly the date had been decided upon by religious astrologers, so perhaps it was not so surprising after all. I felt an inner feeling of contentment and joy, and was very excited about the prospect of witnessing the events set for that day. I truly felt in touch with Bhutan and its people, a feeling that I knew bordered on love, and I was consumed with feelings of inner happiness. It was to be a joyful day too, even though I did not actually get into the Doebumlam (the extension to the tsechu ground at the Tashichoedzong) to actually witness the public coronation. It was just content to be there though, especially during such an important moment in the nation's history and I would certainly not have wanted to miss it. I bumped into the photographer and author, Michael Hawley, from Boston Mass. who so aptly observed: 'just look at the mass of just beautifully dressed people walking towards us, wearing such happy smiles, there is simply nowhere else on Earth like this.' He was right, though perhaps he should know, as he was author of the world's 'largest book', (measuring five by seven feet) and which, needless to say, was about Bhutan.

It is truly a unique place, although change is afoot, and indeed may be presaged by the arrival of a new king. The people, as I had expected, were suitably dressed for the occasion. Wherever I looked there were beautiful groups of people – families, friends, kids, and monks – and they had all made a supreme effort to appear at their best. Pema had been right to counsel me to wear western dress and this was confirmed by Michael Hawley, who although wearing a gho himself, observed that I had done the right thing. Tourists and Bhutanese alike mistook me for a member of some foreign government but, sadly, this held no sway with the security forces at the gates despite my futile assertion: 'British Embassy Old Boy, dont'cha you know!'

As already mentioned, Thimphu had tried very hard and it looked very special, particularly at night. In the lovely daytime sunshine, it looked just brilliant too. Logistically, I felt that the authorities had got it right: all roads in the centre were closed (except to VIP and tourist traffic). Pema loved his special tourist permit sticker on his 4x4, which allowed us through most checkpoints. There were park-and-ride buses available, which were free for all locals. The cell phone network in the centre of town, and indeed anywhere near any of the main events, had been shut down, which was an inspired move, because it forced people to concentrate on the events at hand. Unfortunately, no cameras were allowed in the Doebumlam – a fact that had not been announced previously. Also, even the enhanced space could in no way cope with the crowds that did turn up. There was room for twenty thousand people, but that was not nearly enough. A bemused, and amusing, coronation official announced over the tannoy speakers: 'we cannot even parachute you in!' There was a tourist presence, but it did not appear to be particularly large. Most of them had donned national dress apart from that 'Man from the Embassy'! The suit had indeed seemed to be the right choice, particularly as there did not appear to be many others similarly attired.

These events were being staged for the people, and they had come in their thousands from far and wide, many having taken long and difficult journeys, simply to be there, in Thimphu, at that time. My first attempt at entry into the coronation arena failed. Pema tried hard at the security gate, which was complete with metal detectors, presumably shipped in from India, but all to no avail. We went back to the hotel briefly before returning, this time with my driver Wangchen, to the fence line. There I did manage to see the king after he had emerged from the coronation ceremony, when he came out to speak to his people and publicly address those who had assembled there. I also saw him receiving Bhutan's oldest inhabitant, a 107-year-old lady, who had witnessed all four previous kings of the Wangchuck dynasty being crowned. Although I was not particularly close, I nevertheless had a reasonable view of the key events, and my excellent long camera lens proved very useful. The thrill and emotion of the proceedings, which the king and government had insisted would not be lavish, was indescribable. It had been a long journey to get there, but there was no question in my mind that it had been absolutely the right decision, I simply *had* to be there and I was so glad that I was.

Back at the fence line I had caused much amusement with the conversation I struck up with a lovely local boy, who spoke impeccable English, and who seemed to know everything about the British Royal Family, though not, apparently, the age of his new King. (I did, he was twenty eight.) I was caught out by him later though: 'is that the king's wife' I had asked, 'no, that is his sister!' He then asked: 'do you work for your government, sir?' This was followed by the even better retort: 'does your government have a defence minister as I would like to do that!'

I suspected that the boy would go far in life, except that I heard he had apparently actually managed to get inside the Doebumlam earlier that morning, only to go out to find some food, and was not allowed back in again.

After all the excitement of the day I spent a quiet evening at my lodgings as we were going to try to get into the Changlimethang Stadium early the next day. This was to be the final day of celebrations, and probably the most informal. Various displays were planned and the king was expected to mix freely with the people there. There was a brief – and I thought slightly patronising piece – on the BBC World News about the coronation. It was concentrated on the weight of the 'Raven Crown' itself and the fact that K5 had just become the world's youngest monarch. However there was great coverage on the local BBS channel. Despite being a poor country, and without the means to put on a lavish ceremony, the events had been simply spectacular. I was forced to mentally step back and see where all this was happening: in the last 'Shangri-La'. These people could really teach us something about simplicity and gross national happiness was the key. The fourth king espoused the concept, and it was clear that the fifth king was going to champion it in a comparable fashion. K5 had so wisely observed, during his acceptance speech in front of the thousands of his subjects at the national stadium: '[GNH] is our bridge, and we will build that bridge and cross it together."

The man may only be twenty-eight years old, but he already had a saint-like demeanour, which he clearly displayed with the common touch he had with both young and old alike. The young were moved to spontaneously kiss him and the old were clearly moved in his presence. The politeness of Bhutanese society, particularly their respect for each other, was something I strongly believed at the time we should try and emulate. The country may be hidden away, high up in the Himalayas, but the message flies out of that magical kingdom, borne on the wind from the prayer flags, and blesses the world. Once you have discovered this country you will surely fall in love with it, and will feel the need to return often, simply to gain that much needed karma boost. As the vast crowd, including the many mesmerised tourists, at the stadium had shouted, accompanied by three very loud cheers: 'long live the fourth and fifth *Druk Gyalpos!*' ('Dragon Kings')

Yes, it did shine brightly on the first of the two days of public celebrations. We were in the newly refurbished Chanlimethang Stadium, which was the historic site of a battle in 1885 that effectively sealed the status of the first king and established the Wangchucks as the ruling dynasty. I donned my gho properly for the first time. 'God, this belt is tight!' I mused. 'You look the part, Mark' observed Pema, 'a veritable Bhutanese dasho (lord)'. I joined the men-only line that led to the stadium entrance. The people were polite but very keen to get in. Again no cameras were allowed inside, though no prior announcement had been made about it. Wangchen had the answer though: he simply deposited mine in a nearby little shop for safe keeping! We realised pretty quickly that tourists could go to the front of the line, but I did feel uncomfortable about that privilege. We successfully made it through security, but the gates were not yet officially open, but all of a sudden they were opened and pandemonium ensued. It really was quite frightening, a real scrum, and I was very worryingly told that a little boy was crushed to death in the ensuing melee. There were already masses of people in the stadium, though Wangchen found the tourist seating for us, but the place kept getting fuller and fuller and hotter and hotter. 'Would we be able to escape in four hours time for our lunch and our important afternoon appointment?' I wondered.

However all those thoughts were put aside once the pageantry commenced. The announcer explained that the sutras and prayers would banish all negativity, which they certainly did. Eventually, Wangchen nudged me to indicate he could see the king's cavalcade on the upper road opposite on its way to the stadium. When his procession actually entered the stadium, a wall of emotion completely overtook me. Tears of emotion streamed down my face. It was the culmination of the long journey there, the sheer brilliance of the whole occasion, and the hugely privileged position I felt I was in by simply being present. Talk about banishing negativity, the vibe and the spectacle were overwhelming. The colours on show beneath clear blue skies made me wonder whether Obama's own inauguration would surpass this event. It was a simply incredible display for such a small country. Frugality may be the watchword of the king and government, but what Bhutan put on show that day was impeccable. The centrepiece of the early displays was the mass of armed forces, and I felt their drill moves would compete with the U.S. Marines any day, and even Wangchen seemed impressed.

The king's address to his nation, which I saw later on TV, was pitched perfectly for the occasion. He appeared to give the speech with no prompting notes and certainly no support from an autocue. However the stifling heat was getting to me and, not without some difficulty, we managed to exit the stadium. Sadly we missed the afternoon's entertainment, including the presentation of gifts to the new king, which included two elephants and a calf that had come all the way from Guwarhati, India. More importantly, we had missed the king's informal walkabout in the crowd. However before I left, I joined the crowd in raising a cheer, 'Gyelo', three times in the king's honour. His clenched fist conveying his pride said it all – as did the sight of the tens of thousands of flag-waving subjects when he got into his jeep to circumnavigate the stadium to inspect the parade. The sight was simply overwhelming.

What I missed there that afternoon, I more than made up for with my visit with Samdrup to Dobji dzong. The majority of my charitable funds were channelled through Samdrup, and in the main they were given to this one cause. The lama (abbot) there had established a home for destitute boys from across Bhutan, usually from families damaged by divorce. The ancient dzong at Dobji was once a fort and latterly a gaol. The government gave free use of the building to the lama, but they did not give him any funds to run it. There were twenty-five boys, four teachers, and plenty more knocking on the door and wanting to be taken in. It was situated on the road to the Haa Valley, the ancient route into Bhutan from Tibet. As with nearly every dzong in Bhutan it was set in a spectacular location.

Upon arrival, we were shown to the lama's quarters and served lunch on exquisite china. The slight awkwardness I felt with this undoubted honour started to dissipate during our tour of the dzong itself. My funds had helped buy beds for those boys who needed them and food for their monthly rations. The beds were rudimentary, and the dormitories in the main tower were cold and breezy, even on calm days. Although the location was just stunning I did not much like the approach road which entailed passing through a quarry where the precipitous access road had only just been reinstated following a monsoon landslide. Apparently it had been prepared especially for my visit. I was also very privileged to visit the small temple and see their most precious relic: the one-eared representation of Guru Rinpoche that allegedly spoke. That might seem strange and somewhat unbelievable to a western mind, but to the deeply religious monks this was real. I was blessed with locally sourced holy water and then the trumpet indicated that it was time to say farewell. It was a heart-wrenching moment. I hoped that the young monks, just kids really, were looked after well, albeit in a strict monastic environment. The place appeared to be clean and well kept, and there was a new toilet block being built nearby. The kids were being given three days' holiday to join in the national coronation celebrations, and there were quite a few smiles to be seen. Certainly, they needed to be fed, and I was grateful I could help a little in that respect. It was a sad departure, but I promised myself I would return.

On the way back into Thimphu, Samdrup invited me in to his apartment for tea with his family, which was a rare privilege. We then had a quick drink downtown with Pema and Wangchen to discuss my exit arrangements overland, because, as anticipated, there was no space on any of Drukair's flights. It was the end of a long day – and indeed, a long five days. Long live Bhutan, the fifth king, and gross national happiness! I noted that the highlight of the TV coverage was the ease with which the fifth king interacted with his people. He even pointed to his cheek so that a young girl could kiss him after she had presented him with a gift. He is a monarch who loves being with his people and is totally at ease with them. Whatever doubts people might have had about the fourth king's decision to step down, everyone seemed to realise that this man is a worthy successor to the century-old dynasty.

Wangchen turned up early the next day for the start of the long drive south to the border with India at Phuntsoling / Jaigaon. I was not in a happy mood, but the sun was out again and the mountains looked majestic. The first part of the 180 km journey was pretty good. The new road extended quite a way out of Thimphu before narrowing to single lane Isle of Lewis proportions. The journey was made even more entertaining by the amusing roadside signs such as 'restaurant cum bar', 'Wangkha' and the many warnings of 'shooting stones!' Then, as predicted by Pema, who had gone off separately to Paro to pick up a new Wild Frontiers group, we hit the next stage of the five-year road improvement plan. It lasted for 50 km, which was a nightmare, because I could see the hugely precipitous drops made worse by the lack of barriers. I felt reasonably confident with Wangchen's driving skills, but the drive was still rather hair-raising.

Whole sections were dug up, leaving no road surface during the blasting and widening process. As mentioned earlier, the Indians mix highly modern machinery and techniques with seemingly mediaeval methods. State-of-the-art rock splitters and crushers are seen alongside hordes of the Indian underclass literally breaking rocks on the carriageway. They build retaining walls out of cement bricks manufactured on-site, which seemed incapable of withstanding the monsoon's deluge. However the people seemed confident it would work, and I recalled seeing the finished section near Thimphu, which is most impressive, though it was not in the mountainous route. I had some relief when we stopped for lunch at Gedu village before proceeding to the next hair-raising section. The two Bhutanese music CDs I had bought in Thimphu calmed me down a little though and even Wangchen seemed impressed with my choices.

There were expected and unexpected tears of emotion. Wangchen suddenly explained that he and his wife, Serita, had a fourteen-month-old daughter, Chi, who had one foot amputated at birth. The wooden prosthesis was too heavy for her though, and he wanted to take her to India for treatment. He clearly loved her dearly, and I felt sorry that such a thing had happened to such a nice man and his family. I did not think I was being beguiled; at least I hoped not.

As the journey progressed and the plains of India came into view, the thought of leaving Bhutan was just too much. However we were able to make a brief stop at Kamji School, but unsurprisingly the students were on coronation holiday. I was able to give my letter, together with photographs from my last visit, to the head by way of the vice principal. He desperately tried to clean himself up when I arrived because he thought I was from the World Food Programme conducting a surprise inspection.

We eventually arrived into Phuntsoling though immediately met with some trouble at the Bhutan Gate. Fortunately, we were saved by the dasho in charge of immigration. There was a moment's panic, but the necessary exit stamp was acquired with the assurance that I could head back into the country to stay the night at the nearby Druk Hotel after I had crossed over to the Indian side of the border to obtain their entry visa for my journey in India tomorrow. We walked through the smelly, dirty Indian town of Jaigaon – it was certainly not a place I wanted to stay in overnight, and I was glad I was returning to Bhutan for my night stop. Pema's Indian friend had joined us to assist at the Indian border post. I had visited this post on a previous trip, but we found it had been locked, closed and apparently relocated. A nearby beggar told us where it was now and thankfully, we found it. Fortunately, it was also manned, and after the usual Indian bureaucratic hiatus, the requisite entry stamp was obtained. This was all very necessary because the office would not be open at the time of our early departure the next morning. It was very hot down here on the gangetic plain, but the BBS television coverage of the coronation helped me relax in my hotel room. The fireworks that closed the celebrations at the Chanlimethang Stadium were mightily impressive.

At 6:00 a.m. Bhutan time (5:30 a.m. Indian time), we walked through the closed Bhutan Gate on foot. Wangchen had driven us down there because my case was pretty heavy, even without my gho, which I had bequeathed to Pema to dispose of to others as he saw fit. After an emotional goodbye to Wangchen, I crept through the gate on foot. I felt that it was slightly a 'Midnight Express' moment as my Bhutanese visa had expired at midnight. However I made it through and immediately saw Pema's Indian friend and driver waiting for me which was quite a relief. We drove off into the early dawn and West Bengal's many roadside villages. The roads, to begin with anyway, were atrocious. I reckoned it was about 200 km to Bagdogra airport, and given the condition of the roads, I wondered whether we would make it in time for my flight. The tea estates looked lovely though, but I donned my sunglasses to avoid the inevitable stares. We stopped at a wayside cafe for an omelette and some very welcome chai, then drove through the stunning national park section, complete with its hordes of monkeys. Finally crossing the Coronation Bridge again, which I had been across on my trip in 2006.

Eventually, we arrived into Siliguri, where we briefly caught sight of the Darjeeling Himalayan Railway again and the mad hubbub of Bagdogra town itself. We eventually turned off onto the airport road which was with some relief as I was still wondering whether I would get there in time. Bagdogra airport (IXB) apparently had a very short runway, as a doom-laden man from Melbourne was insistent on telling me, further observing that this caused all sorts of delays and dangers. However I did get there in time to check in for my Jet Airways flight, although the journey had taken much longer than the anticipated four and a half hours. I noticed a family group who looked as if they had just been transported in from the days of the British Raj. They were loud and obnoxious, with a son who was insistent on barging in front of everyone. I so longed for a return of Bhutanese manners.

The usual Indian madness prevailed, but it was good to see that security was thorough. A smart B737-800 arrived, and we hopped on for the half-hour flight to Guwarhati, which actually meant flying in the opposite direction to our final destination: Delhi. Whilst on the ground there we waited for forty minutes so that other passengers, including an obvious bigwig accompanied by a high ranking army officer, could join us. With the recent terrorist attacks in Assam, which included some in Guwarhati, I was a little troubled, but thankfully we made it out unscathed. I had a right-hand seat again, and so enjoyed viewing the Himalayas on the way back to Delhi. I wished a fond farewell to these new found 'friends', and to Bhutan in particular, from 36,000 feet. To begin with, we appeared to be flying directly towards Everest before finally turning and heading west. I had an absolutely clear view all the way; it was an incredible and inspiring vista. We arrived into a very smoggy Delhi airport (IGI), for the domestic terminal, but we took a very long time to reach it in view of the seemingly never-ending taxi-ing. We even appeared, at one point, to enter an active runway: I held my breath and looked away. After our eventual arrival, I went back to the Radisson for six hours before catching the night flight back to Heathrow. During that brief spell I shared dinner with businessman Geoff, from Belgium. Arriving back into London I felt tired but full of spiritual karma after the privileged, incredible and unforgettable experience I had just experienced. It also felt so surreal to be back home.

Many of my friends in the United Kingdom had been bemused by what they had perceived as my personal invitation to attend the coronation. One had even sent a good luck card depicting me apparently being conveyed to the Himalayas on a sedan chair, supported by flunkeys in the style of the court at Versailles. Nothing, of course, could have been further from the truth. This was a country where, on the surface, everything was less; but deep down, everything was more. This was absolutely the case with the coronation arrangements. The last time there was such an event was in 1974, for K4 the current king's father. At that time tourism was virtually non-existent, and in reality, the country was almost closed. There was no airport, and journeys overland were tough and time consuming.

Now, thirty-four years later, tourism thrives, albeit attracting a largely niche foreign market. Tourist numbers had recently been increasing from the United Kingdom, largely due to Michael Palin's 'Himalaya' television series, which had shown him attending the colourful Paro Festival. The infrastructure was now much improved, helped along by the coronation events, and travelling around the country was much easier. However journey times were still very slow, but this may shortly change with the construction of two regional airstrips, one in the Bumthang Valley in central Bhutan and the other near Trashigang, in the east. Although hotel space can be stretched to the limit during the busy festival times, there generally seemed to be much more availability than there used to be.

The Bhutan experience was not just about infrastructure and tourist resources though. The people do not feel the need to prove their place in the modern world, though they are surely part of it. I did not witness a 'country of hermits' as they were clearly in touch with the modern world through television and the Internet. What they have was unique and very precious, and they were justifiably immensely proud of their nation. This fact seemed to be underscored by the very limited exodus from the country, especially amongst the young. Many did leave, particularly to India for tertiary education needs, but most came back, ostensibly because they missed the mountains and the strong religious and family traditions. It went far deeper than that, though of course the country's well-being can partly be explained by the concept of gross national happiness and the reality that it is a beautiful place with beautiful people who have a beautiful culture. But the people truly want to be there, and indeed, given a blank sheet of paper, many from outside the country would join them I am sure. It was certainly not perfect: it was obviously very poor, and they could see what was available in other countries, but they believed that their way was the best path. There simply must be something to that belief, and we could all do well to give it a second thought.

There were naturally exceptions to that idyll, especially amongst the young. Pema had recently commented to me that GNH was probably now running at eighty per cent within that group. However, virtually everywhere I went in Bhutan, I was faced with well-dressed people, who were courteous and polite, who asked for nothing and who displayed the most winning of smiles. One cannot help but love them and to have seen them at that most momentous time in their history, in their country, on their terms, was an unspeakable honour. It was a privilege for which I shall always be grateful and needless to say I shall never forget.

'Gyelo' to K5 and the Bhutanese people, and I sincerely trust that good karma goes with them always.

Thank you and Tashi Delek!

It was not like this!

Everest west of Bhutan

Jhomolhari on the port side, Bhutan below

*army squad prepare to
practice for the Big Day*

Masangang from Dochla

*the stadium awaits the
Coronation celebrations*

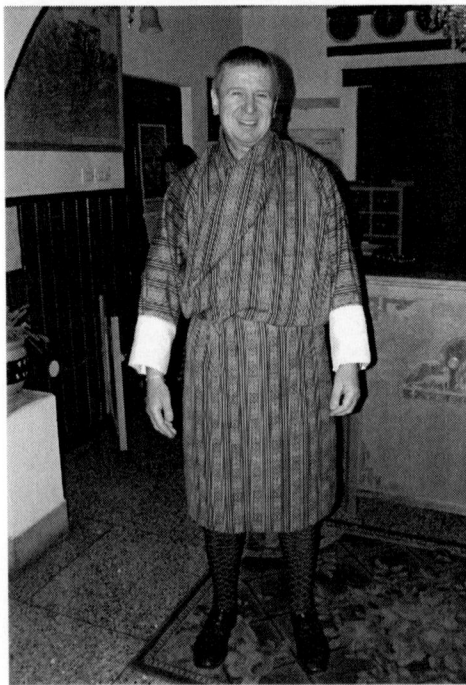

guests get ready

newly crowned K5 addresses His People

pipers at the gates of dawn

class of 2008

you need nerves of steel

CHAPTER 7

THE DEEPER CONNECTION AND THE RISE OF SPIRITUALITY

'Going to school is one thing, getting educated is another, although they coincide at times. Learning from a teacher is preparation. Learning from life in the world is observation. Learning from oneself is intuition.'

Paul Brunton, Perspectives Vol 1

A sense of duty was instilled in me from quite an early age. I think I am from a generation that still believes, even though perhaps we were *made* to believe, that this was the only way to live. It may perhaps be a sort of remnant from the days of empire. Indeed, those Edwardian values were instilled into me at preparatory school, before going on to Bloxham. There were early morning cold baths and marching drills in the schoolyard before having a breakfast of stodgy porridge and overcooked eggs. Above all, we were expected to learn to *lead*. It was a regimen our forebears could fully relate to, I am sure! That said my secondary schooling came at the right time. Somehow, the vast changes presaged by the swinging sixties invaded even these closed establishments. The winds of change were blowing through the land, perhaps not in a totally equal way, but deep changes were nevertheless afoot. During my secondary school years I was enrolled into the Combined Cadet Force, or 'playing soldiers once a week', as some would have it. Bloxham had been the alma mater for two of my uncles on my mother's side. John had joined the RAF and was eventually posted to Malta during the Second World War. He was lost under slightly mysterious circumstances when commanding a modified Wellington aircraft whilst hunting down German shipping attempting to supply Rommel in the North African desert. Phil also joined the RAF and was a navigator on Liberators for his war service. He stayed in the RAF after the war, but subsequently emigrated to Australia to join the RAAF in December of 1966. I remember seeing him off, together with his wife and very young son, from the tented encampment that was Heathrow's North Terminal at the time.

Given that background, I had an interest, more than just maudlin, in matters relating to the Wars. A great friend, Graham, was absolutely on point with his knowledge of World War Two. He likely gleaned his knowledge and interest from his late father, who had served in the RAF as a squadron leader in the North African desert and later by training others on Wellington aircraft at, coincidentally, Abingdon, where I was later to be born. It was during the latter posting that his father famously faced down none other than Douglas Bader, who had dropped by demanding an aircraft that he could use to impress his filly of the day. That request was politely but firmly declined.

Graham had accompanied me when retracing my late father's wartime journey to Nijmegen Bridge. We retraced his steps from his landing on the Normandy Beach (code named *Juno*), and used by the Canadians on D-Day, though Dad had in fact landed there on D+5. Graham and I re-traced his steps along the infamous 'Hell's Highway' route through Belgium and Holland to Nijmegen, where the very same bridge he had been ordered to defend was still there. I took along his medals, including the MBE awarded for his services there, as a mark of respect and tribute. Needless to say that was a very special moment.

My knowledge of World War One was much less deep. I had no relatives I was aware of who served in that war, though doubtless there were some. My friend, Ed, on the other hand was very well aware of the history because he had lost his great-grandfather, Gunner Thomas Dowd of the Royal Garrison Artillery, at Hersin in the Pas de Calais. Thus it was that he and I, together with other friends made a number of very moving visits to the Western Front, particularly the Somme. It was during these visits that we attended the playing of the 'Last Post' at the Menin Gate in Ypres, Belgium, an experience that I sincerely believe everyone should witness at least once. We also visited some of the countless Commonwealth War Graves Commission cemeteries, many set in the middle of fields, where many of the soldiers were buried, quite literally at the very spot where they had fallen. All are immaculately maintained by the CWGC, and it is not uncommon to see messages proclaiming peace and bouquets of flowers on individual memorial headstones, often laid by later generations of the soldier's family. Each message we read told a story that drove a stave of emotion through my heart. These were difficult trips, but they were so emotionally rewarding and I would not have wanted to miss the sheer learning experiences that they were.

Ed had observed when I had returned home from one of my early visits to Bhutan: 'you have come back somehow very different. You seem otherworldly, deeply affected, and in some ways, you are not here (in London), you appear to be still there in spirit.' He was right of course. Ed knows the meaning of places, and he thinks deeply about such matters. We have shared diverse, yet common interests, including hard rock music and World War One. While paying our respects, we have twice shed tears at that service held every evening at Ypres's Menin Gate. I suppose – correction, I know – Ed was right in terms of his observations following my return from the coronation of K5 in 2008. I had thought about living there, and the same idea had been suggested by fellow travellers during my first visit when they had witnessed my initial reaction to the country. That move to live there had been made by some, but not many, though notably some Swiss who had brought their dairy farming skills some time ago. More recently some ex-pat pilots from Europe and New Zealand, and closer still, from India, had taken the plunge. Apparently it is not an easy or straight forward process, but not insurmountable. As in most places it is a question of knowing the right people. Luckily, my driver on my 2009 and 2011 trips said he could help. In fact, I know that he would like me to move there, but it is an unlikely dream.

I believed that past and future visits would satisfy my soul. After all it was my soul that had been so deeply affected. The spirit and karma of Bhutan had seared into my being. For sure the sights and vistas are impressive; and the Himalayas, even from a distance, are awe-inspiring in a way that no camera shot can really ever completely capture. But even more beautiful are the people who are so very special, perhaps even unique. Their underlying deep and all-consuming religious backbone, nurtured by their version of Tibetan Buddhism, drives deep into their lifestyle and all that they do. It is the basis and true foundation on which they live. I was beginning to find that I could not get enough of the country, and I realised that I was proselytising about Bhutan at every opportunity: to my family, my friends, and indeed complete strangers at times. I must have made an impression as quite a few suggested that they would like to join me on a future visit, and, as will be seen, that came to pass in 2009.

Part of the Buddhist religious tradition is the strong belief in a multiplicity of deities. They are ingrained into both the faith and day-to-day Life. Belief in such deities is alien to most westerners, who at best would steer clear of any comment or view the idea with a strong dose of cynicism. However, seeing and hearing the Bhutanese talk about such concepts seems perfectly natural.

The most famous, if that is the correct word, amongst these deities is the Guru Rinpoche, who allegedly had brought Buddhism to Bhutan from India. Famously, during part of his journey, he allegedly flew across Bhutan on the back of a tigress to the 'tiger's nest', where subsequently the Taktshang Monastery was built. This is certainly the most easily recognised and most visited place in the country, and photographs of it often adorn travel books and articles about Bhutan.

There are many other deities, and their thoughts, words, and sayings have the same impact on the Bhutanese as the words of the Bible or the Koran have for adherents of Christianity and Islam. These words from one, 'Jampa, The Future Buddha' should interrupt this chapter because to my mind they succinctly express what this deep faith, in this wonderful country, is all about:

'My Love shines equally upon persons, groups, cultures and worlds
I call upon them to live in universal love and compassion
I am white and golden, harmonious and full of richness
Life (is) a symphony, I write the compelling thesis in the universe

I am found in optimism, in hope and in faith
and in those who look for a better tomorrow.
I bless the discouraged and the lonely,
the fearful and the mournful.
I offer them a way out of the prison of their hearts
I liberate beings from confinement
And show them a brilliant and infinite future
both in the spirit and in the letter of it.'

I cannot compete with that, and I am not sure anyone with a western upbringing and understanding truly can, although I think Van Morrison came pretty close with his lyrics in 'Astral Weeks'.

'I'm nothing but a stranger in this world
I got a home on high
In another land
So far away
Way up in heaven.........'

So why do I go to Bhutan time and again? The world has many treasures elsewhere, I am sure, and indeed I have been very lucky to have seen some – especially those with deep history and spirituality, such as the Kakadu and Red Centre in Australia. One of the best reasons I can muster is the journey itself. As can be seen from my travel diaries, I have been in and out of Bhutan by both road and air. When travelling to the Western Isles and Lewis, the only 'real' way to go is by sea. That way, one sees and feels the sense of location, far from the main conurbations of Scotland and further still from the home counties of England where I live. Even if travel by sea is not one's preference, the voyage within the sea loch (Broom) and then the views of the main-land's mountains from the main channel, are simply spectacular. You see the landscape in its proper context and in the case of the Western Isles, travellers are, whilst taking the main ferry route, some sixty miles, and just under three hours journey time, off the west coast of Scotland, but are less than an hour away by plane from Glasgow or Edinburgh. That flight makes short shrift of what is a very long road journey even before the ferry port is reached.

The sea journey to Lewis can be tough, as can the road journey into or out of Bhutan. Such journeys are rare in these days of 'no time', so I thank Wild Frontiers for the opportunity to travel by road into Bhutan in 2006: it truly was the only way to go. If time, or choice, dictate one's plans, then using Drukair, the world's smallest international airline, is the only alternative option. The company now has three Airbus A319s and an ATR 42 for shorter routes and the currently partly suspended internal routes. It is hoped that these can be restarted soon. The A319s have uprated power plants to deal with the high and constricted location of the airport in the Paro Valley (PBH). They fly the main international sectors to Delhi, Bangkok, and more recently, to Singapore and Hong Kong. Intermediate destinations, such as Kathmandu, Bagdogra, Gaya, Guwarhati, and Dacca are also served. In late 2012, Air India sent a delegation to Bhutan to investigate the possibility of flying there. More recently, in 2013, a new airline, Bhutan Airlines, which is funded by Taishi Industries, the producers of Druk11000, was to commence flights, though initially only on the Bangkok route. I am not convinced that travelling with a new airline is wise though. I think it perhaps best to stick with those who know the area well and have good karma. Nerves of steel are required by the flight crew who, luckily for the passengers, are the only ones who can actually see ahead and thus view what is all around as Paro airport is approached. If you want to see that unnerving view for yourself it is of course available on the Internet. At present, journeys to Bhutan usually include at least one leg of the journey on Drukair, and tickets for those flights cannot be bought without a visa, thus facilitating journeys there can be convoluted, and certainly an exercise that needs plenty of pre-planning.

For those who have been lucky enough to have flown the sectors to or from Delhi will know that the left-hand seat (from Delhi) probably provides the finest view from any aircraft seat in the world. Eight of the ten highest mountain peaks in the world are on show, especially when there is clear weather. Interestingly, the sector back to Delhi seems to be even more spectacular than the outward one even though it is the same route. I think that it is the twisting up and out of the Bhutan valleys, and skimming the ridges, before the full might of the Himalayan range hoves into majestic view, that clinches it. The actual approaches and departures to and from Paro are both just as spectacular, and unlike most other airport approaches in the world, so to say the experience is sheer exhilaration is an understatement. There is much talk about which is the most difficult civil airport approach and exit in the world. As I am not a pilot, I cannot say, but it would not surprise me if Paro took the prize. I know that there are a number of difficult approaches into mountain valleys, particularly in the USA, Europe and Scandinavia, however none of those are in the Himalayas, the highest mountains in the world.

The steep descent by plane into Bhutan starts shortly after passing Everest and its acolytes, Lhotse and Makalu. One of the early English explorers in this region, George Younghusband, aptly described Everest thus: 'a singularly shy and retiring [peak]; it hides itself away behind other mountains.' The adjacent peaks, in many ways, make Everest appear almost insignificant in height because they are not far short of Everest's height in their own right. For their part however, the highest mountains in Bhutan, Jhomolhari and Gangkhar Puensum, stand alone. They rise majestically to over 24,000 feet, which is only around 5,000 feet lower than Everest itself.

At the border with India, Bhutan is virtually at sea level, whilst Paro airport is at 7,500 ft. The nearby passes rise up to twice that height and more, and with its high peaks, Bhutan is truly a country of contrasts. The setting of Paro airport never fails to impress me, especially when I am on the ground, watching the aircraft come in.

Aircraft fly in overhead before suddenly descending below the top ridge of the valley and executing a 180-degree turn within the valley. The aircraft twist through the valleys like fighter planes, whichever approach is taken.

Tremendous flying skills are required of the few pilots that are accredited to fly this route. Most are expats are from India, Europe, or the Antipodes. The exhilaration they must undoubtedly glean from their day job must be immense, and not to say challenging. I am a naturally nervous air passenger however, and I am not sure if this is solely because of where I am headed, I always seem to have total faith in the Drukair flight crews, and I simply relish, and actually very much enjoy, my journeys to and from *The Land of the Thunder Dragon.*

As Bhutan is in the Himalayas, weather is critical to safe flight, and it is as variable and unpredictable as anywhere else. In view of its location, no night or bad weather flights are possible. They always operate under VFR (visual flight rules). If the crew cannot see the immediate mountain ridge tops around the airfield, they will not attempt to fly. This can and does cause flight delays, and Drukair always underscore the need for flexibility with connections to other flights when flying to or from Paro. Although it is a challenging environment you are in good hands and my lord Buddha will look over you. After you have landed in Paro the exhilaration is almost overwhelming. A commonly heard comment from fellow passengers is: '*that* is the way to come into a country!' The tarmac is then often lined with groups taking photos beside the aircraft and flight crew; this is a scene almost unheard of anywhere else. In 2011 *Conde Nast Traveller* magazine voted Paro joint international airport winners along-side the mighty Changi airport in Singapore. The main reason given in the citation was that Paro airport: 'gives a sense of place which most others fail to do, whilst in most others you feel you could be almost anywhere.' Not so at Paro, you only have to look at the airport terminal buildings, which are based on the traditional Bhutanese style, to see that. Another recent observer commented: 'simply arriving at this place gives me goosebumps and a permanent smile'. Welcome to Bhutan indeed!

Once one has landed safely you do certainly feel, and instinctively know, that you are somewhere very different. You may already have a sense of that location, you will certainly sense that you are a long way from anywhere more familiar, high up in the mountains, where you will find that all journeys are going to be very slow when compared with what most are used to. It is also immediately noticeable that it smells different and the air seems to be much cleaner, as is the case when flying into Stornoway in the Western Isles from the polluted south of the United Kingdom and it seems somehow magical too. The Bhutanese people smile a lot, and visitors will be doing that a lot too.

Why does it have such a hold over me and indeed a growing battalion of people from all around the world who are also so deeply affected? Many of those who travel to Bhutan will not return. It will have been ticked off the to-do list or by-passed for different adventures. However, more and more are smitten and have had instilled in them a homing beacon sparking deep seated feelings, which makes future visits inevitable. I know that I am not alone in having exactly those same magnetic feelings about this nation.

Whilst travelling in Australia in November 2012, some friends there pointed to an article on Bhutan in the *Australian Wish* weekend magazine. Such articles are becoming more and more frequent, particularly in Western publications. This particular article concluded with these very appropriate words which I can totally relate to: 'I leave with indelible memories, knowing that I will return to further explore this charming Kingdom. It has been the pilgrimage of a lifetime and I feel most fortunate.'

So what *was* that difference in me that Ed had noticed, and why had Bhutan seared into my soul. Many of my friends, including those who were not as interested in such matters, realised that it was the place where I received a spiritual boost. They were right, I suppose, but even as a spiritual person, I am not sure that I truly recognised that that was happening at first. I certainly do now. I often intone Himalayan karma to help myself and my friends in times of need, though this in no way diminishes my Christian faith. Subconsciously, I believe that the respect I have for duty, fairness, and focus all come together in Bhutan in a way which I thought was being lost elsewhere in the world. Many would, I think, describe these virtues as old-fashioned values, but like many others, I still hold them dear. Generational or not, I believe that they are important.

One of my many interests is popular music in all its various forms. Of course, being a child of the sixties, I am often described as a rocker or metal man. Both those descriptions are, as it happens, only partly right. I recall feeling slightly disappointed when the late Rick Wright of Pink Floyd described their music and pop and rock music in general, as ephemeral. When I am at the height of being *into* a band or album, nothing seems further from the truth ... well not until the next one appears on my radar. I guess, in that sense, Rick was perhaps right after all - no pun intended!

More significantly though, I think that modern life has become more ephemeral too. An American expression I particularly loathe is: 'what's fresh?' It is not just the sound of the words which irk but more about what the phrase implies: what is *new*, as if yesterday and even the present moment are irrelevant and should be forgotten. I certainly agree that sentiment can be maudlin and some things, as we press on through life, should indeed be forgotten. But at some level, we ignore the past and the present, which history has shown oft repeats itself, at our peril. The lessons of history must be recalled. Much of the current strife in the world could have been avoided, or at least better understood, if that seemingly trite advice had been heeded. Though, according to that great traveller and raconteur, Bill Bryson, the Aboriginal language, which is probably the oldest in the world by far, has no words for 'yesterday' or 'tomorrow'. Perhaps they are trying to tell us something!

I am not sure whether Bhutan has had any great world philosophers in its history, but I have mentioned their respect for deities and their wise and perceptive teachings. These are deep-seated lessons that are ingrained into Bhutanese daily life. Life in Bhutan, therefore, does not seem as ephemeral or materialistic as in other nations. To my mind, the two go together. As K4 so wisely observed, we all have nothing of material significance to give to the world, but we have much to take from it. We are, on the one hand, individually poor, but we all have the potential to be rich in spirit and culture. We have nothing to give to the world except this spirituality and culture. And our individual GNH is more important than our own GDP. Variations on this theme, first espoused by K4 in the 1980s, now invariably crop up when one looks up 'Bhutan' in an Internet search engine.

'Perfect' and 'love' are overused words and their true meaning has become really quite diluted. We say them, but we often do not mean what they imply. Bhutan is most certainly not perfect, but on many levels, it comes pretty close. That I love the country is a certainty in the true sense of that often ill-used but wonderful word. Sure, I expect that my love has blinded me to the realities there, but that is in the context of what I have been lucky enough to see and experience elsewhere in the world. On a somewhat trite but pertinent note, the small green character from the 'Star Wars' films wisely said on more than one occasion; 'teach you, we will.' Bhutan certainly can!

As ever in life, there is absolutely no reason why everyone who travels there could or should experience these feelings which I have tried to express in these pages. Humankind is far too diverse for the reaction that consistent. What I have found unique about Bhutan, however, is how deeply and keenly these feelings are for those who do 'get' it. Upon arrival in any far-off land, our minds will be affected. Our souls may be affected, too. My trip to Bhutan allowed me to experience profound happiness and somehow, unselfish satisfaction. Although other places might elicit similar responses, this country seems profoundly unique to me. That is epitomised by the deep sound of the men speaking their local dzonghka language, which is enchanting. Their voices come straight from the dzongs, where the language began. And it is as sonorous as the Tibetan horns used to summon the people and deities to prayer. When you hear it, you feel it!These feelings have been felt by some I have travelled with and many western authors who have written about their own experiences in Bhutan. Many have travelled there more than I have; some have lived there, and some have married Bhutanese partners. And I understand the draw: they seem to have a strength and resilience more than most other races. Whatever your feelings are about the country, you simply have to admire and respect them for their force of will and grace. As I have often observed, we can truly all learn from these people.

It is not overly dramatic to say that the spell cast over me by this place is a web from which I cannot escape, nor do I want to. It has broadened my mind, deepened my soul, and uncovered within me a peace and sense of karma that is new, exciting, and quite unstoppable.

So gird your loins and set aside your fears: the Himalayas are calling. Come along for the ride – it will reward you beyond your wildest dreams.

CHAPTER 8

SPREADING THE WORD, TAKING FOLK WITH ME

'If you live inwardly with love and harmony with yourself and with all others, if you persistently reject all contrary ideas and negative appearances, then this love and this harmony must manifest themselves outwardly in your environment.'

Paul Brunton, Perspectives Vol 1

It was by now November 2009, and I was engaged in a journey that was to be the culmination of all the celebrations of my *soixantieme annee*. I have mentioned previously that friends had started to ask if they could join me. Thus, I decided to travel with my brother, Robin, who had been an absolute star during my rather lavish and somewhat over the top birthday celebrations. I also took Jon, of PL1 fame; a long-term, dear friend whom I knew from my business career in London; and James from Lewis and Florida. I had known James since he was five years old, and I often referred to him as one of my godchildren. I was not his godfather, but in view of our relationship the description seemed apt.

Flight BA257 (LHR–DEL) had been delayed by a stormy Saturday in London, so a good session at a Heathrow T5 bar ensued. We had a good flight to India though and we landed early in the morning into a murky Delhi. We straightaway transferred to the nearby Orchid Eco Hotel. It was not bad, but I felt pretty jet lagged. After an Indian breakfast, we adjourned to our rooms for some rest. James, though, as all young people do, headed off to the business centre to gain access to the Internet.

Later we left with our charming local guide Sanjay Malik and headed to Lutyens' New Delhi. We then went to the much more exciting Old Delhi, where we took a tricycle rickshaw ride through the market streets near the Jama Majid Mosque. 'Velly hard work, 500 rupees' cried my rickshaw wallah, as he struggled around the narrow bustling streets. It was simply stunning, and we all seemed to experience a sensory overload in our different ways. Robin and Jon were the most affected probably because this was their first visit to the subcontinent, James having been to India during his post-university tour two years previously. It was a wonderful experience. It was then an early night after the regulation visit to the hotel bar as we were off quite early the next morning to the airport to join our Drukair flight. I was thinking; 'tomorrow is going to be a very different kind of day for us all'.

As it turned out the flight was delayed until early afternoon. This had something to do with the fact that half the fleet was unavailable, that was one aircraft, as it was on planned maintenance or some such. Anyway, the check-in was eased by our lovely Brazilian friends from São Paulo who we had met in the line. We all stood on the business-class carpet and admired flowers on the desk, feeling just a little pampered and 'special' already. We also had the attention of the ever-friendly and helpful Drukair station manager at Delhi before finally boarding. At long last, we were away, but not before a brief chance meeting with an engineer who had helped build the west–east road across Bhutan. He was going with family and friends to have a significant birthday dinner at the Uma Paro, I admired his style!

Clouds covered the Himalayas but, as we approached Bhutan, the skies began to clear. Mount Jhomolhari seemed to rise up ethereally and the ride in was as exciting as ever. How blessed we were to have those beautiful clear blue skies. This time we passed by Paro dzong as we approached runway 15 at PBH and experienced quite a sharp reverse thrust upon touching down, it was so exciting though! Thanks once again to God and my lord Buddha for happy landings, it was so good to be back. Jon had understandable tears on the tarmac, and after the lengthy immigration procedure and swine flu checks, we met Pema and his drivers, Leki and Banjo, and then we were off to the Olathang Hotel cottages. 'Only three rooms Pema, I think we needed four', but the hiatus was quickly resolved. After stashing our bags we headed off back down to main street Paro for tea and coffee. Instead, though, we had our first, but certainly not last, taste of the very strong local beer 'Druk11000'. ('Druk' means 'dragon', so it was clearly its strength was all in the name!) Pema was in great chatty form and we talked before having dinner back at the hotel along with a nightcap and the first of many card games.

Ah, Druk11000! It is actually brewed in Bhutan, on the southern border with India, and it certainly powers the nation! It is freely available throughout the country and at 8% ABV it seems to work wonders in the thin mountain air.

I was pleasantly surprised to see how quickly the 'party of three' had understood the special place that Bhutan is the moment we landed at Paro. Jon said that his wife, Rosie, would simply love the obvious spiritual vibe it exuded; Robin said he wanted to travel to Bhutan with his wife Moira after his daughters' education was complete; James simply wore a permanent karma grin. 'Thank you everyone' and I thought 'this is just the ticket'.

The next day as the party of three went off to the national museum, I ineffectually tried the shops and bank in Paro. By way of compensation I found my favourite local tomato crisps in one of the stores and furtively consumed them in one of the side streets. I took a quick look at the local *kuru* (darts) competition, and I was eventually re-joined by the others before we all drove off to Thimphu to have 'the lunch' and collect two bicycles for Jon and James. Where else would the bike shop be but three floors up in a building and with no lift?

They were pretty good bikes though, coming complete with all the necessary spares. *'The lunch'* was a term coined by Pema, who had a pretty solid grasp of the English language. This slightly incorrect usage appealed to me though and I felt that this expression should be adopted for our journey. Indeed it was and on subsequent journeys too! In fact, 'the lunch' was particularly important to Pema because it gave him a rest from his guiding duties as I am sure his charges become wearisome at times. Also, and perhaps most importantly, the break allowed him to indulge in his illegal habit of smoking cigarettes, or 'taking incense' as he termed it.

We also found a proper bank after my failure to do so in Paro and made the obligatory visit to the post office to buy some of the beautiful Bhutanese stamps. This all took time, so we had a later than planned start for Wangdue, via the Dochu La Pass. This section was to be the group's first journey at altitude and rather sadly it turned out to be a little bit cloudy up there, though Jon and James were still up for riding down the other side to Wangdue. Meanwhile, Robin was struggling somewhat in the thin air.

So the bike riders set off, and that was the last we saw of them until it became worryingly dark. Around two hours and forty clicks later we came upon James negotiating his way round some cows. And then we saw Jon who, had we not stopped him, would have kept hurtling into the darkness. The ride down had seemed to have been quite an experience for them. Jon amusingly explained that they had founded their own version of the 'Himalayan Cycling Club'! We then completed our journey, with the bicycles safely loaded into our vehicles, and we checked into the Dragon's Nest Hotel, just outside Wangdue, where we enjoyed some celebratory beers, dinner, and yet more cards. Coincidentally, we met up with our Brazilian friends who had also loved the Drukair hair-raising landing into Paro.

The following morning I enjoyed the 'great plane [sic] omelette' for breakfast. We then travelled onto Punakha dzong under the strikingly blue skies, with the two boys riding on ahead. They had come across some ponies just before reaching the dzong, who were quietly eating grass overlooking the river, a photo opportunity if ever there was one! The itself dzong looked simply glorious, and Pema observed that the boys were likely to have been the first cyclists to have crossed the bridge into it. After climbing the very steep ladder style steps we went inside and Pema gave us the great tour I had been lucky enough to experience previously. He explained simply and clearly the life of my lord Buddha, the Shabdrung, and the Guru Rinpoche. It was all very emotional, particularly in the gilded grand central hall, where beautiful colourful murals depicted the various stages of Buddha's life, which drew yet another tear in Jon's eye. Pema did a superb job, especially describing the Buddhist concept of 'the circle of life', in clear and understandable terms. I simply love Punakha dzong because of its location, striking red and white colours and its spiritual significance and after the others had seen it, it was clear that they thought so too.

The Marquess of Zetland, responding to C. J. Morris' address to the Royal Geographical Society in 1935, commented:

> I have travelled over much of [Bhutan … and] there are two things which immediately strike one in Western Bhutan [: …] the solidity and massive character of the chief buildings [and] the social system [that] corresponds […] with a feudal system.

> (C.J.Morris, 'A Journey in Bhutan', *The Geographical Journal,* Vol 86, No.3, 1935).

Perhaps the latter observation was a little less obvious now than it was then, but the feelings of both these comments are still felt by visitors today. Before finally departing this area, we went to the nearby suspension bridge, which I had not been to before. It is set in a very impressive location, and there was much cycling bravado to be had on it by the boys, and also, somewhat worryingly, by our driver Leki too. We were all very fearful that he would tip over the precipitous edge.

Afterwards, we drove into Wangdue town so that James could try to purchase some Druk11000 before the long drive over the Pele La Pass to Trongsa and the Bumthang Valley. Although I had travelled that route twice before, I had not previously had the privilege of seeing it in glorious sunshine. The high mountains could be seen clearly offering a breathe-taking vista. As Robin observed; 'the mountains sparkle, and it does truly feel that we really are in the Himalayas!' 'Yes you are, Robin' I replied, 'or should I call you Tintin, after that great detective's adventures in neighbouring Tibet?'

As we stopped for *the lunch* the clouds started to set in which was a shame, but great food and a very good artefact shop made up for the lack of sunshine. When we reached Trongsa it too was covered in clouds, so not seen at its best. Soon it became quite dark and we still had two and a half hours travelling ahead of us. A further problem was that it had also become very misty and as we had yet another pass to go over at Yotong La (3425 m), the drive became pretty alarming. However I gave full respect to our drivers, Leki and Banjo, who did a terrific job driving in very restricted visibility. Eventually, Jakar came into view and we soon reached the Rinchenling Resort. 'Was it what we had all hoped for?' It was a resounding 'yes' all round! I knew immediately that I had made the right decision to go to the true heart of Bhutan despite the protestations of the two Jonnys from Wild Frontiers and indeed Pema. We played more card games before retiring to bed, and Jon finally won after James and I had done so on the previous nights. I think it took the return through Delhi and the Orchid Hotel before Robin finally regained some pride and won a round himself!

An inspiringly beautiful and warm morning in the Bumthang valley greeted us the next day. I attended a Buddhist ceremony service in the main house for a short while. Then the boys rode on to Kurje whilst Robin and I walked there with Pema. James apparently had a slight fall whilst crossing a bridge, although he seemed okay, before we had a short history lesson about this special place from Pema. We climbed the steps to the guru's cave and received the holy water. Rather embarrassingly I spilt rather too much of it onto the floor, but it was a powerful experience. Then the 'bike boys' and we pedestrians set off on the circular tour to the other side of the valley and the return to our lodgings. Whilst en route we were dallied at the suspension bridge, where James bravely went swimming in the freezing river (Chamkhar Chuu), much to the bemusement of the locals who were watching from the safety of the river bank. Although it was a brave feat, I felt it was also a little dangerous, but he survived the chilly experience with his usual 'joie de vivre'.

After the subsequent walk and drive, it was back to the Rinchenling for *the lunch*, beers, footie with Taishi (the owner's four-year-old, adopted son), and acrobatic displays on the part of Jon and James. In the meantime, Leki and Banjo had made some improvised *kuru* darts and target boards. They had been most ingenious as they had made the *kuru* dart fins out of X-ray paper from the nearby hospital! We collected up everything and walked down, via the Wangdicholing Palace, to the *kuru* ground, where, watched by a few local kids returning from school, fun was had by all. Banjo and James even had some direct hits – though boy, did James in particular, let us know about it! I had no aptitude for throwing the darts at all, though Robin was reasonably successful.

We all then briefly watched Pema performing on the nearby archery range. He successfully fired his arrows across seemingly impossible distances before we all went back to the Rinchenling where, Robin and the boys, enjoyed the much vaunted experience of a Bhutanese hot stone bath. Usually set outside, very hot stone pebbles are placed in a protected end section, thus heating the water to a very high temperature. Apparently relaxing and rejuvenating, I remained unconvinced and steered clear, and anyway, Taishi simply wanted to play some more football!

The temperature during the afternoon had dropped quite markedly and the wind had risen up, so the Swiss-style wood-burner in my room was enjoyed to the full despite my setting a drying towel alight. I am sure the boy had told me it was alright to place things on top to dry! The trip together was not yet over and we had all enjoyed a lovely, restful, and relaxing day in the Bumthang Valley (rather amusingly expressed in a New York accent by James). I felt really glad that I had chosen to come back here and especially to the Rinchenling Resort. I privately hoped that the area was not going to be spoiled by the new airstrip, apparently due to be opened the following year, though I do not believe it will. Having the bikes with us here was just a coup, an excellent suggestion on the part of Jon. James kindly commented 'I am having an awesome time Mark, it is not what I expected at all; it is a very special place and it goes without saying that we have a great group to travel with. Pema is a very good guide – you can dive in and out of his tour narratives.' I replied: 'enjoy every second, because it will all pass by so very quickly.' After of two years of planning the trip I was inwardly hoping that it would not pass too quickly, though James confirmed my spoken sentiment.

The next day was to prove to be a very long one, though as ever, there would be many highlights. I was very sad to be leaving Pema and Sonam, the pretty and always smiling lodge staff, and I knew that I would very much miss staying at the Rinchenling, particularly with the glorious sunshine we had been blessed with. The girls seemed to like the toy teddy bears I gave them, which I suspected was probably a first for them of that type of gift. It really was such a very special and relaxing place with an almost ethereal atmosphere, which appeared to pervade the whole area. However it was time to leave and after our sad farewells we made the first part of the journey was back as far as Trongsa, which this time was bathed in sunshine too. We visited the excellent 'Museum of the Monarchy and Buddhism in Bhutan' in the *Ta Dzong* (watchtower). The precious objects were beautifully laid out in a subtle understated manner. There was some great photography in the short introductory movie, in the fantastically restored building, and just the right number of exhibits, together with a beautiful small temple right at the top overlooking the valley. We all agreed that it was one of the many highlights so far and we were glad that we had dropped by. Although seemingly not that popular with the group, we also made a quick tour of the dzong itself, but not before taking our best photos of the group on a ledge overlooking the dzong. Trongsa is the spiritual home of the Wangchuck Dynasty, and no one can become king unless they have held the title of 'Penlop of Trongsa', a title akin to the 'Prince of Wales' in the United Kingdom. Then, all too soon, it was off again, this time towards the remote Pobjika Valley, where hopefully we could spot some of the very rare black-necked cranes. I am not naturally a 'twitcher' but I knew they would be a fantastic sight.

Arriving in the valley we took *the lunch* at the 'baked potato' farmhouse just as I had done in the previous year, when Obama was elected, and I had met the two lovely, democrat leaning, ladies from America. Sadly though, we could not get close to the cranes and it was using the nearby conservancy centre telescope and long camera lenses that the 'party of three' were able to view them from afar. As I had started to feel distinctly unwell I sat that visit out.

This is a particularly remote valley in this remote country and, as with Bumthang, we felt that it had a special vibe which was difficult to pin point. Before departing we had a little fun with some local school kids near Gantey Goemba. Robin had cleverly remembered to pack some sweets and pens and so it gave him huge pleasure to distribute them to the kids, who were very polite and charming. The ubiquitous smiles on their faces said it all and made the long four-and-a-half-hour drive back to Thimphu, mainly in the dark, a little more bearable. This disconcerting situation was not aided by the fact that our driver, Leki, appeared to be very tired and very alarmingly appeared at one point to be nodding off. Jon was suffering from Robin's brandy ministrations from the night before and feeling decidedly car sick, making this part of the journey even more of a chore for him. Eventually the lights of Thimphu appeared and we arrived at the Jhomolhari Hotel, which was located right in the middle of town. Jon had had enough by then and retired straight to bed. I took supper with Robin and James, who both seemed to have every intention of sampling the karaoke and nightlife. However I followed Jon's lead need and I suspected that the other two would in fact probably not be too far behind despite their ambitious bravado!

The next day turned out to be very special too: a beautiful, sunny start before setting off to the King's Royal Thimphu Golf Course, which was one of only three in Bhutan at that time, and it was the only one open to *chilips* (foreigners). Where else could you have golf course with a dzong and palace as a backdrop? Robin and I were paired against James and Jon, who had not swung a club in ten years. It was a great challenge, and the boys stormed into the lead. Jon did not look rusty at all! However, the two brothers rallied on the back four holes. Finally, when it was down to the last hole, the two boys were victorious, well played! We followed the game with a great *the lunch* in the clubhouse and afterwards were rewarded by a brief handshake and greeting from the Bhutanese Communications Minister. A little shopping expedition followed, before we went off to meet Samdrup.

Our arrival in Dobji Dzong can only be described as a precious moment in time. Two trumpeters, the lama, and eighteen of the twenty-eight monks were lined up to greet us. It was all very emotional, and our breath was taken away, especially for the 'party of three' who were visiting for the first time. Tea and special rice was served on the best china in the lama's guest quarters, followed by a tour of the tower, which was now converted for classroom use, and the new dormitory accommodation. More tears and high emotion followed with the lighting of the butter lamps in the temple, a great honour for us as this was not normally allowed due to the fire risk. Afterwards, we distributed woollen fleece jackets, dyed in a suitable deep red colour to reflect their monastic robes, to the young monks, which I had procured through Samdrup's good offices. I very much needed Jon's assistance in particular with this task as I was fighting back a wall of emotion. Meanwhile Robin distributed more sweets and pens. It was a very precious moment and such a privilege, an unspeakable moment of joy, honour, happiness, and wonder.

A chat or two with the monks outside was followed by a short but very intense soccer game, especially for Jon, who was in goal fending off a fiercely contested penalty shootout. Samdrup, Leki, and Banjo joined in, and James impressed us all with his backflips and then picking up a very small monk who he accidentally dropped to the floor just like an egg! It was a very funny moment and the young monks just loved all the fun; words just cannot explain it.

Sadly, it was then time to depart. There were emotional 'goodbyes' all round to the lama, monks, and my dear friend Samdrup, before setting off for the Uma Paro. It was salutary to think about how the different worlds we had seen that day collided: Jon, in particular, after having had such an amazing time at Dobji, found the comparative luxury of the Uma resort a little hard to take. In fact I too had never stayed in a five-star hotel in Bhutan before this trip - the daily tourist rate levied usually provides for rather more modest, though perfectly acceptable, accommodation.

The place was just unbelievable, perched high on the side of the Paro valley, and set in its own grounds. If Aman Resorts hotels were apparently better, then let them be! It was perhaps a case of too much personal attention from the staff for James though, but we had a lovely evening complete with a reflective chat about the day's events and some more card games. That night, some more personal reflective thoughts came to mind: 'thank you, God. Thank you, my lord Buddha. Thank you to the lama and the monks at Dobji dzong. Thank you, Samdrup. But especially thanks to: Robin, Jon, and James, simply for being there.'

The next day, the weather was again stunning and remained perfect all day. The clarity in the air in the valley was striking. Although 'only' at 7,500 feet it felt higher and the karma that pervades Bhutan is always particularly palpable here. Perhaps it is because it is the 'gateway' to the outside world. After breakfast in my quarters with the 'party of three', served by my charming butler, Bhawani, it was time to drive up the valley to view the snow-capped Jhomolhari and the other high peaks. Jon and James dashed up to see Drukygel, the ruined dzong, whilst it appeared that it was Robin's turn to feel a little queasy. And then we were off for a walk up to the Tiger's Nest. I was thinking: 'surely it should be the *Tigress's* Nest because the guru flew in on one! Jon, James, and Leki ran up via the short-cut route in less than an hour, apparently a record for Leki, who is a very fit man. Robin and I adopted a more leisurely pace together with Pema and Banjo ... at least until the halfway cafe. As Robin and I progressed towards the viewing platform, we met the boys coming back down. They nobly turned back for the obligatory photograph overlooking the Tiger's Nest, and what a picture it was; thanks, everyone! They had, in fact, made it to the temple at the Tiger's Nest before the lunchtime closure. Visiting it, and going inside, was apparently yet another highlight for them.

The food at the cafe was pretty good on the way down, and then we headed back to Uma, but with a stop in Paro Town for final shopping. Sadly, arrival at the Uma began the parting of ways for us all: I said my goodbyes to Banjo there, but not before we had taken one last and, probably only, photograph of the whole group together with our drivers and guide. We had all agreed to rendezvous for drinks before our final dinner together. Everyone was tasked with bringing a list of the 'top five' highlights of the trip. The exchange of those was fun, but saying goodbye was not. However, everyone was departing very happy! Those farewells effectively marked the end of my sixtieth year celebrations, and to be honest, there was nowhere I would rather have been at that time. The tour had been a success, though I was not that surprised, though as ever in life, you can never be sure. I was so proud of how it had all gone and what everyone had appeared to have gained by simply 'being' there. Some will doubtless return, but in the meantime, *Tashi Delek!*

The following morning was yet *another* beautiful day in Druk Yul! Waiting for, and seeing, Drukair flight KB204 departing for Delhi with my 'party of three' was both exciting and sad. Certainly, there was a tear in my eye as I heard the sound of the departing aircraft echoing around the valleys for some time, whilst weaving its way out of Bhutan. Those thoughts were left behind after a lovely breakfast, again served by Bhawani, and accompanied by some of the songs from my recently purchased new Bhutanese CDs. I was then off with Pema and Leki to travel to the Haa Valley, which was a fresh destination for me. We would be going via the highest pass in the country at Chela La. Pema took the wheel for the first time, whilst Leki rode in the back for a change.

Meanwhile, 'naughty Banjo', as the two boys had nicknamed him, had dropped the 'party of three' off at the airport before returning to Thimphu to see his wife, and I believe, his children too. Anyway, we were soon high above the Paro Valley, and we saw the second Drukair aircraft fly out *below* us. We enjoyed just spectacular views of the PBH runway and dzong beyond. The air was very clear and still as we drove higher and higher. There were hardly any other cars or people about, apart from a few folk working re-laying a section of road surface, which looked like a scene from Hades. Huge vats of bitumen were being melted for the process, and thick, black smoke was everywhere.

Yet higher and higher we went. Finally, we stopped for a fruit break, care of Leki, and we saw Mount Jhomolhari in all its glory, together with its attendant peaks. In the 1930s, C.J. Morris had obviously had a whale of a time in this area:

> 'No sooner had I arrived than the Penlop's representatives were announced. They brought with them considerable quantity of liquor and oranges [...] Hardly had we covered a few miles when I found a meal spread out for me by the wayside and a further supply of spirit and oranges. This remarkable display of hospitality was repeated at intervals along the route.'

> (C.J. Morris, 'A journey in Bhutan', *The Geographical Journal*, Vol 86, No.3,1935)

Leki's gesture of producing fruit for his traveller was certainly in the same vein, even if it was not accompanied by the same spirit!

Higher and higher still we drove, past a nunnery clinging to the mountainside just like the Tiger's Nest. Finally, the highest point on Dantak Roads was reached: Chela La (3810 m). Prayer flag city it certainly was, and all of Bhutan was laid out before us in a simply stunning vista. Behind us we could see the west of the country, and the nearby border with Sikkim; to the north was the old way in from Tibet. Perhaps most spectacular of all was looking towards the east, where we spied rolling ridge after rolling ridge and associated valleys, seemingly disappearing off into the distance. It was breathe-taking, and indeed I was breathless in the comparatively thinner air. I instantly felt that anyone visiting Bhutan should stand on this spot, hopefully on a clear day, just to marvel at the sight and understand the true location of the 'last Shangri-La'. I felt this was the *real deal*. I was in the place where it had all started for me, I suppose, because this route was featured in Joanna Lumley's TV programme and book, 'The Land of the Thunder Dragon', in which followed her grandfather's journey from Calcutta, the Raj's capital in India, to Kurje, the sacred spiritual centre of Bhutan.

It was the area where the mountaineers, Mallory and Irvine, must have just skirted while en route from Darjeeling to Yatong, and beyond, on their ill-fated attempts to climb Everest. And it was probably much as C.J. Morris described it earlier:

'After leaving Paro I retraced my path to Ha and from the latter place crossed over the Ha La pass at 13,900ft to Chumbi and Yatung. Although it was now mid April it was bitterly cold [...] and decided to push on to Sikkim. It was raining when we left Yatung and still exceedingly cold. Very soon the rain turned to snow [...] by the next night there was about 4ft all around [...] it seemed impossible to go on. We set off in a gale, it was impossible to see for any distance in front [...] snowstorm most of the way. We eventually [arrived] in Gangtok [Sikkim] whence I continued by motor to Darjeeling.'

(C.J. Morris, 'A journey in Bhutan', *The Geographical Journal*, Vol 86, No.3, 1935)

This was the stuff of heroes, and high up in that remote spot I felt deep feelings of history and imagined stories of derring-do all around me. Then I walked with Leki to a prayer flag-draped stupa on the old route, and listened as he discussed, in his imperfect English, the Buddhist difference between heaven and hell. All the while I continued to strain for breath in the thin air. Leki was a studious, somewhat earnest, and very well-intentioned man. (See appendix 2.) His command of English, though faltering, was nevertheless very impressive as he was largely self-taught. He was also a very committed Buddhist, and his religion meant everything to him and, for my part, I was very keen to learn more about his faith. However the thin air and his faltering command of English was sadly getting the better of us, but not before he had shown me a book which he said would help with my understanding. It was called 'The Heart Treasure of the Enlightened Ones' by Dilgo Khyentse, and whilst reading it later I came across this pithy and salutary entreaty:

'Root text 68
What use is all you have eaten?
It all just turned to excrement
Look how insatiable your appetite has been
Now you had better nourish yourself with the food of Samadhi
[meditative contemplation]
Quit all that eating and drinking and recite a syllable mantra'

I felt suitably chastened and humbled, particularly whilst in such a humble and spiritually strong country. Although mentioned previously, the Bhutanese belief and commitment to their faith was one of the main reasons I had kept returning to this country. It was an inspiring and quite exceptional place, and I was sure that was one of the key reasons why, although small and impoverished, this country was, nevertheless, considered so rich in spirit.

We were off again, but this time we descended somewhat rapidly into the very narrow and steep-sided Haa Valley. We passed the huge, mainly Indian, army base, established to keep an eye on the border with China. The army has such a strong presence in this area that even the dzong had been commandeered as the army HQ, leaving only the central tower to be used as the Buddhist temple. Captain Morris, again observing correctly:

'The valley lies at an average height of 8,000 ft [...] and is therefore never hot. The surrounding hillsides are high and steep, so that the valley loses its sun in the early afternoon.'

(C.J.Morris, 'A journey in Bhutan', *The Geographical Journal*, Vol 86, No 3 1935)

We soon arrived at the rough track leading to the Rigsum Resort. A Druk11000 soon whetted my appetite for a sandwich, which formed *the lunch* together with a pot of hot water sans tea bag! This, together with warnings from Pema about a lack of hot water for the shower, reminded me why I was in Bhutan. I was thinking: 'If the Uma was nice, this was the *real* Bhutan!'

Suddenly, although still sunny, it became very cold and breezy. Thinking about the Indian army base reminded me of the Romans posted high up in the Hardknott Pass in the English Lake District. I was sure it was not a posting either sets of troops would have relished. Still, cold or not, there was plenty of reading time to be had, and Leki had loaned me that book on Buddhist enlightenment. Soon it was time for supper for one, which comprised a very simple meal of local vegetables. People here are especially poor and life is lived on the (economic) edge, and I again felt the stark contrast with the Uma could not have been more marked. Afterwards, Pema chatted with me about the varying characters in my 'party of three' and said he hoped that they would spread the word about Bhutan, and Pema, in London, Surrey, and Florida!

Although the Haa Valley, sited at 2750 metres, was only a little higher than Bumthang, it felt a *lot* higher. The steep sides of the valley appeared to be very close, and the air is noticeably thin. I was the only guest at the resort, indeed I later discovered that I was the only foreign tourist in the whole valley for the two days I was there. For breakfast the next morning I had the best porridge I had tasted for quite a while, served by two pretty but shy girls. I felt that I needed some of James's style to help break the ice! Afterwards we went into Haa town, which definitely had a 'border' feel about it. In view of the lack of tourists, I noticed I was the subject of a lot of stares, perhaps even more than I had experienced whilst in Radi, back in the East.

Pema explained that a lot of illicit trade from Tibet went through the town, after being carried over the mountains on foot. Apparently, Bhutanese 'magic mushrooms' are taken across to China, whilst cheap shoes and other goods are brought back in return. Later, we drove on to the head of the valley at Damthang, where there was a very large, Bhutanese army camp. Sadly, it was a restricted area, but we got through the gate, but only just enough to turn around and come back out again! Apparently, they were awaiting the imminent arrival of an Indian army helicopter at the landing pad a little further up the road, probably carrying a high-ranking officer or dignitary.

After chatting with the ubiquitous schoolboys, and having a quick tour of the Shamen ground, we drove past Talung village and Yartong Goemba and up one side of the valley to a traditional farmhouse. The mother and daughter there, both somewhat inevitably known to Pema, gave him and Leki *the lunch*, whilst I could only manage drinking their lovely chai tea. Life up there appeared to be very simple, although there was electricity, mobile phones, newspapers and a television in their house, which surprised me a little. However I felt that the house and their life style would not have been unrecognised in mediaeval times. Yet despite this, and its remoteness, the Haa Valley was the home of the queen mother and many other important people in Bhutan society. For me, this was definitely the 'explore' part of the trip. (I had given our trip the title 'Discovery and Explore' as I had felt it was appropriate bearing in mind there would those elements for us all.)

Even Pema, who seemed to know everything about Bhutan, had not previously stayed at the Rigsum resort, nor had he gone to Damthang village, so near to the border with China. We visited the temple at Haa dzong. Although not built by the Shabdrung – it dates from 1915 – you would never have guessed because the style was exactly the same as the other, far older ones I had visited previously. A lone monk, manning the temple, gave us the holy water which continued the spiritual connection.

I had a quick look at the army golf course with its greens made out of sand and the nearby fish farm in which the authorities were experimenting with the introduction of brown and rainbow trout. There would be a slight problem if they were successful because the Bhutanese Buddhist religious beliefs do not allow them to kill animals, including fish.

Whilst driving back to the Rigsum reading C.J. Morris's observations during his visit here in the 1935 again seemed pertinent:

'My sombre garments compared most unfavourably with the magnificent brocades of my hosts. The Dzongpon however was a man of great charm. He had been educated at the University of

Calcutta, and it soon became apparent that [he had ...] considerable knowledge of English. The Ha Valley forms part of the personal estate of Raja Dorji, the Bhutanese Agent at Kalimpong, and to him is principally due a remarkable educational experiment which has been proceeding with very great success for some years. He himself was educated at St Paul's school in Darjeeling, but he early realised that although Bhutan has need of men with modern western education, it must be an education adapted to the special needs of the country and given primarily through the medium of the people's own tongue.' (C.J. Morris, 'A journey in Bhutan', *The Geographical Journal*, Vol 86, No.3, 1935)

These thoughts seemed to me to be the very template for the third and fourth king's future educational reforms.

They certainly have quite a ways to go out here in this very remote valley in order to attract the non-trekking tourists. The accommodation was alright, modest in the Bhutan way, though the food was a bit thin and even Pema had agreed with me about that. We were leaving the valley that day, via the longer route back to Paro, a distance of around a hundred kilometres. We got to see the other end of the valley, which was heavily wooded, still steep, and very beautiful. It looked simply magical in the sunshine. And, just like in the East, most of the kids and younger people had been taught to be polite towards passing tourists and local VIPs. So when passing individuals or groups of them, their hands and arms were outstretched in supplication as the 'dasho Mark' passed, much to the amusement of Leki in particular. Pema told me 'respect' was respected out here; he was right and it was simply wonderful to see.

There were masses of red chillies drying everywhere, much more than I had ever seen elsewhere in the country. We passed the ancient dzong at Belika, which was very much like the one at Dobji. We then stopped near Wanaka for tea at a farmhouse where yet another of Pema's aunts lived. Her kids were around after school with one of their friends' who appeared to be about fifteen years old, and was reading about soil erosion in an English textbook. Obviously the homework had helped because he told me had just passed a recent exam. However, upon pointing to a map of Bhutan in his textbook, it was clear that the furthest he had travelled from here was the Paro Valley. He had not been to Thimphu, Wangdue, Punakha, Trongsa or beyond, as I had been so fortunate to do. Likewise, he had not been to the Radi Valley, where Leki came from. It was there that Leki had suffered an unhappy childhood causing him to run away from school on several occasions, and suffering harsh consequences as a result. My new found friend seemed to be living a much happier life.

Suddenly, as we drove on, the thick forestation gave way to much drier, more barren country. We soon found ourselves above Dobji dzong. I saw the original path down that was still used when quarry landslips during the monsoon season blocked the normal access road. And then it was on to Chuzzom (Confluence) and thence back into the Paro Valley. The road here was very tightly squeezed into the narrow confines of the valley which caused me to wonder just how difficult it must be for the Drukair aircraft to fly in and out of the valley.

The high mountains surrounding the valley, and the dzong, were looking simply spectacular in the bright sunshine, and so it was full circle back to Sonam Trophel's Bar in Paro Town, where we drank our first Druk11000 for a while. The lovely bar girl was still there with her warm smile, and we had a lovely *the lunch*. It was a wonderful end to that lovely drive on a lovely day in a lovely country: *thank you again, my lord Buddha.*

Finally I did a little bartering at one of the small shops for a couple of temple lanterns before going back to the Uma, finding myself in the room where Robin had stayed and where the outlook was just as Tintin would have expected! The air was so clear, and the room just magnificent, so the way was clear for a relaxing afternoon and evening before the next day's adventure.

There was an invasion of tiny, red ants near my washbag in my bathroom: 'Haa Valley immigrants, perhaps', I thought. The following morning a blocked loo, and only the second cloudy morning of the whole trip, started my last full day in Druk Yul. I waited for a Drukair flight to approach runway 15 from the excellent vantage point of Robin's room and just when I was about to give up, one took off towards the dzong. It flew up the valley before turning 180 degrees to fly over the airfield again; a fascinating spectacle.

I was collected by Pema and Leki and driven a little way up the Chela La Pass road to a farm road. From there, we took a walk to Dzongdakha, which is not actually a dzong as such despite its name. We enjoyed fantastic views of the Paro Valley again and the path that we were taking clung a little precipitously to the cliff side. I had recommended a Bhutan visit to a lawyer friend in London, and she had spent her honeymoon there, and visited this very spot, which was new to me. Near the top, we met two boys who were resting on a large rock overlooking the valley. They were helping their parents carry down timbers from their derelict community of six houses higher up the hill. There was no farm road up there, so they were moving down to live at a lower level.

We then walked down ourselves, negotiating a really quite steep descent, especially at the start. We arrived back into Paro for refreshment which we took at the same hotel I had been to during my 'Land of the Thunder Dragon' trip in 2007. And then I was off to try and spot yet more Drukair flights from the top road overlooking the airport. Sadly there were no flights, but I had great views of the valley. After that, we drove up the remaining spur of the Paro Valley that I had not previously explored, called the Shari Valley. There were fine views of the mountains again, but none of the dzong; consequently, not many tourists go there. Interestingly, Pema's brother-in-law, Dawa, his assistant guide on the 'Thunder Dragon' trip, lived up there. Pema seems to have relatives and contacts everywhere in Bhutan, especially in the Paro area.

And then it was back to the Uma for the last night of the 'Bhutan Discovery and Explore' 2009 tour.

Before settling in for the final Druk11000 and dinner, I had a pretty uncomfortable session of deep tissue massage in the health spa. It was painful though somehow soporific. What a journey it had been, and there was so much to reflect upon.

Thank you: Pema, Leki, and Banjo, thank you to the 'party of three', for agreeing to come with me to the Land of the Thunder Dragon, I simply knew it had been so worthwhile. I had missed them all since they had left, but I had a wonderful time exploring Haa. However it seemed like an absolute age since we had taken the tricycle rickshaw ride around Old Delhi's street markets.Bhutan continues to surprise and humble me in equal measure. The people remain grounded, realistic and seemingly still full of gross national happiness. In fact, the second international GNH conference was being held in Brazil whilst we had been in Bhutan. The prime minister left to attend it on the very aircraft we had arrived on – hence that red carpet on the tarmac.

My own understanding of Bhutanese spirituality has taken a step forward, thank you, Leki. And sitting there in the luxury of Uma's restaurant, supping merlot, having a lovely meal, and looking down on the twinkling lights of Paro Town, I asked myself: 'would I want to be anywhere else?' I thought not, as the magical mysticism of the country continued to pervade even this resort hotel, and the view of the valley at night seemed very special, and I certainly did not want to leave.' So to Bhutan, 'Druk Yul': *Lazhimbe zhu* and *Tashi Delek!*

Although I had observed yesterday that it had started cloudy, it soon became sunny and really quite hot, so I hoped that it would be so for my departure the next morning. Pema and Leki collected me at an early hour and it looked reasonably clear for a VFR exit from the airport. However, by the time we took off, it was already cloudy in the Paro area. 'Give me a hug, Mark' Pema kindly said at the airport and from Leki, the same. I had slightly lost it at the Uma last night when saying goodbye to them both because I hate airport partings, especially so early in the morning.

Anyway, we were soon airborne and flying out and away from the dzong, just like the 'party of three. We twisted and turned over the ridges and valleys just as before, though some of the ridges looked even closer than on our way in; I felt that I could almost touch them. Our pilot, who sounded Australian, but may have been from New Zealand, simply must have had the best flying job. The weather was completely clear, unlike the inward journey, and I hoped that my 'party of three' had also seen Kanchenjunga, Everest, Makalu, and Lhotse when they left. It really is the best flight in the world, and we seemed to be flying much closer to the highest peaks than I had remembered from 2008. Also, it emphasised just how far east and how deep into the Himalayas we were. It is a secret kingdom, hidden away, the last *Shangri-La* perhaps indeed.

The pilot said that very strong headwinds would mean a flight time of around two hours and fifteen minutes, but it ended up being just two hours. I was greeted with a fairly empty IGI airport at Delhi, and I went straight back to the Orchid Hotel and checked in online for my BA flight before resting in my room in anticipation of a night-time departure to London's Heathrow. There was further time to reflect on the past two weeks; it had been a journey of wonderful and priceless memories. As I had remarked to Pema on leaving Paro; 'I simply could wait for my fifth visit.'

Old Delhi

descent suddenly starts!

Discovery & Explore party landed

first things first

11000's will have to wait

Dragons Nest

always special

special inside too

Trongsa fun!

Gantey kids after school

Dobji courtyard

one each, that's it

special moment

soccer challenge!

Royal Thimphu

the Brothers make it!

we left him there

view from Chelala

stupa marks the old route in

Goodbye

CHAPTER 9

PRECIOUS BEYOND WORDS

'It is important to know that there are three kinds of wisdom:
wisdom resulting from listening, wisdom resulting from reflection,
wisdom resulting from meditation.'

The fourteenth Dalai Lama

Om Mani Padme Hum

So where has this journey brought me, and how did it create such
a deep and indelible imprint on my soul? Was it the seed sown
by Joanna Lumley's TV programme or that chance conversation I
had whilst at work with Ryan? I was not searching, but I suppose,
subconsciously, I was *looking*. To my surprise and complete joy, *two*
'promised lands' appeared. Both cast spells upon me in their own
ways, and they still, and I suspect always will, trigger deep feelings
of belonging. The deep sadness whenever I leave either place is
palpable, and I know that these spells have worked their magic on
others, too – maybe as a result of my own enthusiasm and love for
these places. It is more than that I suspect, as the magic is real.

Beyond the wondrous sounds on *The Perfect Girl* album, it was the smell, the colours, and the smiles of Bhutan that won me over and indeed still do win me over. All these sensations are, I am sure, present elsewhere in the world, but perhaps not to the same degree and certainly not with the same kaleidoscope of country and *karma* coming together in such perfect harmony. The Himalayas are unique, and not simply because of their height and imposing majesty. The karma and GNH I have spoken about are also real. The young leave the country to pursue academic achievement, but for the most part they return, mainly to reacquaint themselves with such strong feelings and to feel at home. Why? Because they *miss* it, especially the mountains, and I can certainly see why.

What have I learned through these travels to the last Shangri-La? What has the place taught me? Even if GNH is running at only eighty per cent, that is seventy five per cent higher than most other countries in the world. One would expect material wealth to provide that happiness easily, but of course it does not, at least certainly not in a lasting and meaningful way. For me, old-fashioned smiles, civility, care, support for the family and respect are values largely lost in most places, but they live on there in a very different kind of society. The world can learn that materialism is not the greatest gift; it is transitory and deeply unsatisfying. Though of course, I know full well that such things have allowed me to see and be part of two promised lands. It is not a clash of religious and secular beliefs; it is the lifting of the veil that allows one to see that great simplicity makes us all spiritually richer. This is not to claim that Bhutan is a utopia where crime and unpleasantness do not exist. I am a realist and always have been. Whether my beliefs stem from my family's genes or something else is of no consequence. I am the person I am – or rather, have become. Inner peace gives us outer strength. One of my earliest memories of contentment was playing alone in a school playing field sandpit near my house. The 'alone' piece formed an integral part of who I am. That said social intercourse and new challenges are vital, rewarding, and exciting.

That is what really appeals to me about Bhutan: their society is rooted in their religious beliefs and mutual respect, yet fun and laughter are always present. So often, we see the strictures that religious beliefs can bring about, often due to humanity's myopic view of the world. Only rarely do people implement the spirit of what was intended. There is no blurring of this vision in Bhutan. It is not so much a question of what is right, but what *is*. How refreshing!

The United Kingdom experienced the feelings, support, and emotions generated by the London Olympics in 2012. The most valuable commodity experienced by all who chose to let it in was the *spirit* of the Olympics, which was absolutely free. I think many would agree that sharing these moments was a life-changing event. It also caused some of us to see just how irrelevant the material things in our lives are, despite holding them so dear. Many were sad to see the Olympics end, and I suspect that was more likely due to the loss of that spirit than the ending of the sporting events themselves.

Om Mani Padme Hum

It is a Sunday afternoon in May and it is beautifully calm, sunny, and warm on Lewis. Folk forsaking the Sabbath are out and about in unusual numbers. They are enjoying the peaceful spell while they can. A deep *ha* (sea mist) is visible a little way out in the Atlantic, and it largely obscures any distant views out to sea. The mountaintops, though, are clear. A lost lamb calls for its mother, who is actually quite close by. This spot, at Mealista, conjures up thoughts of that deep and riven past. I recall those words on the nearby plaque: 'others who lived in and loved this place. It was once their treasured home, and that is why it is such a powerful place'.

The clearing and cleansing of my mind is palpable. Depending on one's personal habits, a bath or shower can wash away the rigours of the day or night, but the mind rarely gets such a quick fix. In truth, we rarely let our minds get a similar chance. Our modern world gets exponentially busier and more stressful. Mum's words, spoken at a time when her three sons were growing up and leaving home, are relevant: 'your Father and I had the war to contend with, dear, but I would take that for all the stress you boys are under and will be put under in your lives.'

How to see the wood for the trees is the key, and we all have to find ways through the forest of life. Personal resources are for most finite and not easily or quickly gained. And indeed such resources, once gained, are easily lost. Thus, travelling to my promised lands is not an option for all. And selfish as it is, I would not want everyone to visit my special places. However, what I hope to impart to my readers through this book – which has been part travelogue, part life journey – is that the world out there is a very special place if you are willing to look, and so, as the Bible so pithily exhorts: 'seek and ye shall find'.

The world as it is now, with its access to instant communication and information, can inform you about Lewis and Bhutan in a thrice, but it can only tell you so much. A computer screen cannot tell you what it feels like, smells like, *is* like. For that, you have to *be* there. That break of habit on my part in 2006 (and joining that group tour to a far-off land) was indeed a life-changing experience. That experience was, for me, unique; it was like nothing I had felt before, and it was not a little unnerving and challenging. However, I have not looked back, and a significant part of me has changed forever. I recently heard a comment from one of the doyens on television's 'Dragon's Den' which were so apposite to these feelings: 'some of the greatest and most special moments of our lives are getting swept away with technology.' The feelings I experienced in Bhutan, on the other hand, were real.

Om Mani Padme Hum

I know that I need to return there, and will go back for as long as I am able – maybe with new friends, maybe alone, maybe to places I know well, maybe new ones. I just need to feel the spirit of the place. It is an unlikely place for a Westerner to live, and the fact that it is difficult for someone like me to live there is probably a good thing. Absence makes the heart grow fonder, they say, and that sentiment is certainly true in my case. I quite often yearn to be there, but by the same token, I am slightly relieved that I am not there yet because I have something to look forward to.

A missionary acquaintance with whom I struck up an email conversation was mortified to discover that, as a Christian, I was not banging on the doors of Bhutan to let Christianity in. It is one of the few countries yet to be touched by Christian missionaries. I have no wish to offend or change my acquaintance's deeply held beliefs. I doubt that I could, anyway. But the truth is Bhutan does not need that kind of change or influence. It could be introduced for sure, but it would do nothing for the people; they simply do not need it. As Linda Leaming so wisely observed in her book 'Married to Bhutan': 'The country does not particularly need the rest of the world, but the world needs Bhutan.'

I have previously mentioned that the Bhutanese seem to be quite comfortable with the life-style they lead despite the poverty that afflicts them. The antics of young, red-blooded, Bhutanese males practicing the art of night-hunting, often leads to the practical and virtuous squaring of one of life's circles. Find each other, like each other, sleep with each other, live together: couples in that state are considered to be married, and without ceremony, I like that. Mind you, K4 took that concept a little further when he ascended to the throne during his teenage years and married three sisters!

Unlike their mighty neighbours in India, Bhutanese culture does not countenance begging because their society and religion provide for them. It must also provide that inner comfort I have alluded to. Generally in this world, smiles do not lie: especially when they shine forth so convincingly from Bhutanese eyes. It is a wonderfully natural gift to be able to smile, and it is a very difficult act to fake. The Bhutanese smile all the time … with relish.

Om Mani Padme Hum

The Lewis sunshine is getting warmer, and I watch another transatlantic jet from Europe heading out over the ocean. The land and the isles below that they are leaving behind must look magical. However, the passengers high above cannot hear the gently heaving ocean, nor smell the land, nor see Cracaval and the other Uig hills with their fierce cliffs and inviting walks. Instead they are treated to a hundred channels on a small screen and a pre-dinner aperitif call. Recently, local friends on Lewis met a retired American pilot and his wife. His visit was brought about by very similar thoughts: he had flown over the clearly beautiful islands often en route to and from the United States, and he felt that he simply had to visit them. Apparently he enjoyed every moment, of course I was not surprised. The mental equivalent of a physical shower was having the same effect on my soul; karma was taking hold. It was not an escape, it was a support; it was not a solution, but it was an increasingly vital part of the answer.

My Chicago-born friend, Jori, married a Stornoway girl some years ago, and he has lived on these isles ever since. His big thing outside of work is music, generally the kind of music I like. His mantra, oft quoted, is deeply felt. This community is small, and yet it produces amazing talent of all varieties. He feels it is a secret treasure, and that those who can experience it are blessed. It is a niche market, but his point is well made. Having been privileged to have heard some of that home-grown talent, I know just what he means. Bhutanese music does it for me every time I hear it, but I suspect it is too jingly for Jori's tastes. The music transports me back there, and I treasure it for that.

Om Mani Padme Hum

Is not Bhutan just like any other holiday destination? On one level, of course it is. I have heard variations of the following words often: 'you are very lucky to go there, but we cannot because there is nothing for the kids to do, and what about the food? It is a long way, too, and it is so expensive, so no thanks. We will stick to what we know. Maybe when we are retired we will go there.' I hope that the preceding chapters have dispelled some of those myths. Though in truth, I think that the myths should remain as they are, as some of the mysticism of the country imply cannot, and should not, be dispelled.

I love film because it is a form of escape, as indeed it is often intended to be. It is an art form, of course, and great thespians abound. Everyone has a favourite film. Who can forget the sight of Omar Sharif riding out of the desert mirage on a camel in 'Lawrence of Arabia'? Those lucky enough to have seen it will certainly not forget that image. The scene has a mystical, surreal feel to it even though it ends with a gunshot. As I have reported, Bhutan is a mystical, magical place, full of allegorical tales and their tiny film industry is no exception. 'The Cup', 'Travellers and Magicians', and 'Chorten Kora' all convey a magical theme. Even if you do not understand dzongkha, you can relate to the stories being told. Mainstream Hollywood has been to Bhutan too, in 1993, for Bertolucci's 'Little Buddha' (starring an, at the time, impossibly handsome, Keanu Reeves who played the part of Siddhartha) which was filmed there. Much of it was filmed at Paro dzong, in the days before television reached Bhutan and the tourist infrastructure was still thin. Being on the set then must have been an interesting experience. The producer said that filming in Bhutan had been a real joy.

'The Other Final', released in 2003, sticks to the magical theme too, even though it is about football. Football, of course, is a common language throughout the world. The story was inspired by a young man from Holland who was saddened and shocked that his country had not made the FIFA World Cup final in Japan in 2002. 'The Other Final' was played between the two lowest-listed teams in the FIFA rankings – namely, Bhutan and Montserrat. The latter, probably the better team, lost 4–0 probably due to playing at altitude in Bhutan, rather than a lack of football skill. The key to the film was the build-up in both countries: the very long journey the Montserrat team had taken in order to play in Thimphu, Bhutan. The film was delightful due to the camaraderie that arose despite the two very different cultures and languages. Seeing both teams and coaches singing the Caribbean mantra, 'Hot, hot, hot' in the Himalayas, was unforgettable and indeed allegorical.

Wildlife abounds in Bhutan. At times, one must contend with the annoying cacophony of dogs barking at night, particularly in the capital Thimphu. I learned early that earplugs whilst staying there are invaluable. The Bhutanese have an aversion to killing *any* form of life, so during the preparations to clear up the city, whilst making arrangements for the coronation in 2008, the dogs were rounded up and corralled elsewhere, only to be released afterwards. That is Bhutan for you.

On a more exotic note, Bhutan is home to populations of red pandas, and more especially, Bengal tigers, the latter famously shown to be surviving high up above the tree line, at four thousand metres, in the Black Mountains in the BBC production 'The Land of the Tiger' (2010). Finding them there was an emotional experience for all involved, as well as the viewer. Part discovery, part learning, it was also part of an adventurous campaign to create a 'tiger corridor' along the whole range of the High Himalaya where these beautiful but endangered animals could roam and survive. The discovery of them surviving in the Black Mountain region of Bhutan, at that height, was the key. Then perhaps, there is the yeti, well perhaps not!

Bhutan is roughly the same size as Switzerland, but despite its small land mass, there is still much to see. I have travelled from the far west, the Haa valley, to the far north east, Trashi Yangste, but I have not yet visited Gasa in the north. That is positioned high up in the mountains, and only one road leads to this area, the largest district in the country, but even that does not actually reach Gasa. Many people use mules to reach this village. It is apparently a treasure, though: there are hot, healing springs at the dzong there, and one commonly sees friendly Laya people, who wear faintly comical, and impractical, conical bamboo hats. Serious trekkers to Jhomolhari or Lunana, for the Snowman trek, have likely met them. Government officials cannot be put off by the location though, so it was not a surprise to see photographs of election officials struggling in early in 2013 to get there and back for the national election process. I am sure that they made use of the hot springs whilst there though. I would imagine that the journey there is well worth the effort for interested visitors.

As has been noted in three of the preceding chapters, I have been fortunate enough to visit Bumthang in central Bhutan, and it is certainly one of my favourite spots. Most tourists do not go there because it takes a long time to get there, and back, on a gruelling road journey. The recently opened airstrip will doubtless change all that. Bumthang is where I truly feel the spirit of Bhutan. Our young Bhutanese guide, Dawa, felt the same in 2007. He was aged twenty-two years at the time, and he had never visited the area before. He absolutely loved it and expressed similar feelings about the experience of being there. Other Western travellers have made similar comments. The place is not particularly spectacular in terms of location, but the long journey helps one 'get it'. Steeped in history, there is a seventh-century Tibetan temple at Jampa Laktang and more significant is Kurje Laktang, the burial ground for the Wangchuck Dynasty. The cave in one of the temples there allegedly bears the imprint of Guru Rinpoche, who fought local demons and espoused Buddhism in the area before he 'flew' to the more famous Tiger's Nest in the Paro Valley. Subsequently, another deity, Dorji Lingpa (1346–1405), who discovered the cave, created many of the myths that exist today. The nearby dzong at Jakar is one of the largest in the land, and from a distance it looks like a white bird with its mighty wings outstretched. Chamkar Bazaar, Wandicholing Palace, the valley system, Ura village – are all very special. Upon seeing these places, the mind is cleared and relieved of stress, and a deep satisfaction that comes from actually being *there* will make you feel somehow *at home*.

Om Mani Padme Hum

One of the people I truly admire is An San Suu Kyi, also known in her Burmese homeland as 'The Lady'. Burma, or Myanmar as the stubborn ruling Generals still insist on calling it. They are now reluctantly allowing the country to be dragged, kicking and screaming into the modern world. If you want to know more about this wonderful woman, you should see the film 'The Lady'. Somewhat annoyingly it was released around the same time as 'The Iron Lady' it unsurprisingly became a little lost as a consequence. She is widely revered in Burma, and one can see why after watching the film, though even she cannot seem to effectively deal with the deep ethnic divides there. Her father, widely recognised as the architect of modern Burma, was assassinated before he could properly fulfil his dream and that is why, after many years of house arrest, she is now seeking to fulfil that legacy.

Her late husband was Michael Aris, an Oxford don, who sadly died from prostate cancer in 1999. He was a lecturer at Oxford on Himalayan studies and in particular he was a renowned expert on Bhutan. He had travelled extensively in the region, quite often accompanied by 'The Lady'. His book, 'The Raven Crown', is the definitive history of the early kings of the Wangchuck Dynasty. It is a treasure and a priceless mine of information. Although An San Suu Kyi has an amazingly global profile, she is an insular and self-contained woman – she needed to be to survive those years of house arrest. Even now, although feted by foreign dignitaries visiting Burma, or more recently when travelling internationally, she will not always say what is expected of her, and some would say that she is somewhat stubborn.

Om Mani Padme Hum

K4 is, by all accounts, a reserved and insular man too. He is not easily gregarious. However he hit precisely the right note when he was trying to find a rung on the world's ladder to hang his country onto: GNH. It is so simple, yet so incredibly deep and meaningful. It was based on four pillars: preserving the culture and religion, good governance, economic welfare, and deep care for the environment. Seemingly simple but it works! And unlike so many political initiatives, it actually costs nothing. It is a treasure that weighs more than gold. Many have tried to grasp its true meaning in a western way by turning it into a sound bite, but it is far too deep and meaningful for that. However, the late Martin Uitz heard it described by a Bhutanese writer thus: 'do less, eat less, limit your stress, lose some of your acquisitiveness and be happier.' If a sound bite is required, that will most certainly do, though only time will tell whether K4's vision will outlast his lifetime, and that of his son K5, who has taken up his mantle. The infant democratic process is currently going through the inevitable growing pains, though my bet is that it will survive the test of time.

So go to Bhutan and see for yourself: feel the reality; see those smiles; see some of the best-dressed people in the world; see those heart-melting award winning smiles; wave at the polite groups of homeward-bound school-kids; wish for a return to that long-lost innocence of life. In short, become happy – you surely will!

Om Mani Padme Hum

CHAPTER 10

SQUARING THE CIRCLE AND BEYOND

'Outer peace without inner peace is impossible.'

The fourteenth Dalai Lama

On my fifth visit, in 2011, a largely new party was joining me for two of my three weeks there. It was to be my longest stay in the country, and though I would be travelling from the extreme west (Haa) to the east (Radi Valley), which I had seen before, I would also be going to the far northeast to visit Trashi Yangste and the Bomdeling Valley. Those friends were joining me as far as central Bhutan and the Bumthang Valley, but thereafter I would be on my own (albeit with my guide and driver). The prospect of the far northeast was very exciting as very few foreign tourists make it that far, and that will probably remain the case until they can resolve the technical issues surrounding the opening of the new regional airport there. The journey was to encapsulate and epitomise all that Bhutan had come to mean to me, so I shall describe it in some detail. There was no doubt that the indefinable feelings of inner calm (karma) had instilled themselves into me and my fellow travellers on previous journeys, so I had few fears that it would be otherwise this time. Bhutan was special, exceptional, and quite probably unique; I knew that, and the pleasure and privilege of being there again was simply overwhelming.

We arrived in Delhi very early in the morning as usual, and we found ourselves in the impressive, new terminal three at IGI, which had been completed the previous year in time for, rather unusually for India, the Commonwealth Games. It was an incredible space in terms of its size and its modern appearance and it was in complete contrast to the one it had replaced. Sadly though, it had lost some of the magic of India along the way, the somewhat mad and disconcerting hubbub had gone that was for sure.

This was the first time the complete party had an opportunity to meet each other. Chris had naturally travelled in first class; I had been in business class, together with Nigel and Tina, whilst the Haysoms (hereafter known as *the 24s,* for a rather quirky reason known only to us) comprising Jon, Rosie, Eleanor and Cameron, were in premium economy. It turned out to be a very good early bonding session. The kids were just marvellous, even after the near eight-hour flight. We were met by our local Wild Frontiers rep, Ashish Metha, who took us in a rather shabby red bus to the Uppal Hotel, formerly the Orchid, very near to the airport and where I had stayed on previous visits. Our rooms became ready one by one, and in the meantime we had an excellent breakfast. Afterwards, we met our guide for our Delhi day: Paramjeet Singh, and re-boarded our red bus and headed for the Raj Path and the obligatory short stay in New Delhi. Thereafter we quickly headed towards the Red Fort, and Old Delhi, for our tricycle rickshaw ride in the markets area.

We rode down Chandi Chowk to the Jama Majid, which was particularly enjoyed by the new members of the party, just as much as those who were initiated in 2009. And then, after acquiring two extra rickshaws to deal with the heavyweights among us, we were off to the wonderful spice market, though this time taking the very dark staircase up to the first level. This was an amazing experience, and although prohibited, a great many camera shots were taken! We then went back to the Red Fort, where I became separated for a short time from the main party whilst paying off my somewhat avaricious rickshaw boy. We then had a good lunch washed down with very large glasses of Kingfisher beers, courtesy of Nigel. Many began fading fast with the change in climate, slight jet lag, and effects of the beer, so we went back to the Uppal for rest before an evening rendezvous at the hotel bar. However that rendezvous turned out to be 'dinner for four' as the '24s' slept through the whole night.

We were all up promptly for an early breakfast. The 24s had had their much-needed sleep and, apparently, an early morning swim. Ashish arrived promptly with the red bus, and we were shortly off again to the airport. All the necessary formalities there took their toll, particularly on Jon, but it was not long before we were called to the gate for Drukair flight KB205. The new international terminal three at Delhi's IGI had a surprisingly nice ambience. We were picked up by a passing golf buggy, which was good because it was a very long walk to the gate. Upon arrival there we sent the buggy back to collect the 24s, who duly arrived shortly afterwards. And then, after boarding and an interminable wait on the runway threshold, we were off on the flight to Paro.

Strong winds from the east made the flight a little bumpy, though it was not too bad. The Himalayas soon came into view, and were as impressive as ever. There was cloud cover all around though, and knowing that there were mountains all around us, I found it a little unnerving. Finally, as we began our descent it was suddenly aborted with the engines being powered up, and we found ourselves above the clouds again. The pilot announcing that, due to strong winds, we would be taking a different landing approach. We later learned from Jon, who had spoken to the captain after landing, that he taken over the controls from his female co-pilot during the rather testing descent. After stooging aloft for a while, we wound our way down to the southerly approach on runway thirty-three at PBH. As ever, it was a fantastic ride in and everyone was thrilled and impressed! The obligatory photos were taken on the ramp, which caused us to be the last party through immigration.

We were met with the usual joy on the part of Pema and his new team: an additional guide, immediately titled for obvious reasons,

Pema Two; and three drivers, Pema Three, Dilbardu, and Chimi. I immediately said: 'sorry Pema, but before we go to the hotel we need to visit the cafe bar in Paro Town to have some welcoming Druk11000s!' Despite being closed when we arrived, the cafe was soon opened for us and the strong nectar combined with the altitude very quickly went to our heads.

From there we drove to our lodgings at the Olathang Hotel where, this time, we were billeted in the main hotel. The rooms were clean and warm, which was nice because it had suddenly become quite chilly. This was the first tourist hotel that had been built in Bhutan, at the time if K4's coronation in 1974. Although therefore a little old and tired it was a suitably special place to spend our first night. It was a real joy to be back for my fifth trip to the Land of the Thunder Dragon - priceless, special, wonderful, and as ever already unmissable; thank you God, my lord Buddha and, of course, Drukair!

That evening, we were joined at the bar by a glacial geologist, Erin, who came from Maine. He rather succinctly observed: 'you Brits with your beers, but hey, why not, I will join you!' We subsequently had a great, fun and funny evening, together with Pema who I thought was in particularly fine form but had definitely been cornered into telling tales of his 'night hunting' in the days before electricity came to town. Bhutan, its people, and karma were already definitely kicking in.

We drove up to the national museum after breakfast the next morning. The road was being widened up there, so we had to walk the last bit. The museum itself had been damaged in the recent earthquake which had been centred in neighbouring Sikkim, and so it was closed. Luckily some of the exhibits had been relocated into another building nearby. All were stunned by the sight of a Drukair flight which flew in high above us before descending steeply into the Paro Valley and onto the runway which was situated below us. We then walked down to Paro dzong for a short visit where we took our first holy water in the temple. We also made our first purchase, expertly negotiated by young Cameron, which comprised some delightful bright orange sunki cords.

Pema gave the first of his many cultural talks. In the meantime our drivers had kindly bought us all 'king and queen' wedding badges (minted in honour of the recent royal wedding). We then set off towards the Chela La Pass. Chris continued to be amazed by the constricted location of the airport and openly promised himself that he would come back to this spot to take photos on his return leg. Unfortunately, after the long climb towards the pass, we were met with clouds on the summit. It was cold and we saw the first signs of frost and snow. After a very brief stop we descended into the Haa Valley. Ironically, the sun tried to come out as we drove down, but it was starting to get dark, especially so in the steep-sided valley. So we went straight to the Rigsum Resort where the rooms were warm (even if the bathrooms were not). In the main house restaurant area the rather ineffective wood-fired stove only kept us slightly warm, but the Druk11000 did a better job! We chatted to two 'refugee campers', Andrew and Megan, from Adelaide. Supper was followed by an early night for the kids, Nigel and Tina. The rest of us settled into the first of many rounds of cards (sevens). Pema did his best to outplay a very competitive Rosie. I had a pretty sleepless night due to the Rigsum Resort privations and the anticipation of our visit to Dobji the next day. However, the bottom line was that I was just beginning to get back the vibe of this amazing country, where every traveller you meet says much the same thing: 'The country and its people are exceptional. There is nowhere else like it on earth.'

The following morning I gave a short talk to all, except Jon and the kids, about Dobji and our impending visit there. The ride out of the Haa Valley was glorious and although we did not have completely blue skies there was plenty of sunshine in our minds, especially after the disappointment at the summit of Chela La the previous day. There were the usual surprising and interesting Bhutanese sights along the way: women winnowing corn actually on the road, school-kids taking exams sitting out in the open, and others of the same ilk formally bowing, as they had during my last visit, when 'dasho Mark' had passed by. Everyone was in great form and we eventually arrived at Dobji dzong. I had recently read that this site had once been visited by one of the Bhutanese high deities, *Jetsun Milarepa* (1040–1123). We were met outside the gate by Samdrup and the lama.

We then entered the dzong and were presented with the usual line-up of monks before being escorted to the lama's 'grand quarters'. These quarters had recently been occupied by none less than the Je Kempo, the most senior official in the monastic body. He is second only in rank to the king in Bhutan and so this was a great honour for us. An absolutely sumptuous spread was laid out with tea, rice, cakes, breads served with jelly and fruits which was all far too generous. We were then escorted to the newly refurbished temple, which had also been damaged during the recent earthquake. This was an absolute wonder to behold. It was now slightly larger than before, and it had all been beautifully hand-painted inside with religious figures. We all lit candles, took holy water, and gave our gifts. The 24s gave a football and a basketball, together with the all-important pump. The lama presented all of us with white shawls (*kab-nes*), which was a great honour and definitely presaged tears of emotion in us all. We were then shown their most precious relic, the one-eared representation of Guru Rinpoche, which honour I had been afforded during my first visit in 2008.

We all took a tour of the tower, and we saw signs of the unrepaired earthquake damage, especially in the so-called television room and library. Both were very sparse and only just lived up to their descriptions. Unfortunately, it had started to rain quite hard, and so the obligatory group photos had to be taken inside the temple. In truth this was probably the most appropriate place to gather all twenty-seven monks, together with their tutors, and the lama. Sadly the football re-match that Jon, in particular, had been looking forward to had to be cancelled because of the rain. The new games area looked to be precariously close to the cliff edge in places though, so it was possibly just as well. It was a joyous visit, but the happiness was overshadowed by the news, conveyed by Samdrup, that the lama was unwell. It was suspected he had a heart problem. Samdrup knew a cardiologist who would, if necessary, arrange to have him transferred to India for treatment. May the lord Buddha bless the lama, his health, and all the monks and tutors of Dobji dzong.

We returned to our vehicles accompanied by the usual trumpet escort. I had a tear in my eye, but an elated heart. The new road layout had become very slippery and Chimi, together with Nigel and Tina inside his 4x4, needed help, so we all got out to push, getting spattered with mud in the process. As we rounded the last rock bluff overlooking the dzong, Pema pointed out that all the monks were waving to us from the ramparts. It was a truly fitting end to our very special and emotional visit.

We soon found ourselves back in Thimphu, which was so different from Haa, especially for those new to Bhutan. We got to the bank just in time, and we also visited the GPO next door, in order to purchase the obligatory special stamps. We checked into the Galingkha Hotel, which was a new one for me. It was located right in the centre of town. It was very nice, and there was an opportunity for Rosie to get a massage, Nigel (who was looking more and more like the young Justin Bieber, or 'Justin Beaver' as Cameron called him) to get a haircut, and shopping for prayer flags and other artefacts for the rest of us. We then went back to the hotel for dinner, where we were surprised by the appearance of Leki, Robin's and my driver from the 2009 trip. I suspected the hand of Pema in arranging this lovely surprise get-together.

We repaired to a local bar and exchanged stories of our lives since last we met. It was a somewhat emotional reunion for both Leki and me. He was now sometimes driving taxis in Thimphu or otherwise trucks and buses all over Bhutan. Apparently his son, 'a rascal', aged thirteen and his daughter, aged eight, were both doing well. He clearly wanted to be on our tour, but circumstances (or perhaps local politics) had seemingly prevented that from happening. After fond farewells, it was back to the hotel for dinner. Everyone was tired, especially Chris, so it was an early night. All I all, it had been a glorious day, likely to be etched forever in our memories. All of them appeared to have been deeply affected by the Dobji experience, especially Rosie, Eleanor, and Tina. Also I shall always remember Cameron's polite words of 'kradinche la' to the lama for his hospitality there.

A very beautiful sunny morning greeted us, which was just as well because most of us had been kept awake by the notorious barking dogs. At one point, an obviously territorial fight between them had broken out very early in the morning, and the noise had been simply horrendous. Needless to say those who had forgotten the recommendation to bring earplugs regretted it. Despite the noise however, the Galingkha had been a success. And after a very tasty breakfast, nearly western in style, we set off for the Dochu La Pass (3,100 m). As with the Chela La Pass when we had travelled to Haa, the weather did not play fair, and although the mist largely cleared, clouds blocked the main Himalayan view. We briefly re-enacted, by means of a mock photograph, the start of Jon's 2009 downhill bike ride, but sadly without actual bikes this time. And after the lunch at the nearby restaurant, we headed down to the Dragon's Nest Hotel at Wangdue. Nigel must have excellent eyesight because he had apparently spotted quite a few high peaks in the clearing skies and was suitably awed.

Everyone seemed to like this simple hotel at Wangdue with its riverside location and plenty of birds and flowers in the neat gardens. Eleanor and Cam let off some steam in the grounds, and indeed my room, which they found to be great fun. After dinner, everything was very calm until we were hit by a slew of Druk11000s, as suggested by the very strange Christian from Sweden. What a night it was then, full of laughs, deep conversation between Tina and Pema and general high spirits!

I had discussed a revised itinerary for the far eastern section of my journey with Pema, which now included a further night stop, in order to ease the long journey back from Trashi Yangste. It was another early night for Chris, and I was not far behind, though Pema and Tina seemed set for a very late one.

Early morning mist soon cleared to reveal a near cloudless clear sky. We wondered whether it would last for our special day in Punakha. We set off stopping at the nearby school and the river-side so that Cam could enjoy a glacial river dip (just as James had done in 2009). He plunged into the very cold water with glee. The river waters came straight down from the Himalaya above Lunana via the two rivers which converge in front of Punakha dzong. The Phu Chuu (Man River) comes in from the left, and the Ma Chuu (Woman River) from the right, this confluence adding yet further beauty to this wonderful location.

Prior to going across the rebuilt bridge and into the dzong, I chatted to two friendly schoolboys from the locality; Tenzin, accompanied by his friend also called Tenzin! They had both just completed exams for the day, and they were going home early. As with young kids all over Bhutan they were very keen to speak to someone who spoke English so that they could practise their skills: 'ask me a question, ask me a question!' they cried, so we talked about my journeys to Haa and Bumthang. And then I had more conversation with another student who was revising for his science exam, whilst sitting in a lovely park which was squeezed in between the school and the river. We then donned our white 'kab-nes' and set forth to enter Punakha dzong, which like most, had been built by the great Shabdrung Nawang Namgyel (1594 -1651). It was as impressive as ever, with Nigel ruminating on the simplicity of the setting: the nearby mountains, trees and the constant sound of running water, which all added to the magic.

The Pema tour led us into the inner temple, but not before he gave us his "short history of Bhutan" talk. This was not really for the kids, so I had a nice chat with Eleanor about all that glistens here like gold *is* in fact gold, whilst Cam played nearby! Once in the temple, it was, as ever, overwhelming. The royal wedding had recently taken place, and the grounds were still dressed for the occasion, set off by the plethora of brand new prayer flags. We were all given red sunki cords which had been blessed within the Shabdrung's own private temple. We also took some of the very fragrant holy water, a particular honour in this much revered place.

Pema pointed out the fantastic murals depicting the life of my lord Buddha. Although I had heard this talk before, I was still inspired by it. After a fairly brief visit to the suspension bridge, we went for the lunch at New Punakha. We all agreed it was the best food we had eaten so far. A break was needed, so we retreated to the Dragon's Nest for rest and chores. The morning laundry had been done and returned, and the Wi-Fi was working, though somewhat intermittently. The forecast for Bumthang, our destination the next day, was for bright but cold weather, with temperatures not much above freezing. We planned to meet on my bedroom terrace for cocktails later and then had a quiet dinner, but there was a small drama when Cam was stung on his foot by a bee or something similar, though luckily he seemed to recover very quickly. A lovely chat all round was followed by an equally touching 'goodnight' to everyone individually from the kids. What a wonderful combo they are, and what joy they bring to the party. After gazing for a while into the totally clear night sky we retreated to bed. All had enjoyed the Dragon's Nest, it was a good call to return, good thinking Jon.

After an early breakfast, we were all, somewhat surprisingly, good to go at the agreed start-time. The near two hundred kilometre journey ahead of us would take nine and a half hours including stops. The day was special from the start, particularly enhanced by the wall-to-wall sunshine. Again, there was not a cloud in the sky, and the weather seemed to get better and better as the day progressed. I could not remember seeing Bhutan in comparable conditions, and even Pema seemed impressed, observing that it augured well for a bright winter. We stopped briefly at the Old Wangdue town site, now almost completely relocated to the new site nearby. We saw that the wonderful old shops, which used to appear to cling precariously to the rocks, were now completely demolished. This had been anticipated, but it was a great shame, as something from the past had definitely been lost. I reflected that I was glad that my 2009 party had seen it as it was, even with the dead carcass that being sold off in pieces in the market square.

We drove up and over the Pele La Pass (3,420 m), stopping for Chris in the very appropriately named Nobding village to take photos of the rather graphic phalluses that were painted on the outside of many of the houses in order to ward off evil spirits. We soon started to see Jhomolhari (7,314 m) and its acolytes, Jichu Drake (6,794 m) and Khang Bum (5,198 m) in all their glory. It was a rare privilege as although I had travelled this road twice before, I had never seen these views because of the mist and clouds. Eventually, we were over the top and into the wonderful Black Mountain valley. Although Tina was not travelling in my car, I heard subsequently from Nigel that she had cried with emotion upon seeing it. Sadly, though unsurprisingly, there were no sightings of the very rare Bengal tigers though. We had a speedy, but pleasant, chai stop before setting off towards Trongsa and the very daunting, in view of the sheer drops exposed, road blockage just outside the town.

We had lunch in the Ta Dzong museum cafe, which seemed to subsequently start some rather unpleasant and far-reaching health problems for me, though in all honesty I do not think I could blame that on the food we all ate there. Nigel, Chris, and Eleanor did a quick tour of the museum afterwards, and as with the 2009 party, they were very impressed. We were shortly off again, over the Yotong La Pass (3,425m), but very soon, the consequences of that museum cafe lunch overtook me. Fortunately, our driver found a discreet spot to stop, though I cursed the rigours of being a western traveller in Asian climes!

We had to stop for a while outside the entrance to the Bumthang valley system when we encountered yet another road blockage. We were near the last of the passes, at Kiki La (2,860 m). The arrangements were a little chaotic, to say the least, when traffic from both directions tried in vain to negotiate the narrow chicane, though somehow we all got through. Eventually, we reached Chamkhar Bazaar at Jakar, which showed promising signs of recovery after the two recent devastating fires there. We then embraced the homely comforts of the Rinchenling Lodge after being personally welcomed by the proprietor, Dasho Jampel Ngedrup, his son Tenzin, and their very friendly staff. We had to wait before seeing his adopted son Taishi again, who was now six years old, because he was sleeping after taking his school exams that day.

Despite the fact that I was not feeling a hundred per cent, it nevertheless really felt like a homecoming for both Jon and me. We both boasted big smiles of contentment. We then had a lovely meal and light banter with the 24s, Chris, Pema and the Dasho before departing for some much-needed sleep. For Chris, there was the added joy that there was an active Wi-Fi signal here. We had all decided that a delayed start the next day was called for. Pema had told Nigel the night before that fewer than twenty per cent of tourists visiting Bhutan make it as far as Bumthang. I felt that this was their loss as it was a wonderful place, with a very special vibe of its own.

'What happened to my stove lighting set for 7:00 a.m.?' I wondered, though I was placated by a stunning breakfast of porridge, local honey, strawberry jam, baked potatoes, and eggs. We then asked if Taishi to join us on our day out to be company for Eleanor and especially Cameron. 'Are you sure?' asked the Dasho, 'he is very naughty!' He agreed and we headed out on the familiar (for me) walk to Kurje Lakthang, the revered 'heart of Bhutan'.

We stopped first at the Tibetan monastery at Khaine Lhakhang. The kids loved the prayer wheels, and Cam and Taishi cartwheeled together in the ancient courtyard which was a touching sight to see. We all lit some of the one hundred and eight candles – one to mark each of the books of the teachings of my lord Buddha. It was a lovely spiritual moment, and it quietened the kids for a time, and then it was on to Kurje itself, which was followed by another of Pema's talks, and a trip into a temple. While buying blessed sunki cords and other gifts from the monks, the peace was shattered by two cats fighting each other outside and who came charging into the temple.

We then walked towards the river, somewhat surprisingly past an active film set, and on towards the spot where James had taken a dip briefly in the freezing Chuu (river) in 2009. After quite a long walk, we reached our transport and headed back into town, pausing briefly to gaze at the nearly complete new Bathapalang airstrip. There was as yet no ramp for aircraft to board passengers, and the approach looked as interesting as that in Paro. It will certainly make a huge time saving for those journeying to this remote area though.

On the way into town Taishi fell asleep in the car between Chris and me and had to be woken upon our arrival into town. He soon reverted to his mad self in the restaurant, though Jon did a pretty fair job of trying to maintain discipline. And then it was back to the Rinchenling, for the by now lighted Swiss stoves, stone baths for some, and some good rest for us all. It had been another clear, sunny day, but the wind had got up (as usual) in the late afternoon, causing the air to become quite cold. We were lucky, though, that the magic and peace of Bumthang was working for all of us. Although, in parts, it seemed as if we could have been somewhere in Europe, the big difference was made by the people and the deep feeling of karma. The people were so nice and their spirit just rubbed off on us all. In the evening, we played a lengthy card game (sevens), which resulted in Rosie, as ever, taking the prize. As usual Nigel and Tina had retired earlier, whilst the rest of us listened to a visiting Dutchman, wearing a gho, surprisingly speaking in fluent dzongkha to the locals. Finally it was off to those rooms warmed so effectively by the wood-burning stoves, which we had kept fuelled with logs during the course of our evening.

After another lovely breakfast, which found favour with us all and not just the kids with their less adventurous tastes, we went for a walk into town. We heard that there had been a minor earthquake that morning, but we had all been totally oblivious of that. We walked into town on the opposite side of the river from the new airstrip, which was now clearly visible to us. We wandered into the wonderful old summer palace of the first king at Wangdicholing, the palace that featured those beautiful blue paint hues. All were impressed with those colours and the structure's history. It was just the place for the Bhutan5 Team photograph. The kids were then packed into the vehicles while the rest of us walked into town. We went for lunch, where Pema had arranged for some variety from the usual fare, Rosie actually had a little piece of pizza. In fact Taishi had some of that too, and I think he enjoyed it even more than Rosie! We then went back for individual 'R & R' at the Rinchenling, though Nigel and Tina went back to Kurje to find the lady who was selling bells and trinkets. Meanwhile Jon and Rosie soaked in one of the traditional stone baths, whilst the kids played and Chris worked. I would help him with his photo captions later which was going to be some task as he had taken quite a few.

I was really not looking forward to the parting of ways on the following day, and my emotions were set off by Tina and Nigel's

Taktshang post-card which contained some well-chosen and poignant words. I had been delighted that the Bhutan5 Party had come to Bhutan and that they had all got on so well together. Though the trip had been inspired by one man's love for another country, I was glad that the love and karma had rubbed off on the others too. It made my own journey all the more joyous, but I knew I would miss those leaving very much. Thanks to Chris, in particular, for his company in Pema Three's vehicle. I simply loved ending our trip together with such a lovely meal at the Rinchenling, I felt there was no more appropriate place.

That evening, Leki seemed to appear from nowhere. He had driven straight through from Thimphu, leaving at 10:30 a.m. and arriving at 7:30 p.m. what a star! He was, as Rosie pointed out, overjoyed to see dasho Mark. Indeed, he was full of spiritual joy having auspiciously lit several butter lamps for our safe journey. He was so very kind and had even brought me some briefing notes about the religious stupas in Bhutan, which would provide homework for me that evening.

Inevitably, the party dwindled as, one by one, they went off to bed. Rosie, Jon, Chris, and I played some more, red wine-fuelled, card games. At one point we were joined, during an awkward moment, by an apparently drunk Swiss doctor from the local hospital, where had been seconded for six months. He somewhat pithily observed 'you would not want to need a doctor here.' Observing the state of him I thought 'quite right too'!

So as the first part of the tour ended I wished the departing group good karma for their long journey back: 'enjoy Pobjika, the Uma Paro and the Tigers Nest, and then safe home. Tashi Delek!'

A sunny morning greeted us again the next day when we were awoken early so as to be ready for our respective prompt departures. Certainly the group returning west needed to avoid the road blockages, and associated closures, at Bumthang and Trongsa. So, after the final breakfast together, it was time to part ways but not before final farewell hugs all round, including the drivers and guides. Taishi joined us for this, though he was very quiet for a change, and really quite tearful. The three departing cars were soon through the gate, and I was left to board the new, unregistered Hyundai Santa Fe. Leki and Pema were to accompany me for the rest of my trip, and the first stage was the eight-hour drive to Mongar. We reached the Shertang La Pass (3,590 m) fairly quickly, as well as the much higher Thrumshing La Pass (3,750 m) where we made a stop. It was a simply wondrous view of the Himalayas up there. I had done the route once before, indeed putting up my own prayer flags in 2007, but it had been completely shrouded in mist at the time. I was thinking: 'this is what I came to see'. It was a real joy, and I felt extremely happy.

We saw Bhutan's highest peak, Gangkhar Puensum (7,541 m), on the way up. It was apparently the world's highest unclimbed peak. Impressive as those views were, the sight from the summit of Thrumshing La was something else, absolutely spectacular. The view had taken my breath away in more ways than one. But despite my breathlessness I had felt somehow at ease with the world, spiritually enlightened, and deeply privileged just to have been standing there. We then travelled the long, long route down the other side, descending some 3,200 m in 84 km! However we soon stopped at Sengor at a roadside café, eating some very delicious noodles. We then drove ever downwards, marvelling at the engineering of these roads in the very difficult terrain.

We passed a few monsoon avalanche sites and some hair-raising road-widening projects. We came upon the spectacular Namling waterfalls, which I had only seen in the mist before. There were two very exposed rock-fall sites where the temporary section of road passing by the falls was extremely narrow. Continuing ever on down, the vegetation suddenly turned semi-tropical, and we saw langur monkeys, and we also disturbed an angry brown alpha male monkey, causing him to perform much snarling, barking, and mating!

As ever with these long journeys, the last hour or so seemed to drag, though we were soon making our approach to Mongar. Ironically, the road surface improved dramatically, though we were held for a while at yet another road-widening site. I think Leki was getting very tired after two long days of driving as, curiously and somewhat disturbingly, his sleepiness seemed to cause him to drive faster and faster. Anyway, we reached the town in the fading evening light and went up a short access road to the Wangchuck Hotel which I had seen being built in 2007, and it had looked like a good spot. As with so many other places in Bhutan, it had suffered some earthquake damage and, at first blush, it was not quite as nice as I had hoped it would be despite the good location. There was a spacious room waiting for me though, together with a good shower, which was a relief as I feared that the next three nights would likely be much more spartan. But as Tina had written in that post-card at the Rinchenling: 'as you go east it will become a true adventure into a new and very remote part of this amazing country'. Refreshed I met Pema and Leki in the hotel bar later to discuss our plans for the next day.

As it turned out it was to be yet another day of 'one hundred per cent visibility all over Bhutan', as Pema was wont to say. It was also to be another long, though fascinating and exhilarating day. It had started with a short walk around Mongar town, where Pema bartered for some aluminium wares for his home temple, while I chatted with some school-kids who had just finished their exams. 'Picture, picture' they cried, and what a lovely photo opportunity it was too. Another student nearby just wanted to talk about Wayne Rooney!

We were soon to be off again, but not before discovering that Leki had apprently mislaid the car keys, which could have been a major problem. Pema was not amused, even after he had traced them, seemingly left behind in a nearby shop. We drove up and over the Kori La Pass (2,400 m), which I rather aptly renamed the 'Gorilla Pass', much to the amusement of my Bhutanese friends. Although it was lower than the one at Dochu La I somehow preferred it. There were some magnificent views of the eastern Himalayas, and like Thrumshing La, I felt that it had a feeling of spirituality surrounding it which was exemplified when Leki and I shared the lighting of a holy candle in the lamp room at the summit. Funds raised in the collection box there were sent to the local monks nearby. After that, we had some welcome chai and took a photo of the stupendous display of prayer flags, some of which were strung at a very great height over the road. Our journey then continued on down the other side, and as we travelled, I felt more and more like a dasho whose somewhat regal waves were invariably returned, together with those winning smiles.

I missed so many photo opportunities along the way despite asking Leki to stop many times. I wanted to capture the spectacular mountain vistas, but more especially the people. I had missed a great opportunity at Nartshang monastery where the young monks there, who were not wearing their obligatory red robes, were playing football in the beautiful courtyard. I secretly hoped that I might be able to capture a similar shot when on my return journey through there.

As we headed for the Yadi switchbacks and Yadi village (1,480 m), Pema spotted a new café situated at the top of a steep drive. It was rather oddly named the 'Monkey's Shoulder'. We duly stopped and I was very glad that we did as it was a magical spot, and I could have stayed there all day. Tina would have loved the garden, which was full of flowers and many of which could have been found in England. The fresh food was, in Leki's estimation, 'five-star quality', and I really enjoyed sitting in yet another 'dasho's' chair.

Pema pointed out the precarious site of the new regional airstrip that would serve the eastern region, and Trashigang in particular, situated at Yongpula. It was situated on top of a very high ridge, which I was sure would make for some interesting, and doubtless disconcerting, flights in. However, it would be a great bonus for tourists not wishing to take the four-day journey to the east and back. The weather was clear and hot, and the 'Monkey's Shoulder' was so peaceful that it felt heavenly. I thought: 'thank you again God and, my lord Buddha, I am so blessed to be here. I do not know when I will be back, but when I return, I think I may have to brace myself for that approach to Yongpula'.

And then we were off again, the scenery became drier and sparser, and there were signs of old wild fires. We drove past the longest line of prayer flags I had ever seen, strung across the Drangmo Chuu, and on to the immigration checkpoint just outside Trashigang. Most checkpoints had been dispensed with, so it was a surprise to come across one, though we were now very close to the Indian and Chinese borders. We drove up the hill, past yet more road blockages, and into the town itself where there was some frenetic driving from Leki and indeed other road-users. Once in the town I found that it was slightly more oppressive than I remembered. There were definitely more stares from the locals at the comparatively unusual sight of a lone foreign tourist, but the sight of the dzong was as impressive as ever. This was my favourite among those I had seen on my journeys to Bhutan so far. It was compact, beautiful, and on a splendidly precipitous location. Many others were similarly located, but somehow this one struck me as being very special, possibly because of the remoteness of this part of the country.

We delayed actually stopping in the town until the next day, and immediately took the road to the nearby Radi valley. Driving past the site of the great flood of 2007, when the road had had to be realigned, leaving a large stupa isolated in the middle of the river. The road surface had also been much improved since my previous journey and it now went all the way up to the Goemba lodgings at Rangjung. However the building there looked very different since another floor was being built on top. It was still a magical spot, and I thought that, when it was finally finished, it would provide much improved accommodation. However, the very basic rooms I recalled were still the same, and I was appropriately billeted in room number one, where I was told that, this time, we had running hot water, which was a blessing. It was also perhaps not a surprise to see that I was the only guest staying there.

Leki's wife's family lived in a village in the valley so he wanted to go off and visit them and stay the night, so I agreed a reasonable departure time for the next morning. In the meantime I settled down in the canteen to catch up with my diary and general reading, all helped along with a Druk11000. Pema had recently heard from Pema Two that my returning party had just reached the Uma Paro, and I was pleased to hear that. I was also excited to be heading into entirely new territory the next day.

I awoke to another bright, cold morning, but it felt lovely to be back in the Radi Valley, albeit without the rowdy Wild Frontiers group of 2007. I remembered so well Pema's nephew laughing uncontrollably at Amanda's mock Nepali language. After a breakfast bolstered by a freshly boiled egg which Leki had brought down from the village where he had stayed overnight, and after buying a silk scarf and tipping the old man who was tending to housekeeping duties, we were off.

We soon stopped to allow me to walk through the roadside village of Lungtenzampa, which was built in traditional style and looked, to my eyes anyway, as if it had been there for centuries, and probably much the same throughout that time. I was quickly engaged in conversation by a young man, probably still a student, who ran the local dairy. He also had a small dairy herd, some poultry, and a small holding for vegetables. He invited me into the dairy which was immaculate and very clean. He spoke just excellent English and was very keen to tell me all about his work and life. I would have very much liked to have heard news from this part of Bhutan when I returned home, but I rather foolishly forgot to ask for his name and contact details. Despite all his duties and hard work in the village, he attended a college some distance away at Wamray, which is on the way to Pemagatsel. How he combined these two lives I had no idea, but he appeared to do both brilliantly, which was both a revelation and an inspiration.

We were soon off again and back into Trashigang, but it had suddenly become very hot. Leki and I visited the temple within the dzong, where Leki asked the monk to bless an early draft of this book. Leki had kindly asked the duty monk to bless my endeavours, and afterwards we lit a candle as an offering, which was, needless to say, a very special moment. Afterwards, during a quick tour of the town, I bought a copy of the Bhutan daily newspaper, the Kuensel, and other sundries before setting off again, only to be soon halted for well over half an hour by more road blockages. The Indian contractor, Dantak, was working on this section of the road and as Pema pointed out, the company appeared to be skimping on their duties because they were using the same machinery both for the rock splitting and debris clearance. Two units would have been far more efficient but as Pema noted the contract was based on the time working, so I am sure that Dantak was happy with their strategy, even if the road-users were not.

Whilst waiting for the allocated blockage time to clear, Pema and I walked through the road works where we had to run past the point being worked upon, which as usual, was very near to a long steep drop. Eventually we were picked up by Leki, and then took the Trashi Yangste road after the immigration post. For some reason Leki was driving very slowly, but eventually we reached Gom Kora, which was a very significant place for Leki, due to its connection with Guru Rinpoche. There is an alleged imprint of his face in the cave, just like the one in Bumthang. We did the 'three rounds' at the site and spun what must have been almost all of the one hundred and eight prayer wheels before going into the temple to light the holy candles. Whilst taking holy water from two very young duty monks. I noticed that my lethargy, brought on by our slow journey, had seemingly disappeared, and I offered a suitable prayer of thanks to my lord Buddha. Afterwards, Leki and I went into Guru Rinpoche's cave, before going back outside where he carried a very heavy rock three times around the auspicious holy stone. This was his personal religious offering and I was very impressed by his efforts as the rock was clearly extremely heavy.

Refreshed by the stop in this spiritual place, and after buying some souvenirs from the temple boys, which included a sealed pot full of religious items (see appendix 7), we headed to the nearby village of Duksum, where three valleys meet. This village was particularly significant as one of the original chain link bridges was built there in the fifteenth century by the Tibetan bridge builder, Thangtong Gyalpo. It had long since been washed away, though incredibly part of it had been recovered, and now forms part of a similar bridge in the Paro valley, and another small section is kept in the national museum nearby. Apparently Duksum was originally a place filled with bad karma, and the Guru Rinpoche had had to chase away a bad deity from there. Now that the significant tourist attraction of the bridge had been washed away, it had lost its appeal and had sadly become quite dilapidated. Leki said that it was now a staging post for the buses travelling between Trashi Yangste and Thimphu, a route which he drives from time to time. We took a walk around the village before going to a restaurant. By coincidence the two Dutch guests from the Rinchenling were also eating there. I chatted outside with their Bhutanese driver and guide, who explained that they had just visited Trashi Yangste dzong, further up the valley, and where we were headed later. I was told that they would be staying overnight in Trashigang before exiting Bhutan via Samdrupjongkhar the next day.

As they departed I hung around outside waiting for my noodles, when suddenly, I became engaged in conversation by a passing schoolboy, Jigme, and his friends, Taishi and Pema. They were really nice, smart, polite, and articulate and I had a really interesting conversation with them. 'Would you like to come to the United Kingdom?' I asked. 'Yes, it is our dream' remarked Pema. Taishi came from Paro, and my guide, Pema, wondered why he was living so far from there. It transpired that his father was working on a government contract nearby. So after a nice lunch I took photos of my new-found friends, exchanged email addresses, and insisted that they all should write to me when I returned home, though I suspected that they probably would not. And then we were all too soon off again, amidst heartfelt waves and smiles from all of them, which was a very poignant moment. Apart from unerring politeness and excellent English, the school kids looked very smart in their national dress, despite the obvious poverty in this very remote and rural part of Bhutan. There was no scruffiness in the clothing they wore, even though I suspected that it would have to be made to last for quite some time. They were very well informed, considering the remote location, though I suspected this was helped along by the age of the Internet.

Onwards and upwards we went, towards Trashi Yangste and into the fading Himalayan light, which always created a fantastic, partly diffused, vista. The topography changed again and we saw steep and deeply forested valleys with a farm road visible on the opposite ridge. This particular farm road seemed to be holding onto the steep slopes by its fingernails. I was thinking: 'I definitely would not want to be on that road'. After first catching a brief glimpse, we then saw the incredible spectre of the jagged Himalayas rising up behind Trashi Yangste. The high peaks were possibly Me La or Sherja La, both of which exceeded 8,000m. We passed by the dzong, recently refurbished, and beautifully positioned amongst the valleys and mountains, and which was apparently one of the oldest in Bhutan. Finally, we headed into the town itself and caught a brief glimpse of the Chorten Kora which we planned to visit there the next day.

The town itself is set in a bowl that is surrounded by hills, and behind those are the high mountains. It is spaciously set out, unlike Trashigang, and my hotel, the Karmaling, was not nearly as bad as I had feared. The rooms in the newer section were nice, but as the Lonely Planet guide-book had observed that: 'the mattresses are (very) hard and there are no showers in the rooms, just a hot water geyser and a bucket'. Tina would definitely not have approved. (I suspected that she would also have had a problem with the very basic ablution facilities back at Duksum as well.) As we settled in Leki called Pema Two and I was able to speak to Jon, Chris, and Nigel, who were then at Sonam Trophel's cafe in Paro Town. They were apparently enjoying their final Druk11000s. Earlier in the day they had climbed up to the Tiger's Nest, whilst the kids rode on the ponies. The 24s had made it all the way to the monastery there, together with their driver Dilbardu who, together with guide Pema Two, had kindly carried Cameron up the last very steep section. Just like me, Nigel, Tina, and Chris had only made it as far as the viewing platform. They were all unsurprisingly very tired after their day's exertions, and unbeknownst to me at the time, Chris was not feeling at all well, much to the consternation of my party and the cafe staff.

I was very pleased to hear Nigel commenting on the stunningly clear views of the Himalayas that he had witnessed on their return journey over the Dochu La Pass, which he felt were 'life changing'. I asked him, knowing his love of detail, to look at the map to see just how far east and then northeast I had travelled since we had parted ways in Bumthang, and noted that I had travelled 603 km since leaving Paro. After chatting to him, and wishing them all 'Tashi Delek!' again for their onward journey home, I settled into the very comfortable upstairs lounge. The wood-burner was lit by the very attentive hotel boy, who had also served me with chai and biscuits, and a Druk11000 for later. Meanwhile Pema had been taking his 'incense' outside. It had been another very memorable day.

My breakfast was accompanied by a few small birds lodging in the inside of the dining room rafters! The plumbing was indeed basic, but despite there being no shower, the water was indeed hot. I found that it was best not to look too closely at the electrics though. It was a crisp morning with only the faintest wisps of cloud in the sky. I took a quick walk around the small downtown area before heading for the Chorten Kora. Although not as big as the one it is based upon in Kathmandu, it is magnificently located. Leki and I walked the statutory three rounds of the outside, but we only spun some of the (more than) three hundred prayer wheels before going into the temple, where we naturally lit a candle and took the holy water. Thank you, Leki, for your conducted tour of this place, it was indeed very special. I gathered from him that, although not many tourists make it this far to the east, the annual festival here is one of the best in Bhutan.

We then drove out of town and went north, stopping briefly at the excellent Bumdeling Wildlife Sanctuary Visitor Centre. Much to my relief, I heard that the eight kilometre road to the sanctuary was not at 'height', but it turned out to be very bumpy. It was really lovely driving through the woods after we had left the flag-covered Bailey bridge at the edge of town. The sunlight shone through the trees, and the mountains appeared as well. We saw a beautiful, red-tinged barking deer (muntjac) and passed village folk coming down the track with their produce for the market. Pema hailed an elderly lady, who was walking down the track with her grandson. They were clearly struggling under the weight of their loads. He purchased some of their produce on the spot, much to their delight. The lady was quite a character with a fantastic smile, though both spoke very few words even when prompted.

Gradually, the valley began to open up and the village of Bumdeling came into view. As usual, I found that I interacted easily with the local kids, which was as ever, so rewarding. It also reminded me of that visit to Kamji school in 2006, when Janine had commented how quickly I had become a pied piper' figure to the kids there.

They are such beautiful and engaging people, and as usual, quite a few really wanted to have a chat with a visiting foreigner. As is the case everywhere in Bhutan, the people had jet-black hair, brown complexions, and perfect features, which is the same for both boys and girls. And all were, as ever, impeccably dressed, with those famous winning smiles which helped break the language barrier. We were told, by these kids, that nine black-necked cranes had in fact already landed in the valley following this year's migration from Tibet. They also confirmed that these rare birds are very important to them, as very few tourists that travel this far, probably only around five per cent of the total intake, and mainly do so in order to see these particular very rare birds.

This was surprisingly Pema's first visit to this part of Bhutan, as he had been pretty much everywhere else, including completing the arduous Snowman trek in the far north. We pressed on, and over a couple of fords, and into the open space which formed the landing grounds below the mountain peaks. One peak was Yungha, and it rose to around 3,700 m. We quickly spotted a lone, probably young crane, and I went hunting for it with my camera across the paddy fields. Its parents must have been about, and sure enough Leki spotted them, quite a way off across the river. Continuing to press on, we saw another pair, and so I went stalking again. We had now seen five of the nine black-necked cranes known to be in the area, which was really exciting. This valley was so beautiful, quiet and remote, yet somehow so inspiring. It was just such a fantastic way in which to finish the last day of my outward journey in Bhutan, before we started the very long journey back.

We turned and headed back, dropping by the local papper (sic) factory. This area is known for paper manufacture and handicrafts manufactured from avocado wood. The factory was not open, but the large family was in and roasting recently harvested corn in a hot kiln. Pema asked them whether they could provide refreshment, which was duly produced and served in their very tidy private lounge. Yet again, I was installed in the dasho's chair, and I felt very privileged and happy to be amongst such lovely people, who had so willingly invited unexpected guests into their home.

There were various kids about, including one of their sons, who appeared to be painfully shy. Together with his friend, the boy was stripping corn cobs in the lower field. I made some conversational progress when I asked them to show me how it was done, and needless to say, I was very much slower at the task than them, which they found very amusing! Elsewhere, Pema had found the youngest boy of the family, who was just like, and just as naughty, as Taishi at the Rinchenling. Perhaps not so surprising as they both shred the same name! Before leaving, I managed to obtain some of their beautiful, handmade paper, and then we slowly retraced our route down the bumpy road to exit the sanctuary. We headed straight for Trashi Yangste dzong and passed by one of those archetypal mediaeval cantilever bridges, which was almost completely hidden under the weight of prayer flags. The dzong was wonderfully located, and it looked very old despite the recent thorough refurbishment, which had been orchestrated by K5. It had a less aggressive feel than most others, whose warlike fort structures had a clear historical purpose. This particular one seemed to be more appropriate for a dasho's residence.

We all went inside and up two flights of steep, ladder-type stairs which reminded Pema and I of the tower at Dobji. We took the holy water, which I noted was sadly probably the last time for me on this trip, before departing the dzong and heading into the fading light. On the way we were briefly held up by a lorry being loaded up with some very tall prayer flag poles, before arriving back into town. At the ridiculously overpriced handicraft shop, complete with a surprisingly sullen counter girl, I bought a set of exquisite avocado wood bowls. We were all pretty tired by then, probably exacerbated by the altitude, so we headed straight back to the Karmaling Hotel for coffee and other suitable refreshment.

Pema and Leki came back to the hotel in a pretty happy mood that night, perhaps they might even have been a little drunk. I lost track of how many times Pema told me how much he liked the chillies from the Bumdeling area! In a more sober moment however, he made an interesting observation: 'as successful as the concept of GNH is, he thought it was only fully accepted by around eighty per cent of the population, and was particularly thin amongst the young'. I still thought that rate was pretty good, though it is clear that concept needed to be nurtured, particularly as time passes and the world changes. I thought these were insightful words, and he particularly made reference to the unemployed youth, and I was reminded me of my young friends at Duksum, and their dreams of going to the United Kingdom.

These thoughts were further emphasised upon my departure the next morning, when I tipped the Karmaling hotel boy, Sharab. He had worked tirelessly fetching and carrying over my two day stay. He had kept my room clean and warm, ceaselessly tended to the temperamental dining room stove, produced all the meals, and all provided the all-important liquid refreshments! He was genuinely overwhelmed with my tip and came back twice to say so. I felt humbled by his story: he came from a broken home, worked for his uncle (who owned the hotel), and hoped to start a bakery next year facilitated by a loan. He commented: 'there are so few visitors here, sir, and it is a very poor area; we only have the black-necked cranes and the Chorten Kora to attract people to come here'. I countered by saying that the town had much more than that because it was in such a beautiful place and had such beautiful people. I genuinely wished him a special Tashi Delek, and said that I looked forward to buying the fresh breads from his bakery during my next visit. I also said goodbye to a fellow guest, Kuni, who came from Japan, and was working on secondment for the Bhutanese Government until November the following year. Clearly a bright guy, he had appeared to speak fluent Dzongkha to his Bhutanese counterparts. We had got on very well over some glasses of Druk11000!

Very sadly, it was now time to say goodbye to Trashi Yangste and the unexpectedly comfortable Karmaling, made just perfect by Sharab and his uncle. They both waved very genuinely from the hotel steps as we left. We were shortly stopped at the edge of town for a random driving license check, fortunately forgetful Leki did have his on him. We soon found ourselves back at Duksum, where we had been expecting to stop again, but we abandoned that plan and drove on further up the road, and past the immigration post, and into Rolong.

Sadly there had been no sign of my 'three musketeers' in Duksum, so I had gone along with that plan. By this time the day had warmed up quite dramatically. Whilst in Rolong, we visited the road workers' shop/cafe where we took chai, and where I was, once again, installed into a dasho's chair. This was all very pleasant until we were rather rudely interrupted by a local villager, who had just come down off the nearby mountains, and who was obviously quite the worse for wear!

Rolong was the place where that very long line of prayer flags spanned the Drongma Chuu (river). As we travelled on I rather incongruously heard Justin Bieber on the car radio, and I was instantly reminded of Cameron, who had thought that Nigel's haircut had looked very similar to that of the Canadian warbler. We stopped briefly by the bridge at Serichu, apparently this had the reputation of being the hottest place in Bhutan, and it certainly felt like it. We then drove back up over the Yadi switchbacks to the 'Monkey's Shoulder' cafe, which Pema had rather crudely renamed the 'Monkey's Ass' in view of the ridiculously tight turn needed to access it from that direction. Another great meal followed, which included delicious potatoes and broad beans, which was a nice variation on the usual fare. I was joined in my dasho's chair by a bespectacled toy tiger; though sadly no sight of the real thing as yet.

Pema had spotted some pretty big wildfires and noted that the smoke appeared to be spreading quite quickly, though it still seemed to be a way quite a way off still. We were told that one of the fires was near Lhunste; the other, more worryingly, was near to Mongar, our destination for the day. These fires were usually caused by farmers illicitly burning off lemon grass on their land. The fires are then fanned by strong afternoon winds. It was a real problem, and the government had been trying to tackle the problem by educating the farmers. As we departed though, the smoke haze became more and more obvious. We stopped briefly at Nartshang monastery in the hope of catching those monks playing football but it was not to be, though Leki did his best to imitate them, with a lone chicken joining him in the monastery courtyard during his endeavours! When we reached the 'Gorilla Pass' again, the view of the mountains had already been completely obliterated by the smoke haze. I met two groups up there who had been at the Bhutan/Japan conference at Trashi Yangste. One group was returning to Lhunste, and both groups were amazed that I was already on my fifth trip to Bhutan. Understandably, the folk from Lhunste said I should visit there next time. Conversation with the Bhutanese is easy; they are genuinely interested, and most speak comfortably in English, a direct product of K4's forward thinking education reforms.

So after taking some chai at the pass, we set off on the final leg to Mongar, where the smell of smoke was really quite noticeable. I had the same 'room with a view' at the Wangchuck Hotel, and the bellboy, who I had handsomely tipped on my outward journey, seemed pleased to see me. As there was no lift he had to work hard carrying my heavy bags to my room though. I was somewhat disappointed about the smoke haze, but the outline relief of the mountains as the sun went down was really quite dramatic. I hoped Pema was right when he said that the cool air of the night would make the smoke dissipate. It would be a long, long drive back to Bumthang the next day, and I really hoped that we would get that fantastic view from the summit of Thrumshing La again. I was pleased that Leki had gone to the local, quite large hospital to get his red eye looked at. He came back with some suitable eye drops; I definitely wanted my driver to be able to see clearly! 'An early night and a good sleep was needed by us all' I thought.

Although we had a long day ahead, at least it was another lovely sunny start. There was only a hint of the wildfire smoke, so Pema was proved right. I went online before breakfast to pick up the football results, and I was quickly joined by the bellboy, Tshewang Nangay, who turned out to be a Manchester United fan. They had surprisingly just been held to a 1–1 draw by Newcastle.

Our departure was slightly delayed by the late appearance of a rather sleepy Pema, but we were soon on our way out of Mongar. We entered a lovely, fertile valley and stopped at Thridanghi, where I shopped at a tiny roadside store and met more friendly local people. A very polite eleven-year-old boy was soon in conversation with me while his two younger siblings shouted: 'picture, picture!' Further on in the village, we stopped at the wonderfully named Karma Hotel for some chai. It was a great location and Leki rather cheekily observed: 'the dasho should buy a plot of land here and build a house.' In fact, I think I spotted a site that would also have room for a helipad!

Pema said that the villagers thought that the wildfires had started in the Shemgang area, south of Trongsa, which is where Pema went to high school. We were off again on the long drive up to the Thrumshing La pass. There we saw the first signs of clouds spoiling that 'hundred per cent visibility all over Bhutan.' They were coming up from Assam, to the south in India, where the steamy northern plains caused these changes in the weather. We hoped that the clouds would not hang around for too long, and that Pema would be proven right when he had said the forthcoming winter would be long and bright. It was the first cloud in nearly ten days for me, so I was still happy.

By the time we had passed through Sengor, eaten noodles at the same road-side café, and had reached the summit of the pass, the clouds were all around us. But at least the high mountains were still visible. Leki lit some pine ferns as an offering, which gave off a wonderfully pungent smell. Pema spotted a raven, the royal bird of Bhutan. And then it was down the other side with 'Funky Leki', whom I had nick-named after his mobile ringtone. He was driving very carefully over the frost and black ice patches, which appeared with alarming regularity. It was not what you wanted on NH2, which, at times, must rival the road to the border at Samdrupjongkhar. I had driven over that section before and knew it was pretty scary and was definitely not for the faint-hearted.

The views were just stunning, and to quote Nigel whilst he was at Dochu La, they were somehow 'life-changing'. Pema observed that the views from Thrumshing La beat Dochu La any day, and I agreed. By the time we reached Ura, Leki was flagging, so I called for a nature stop. We were, quite coincidentally, right by a national park loo, a very rare facility, so it must have been karma calling or perhaps it was a *karma karsai!* After handing out Werther's Original sweets all round, we headed down into the Bumthang Valley system and the gathering dark. We stopped briefly in Chamkhar Bazaar to get the dasho a replacement biro, having stupidly left the original of that precious commodity at the Karma Hotel. We soon arrived back at the Rinchenling where I was allocated the rather posh and spacious room twenty-one, which came complete with four very large and noisy flies. I firmly resisted my western temptation to swat them in favour of Buddhist karma.

The stove had been lit, so I felt at home almost immediately. That was good because we had an early start the next day for the journey to Gantey (where there was to be a two-day break). Leki mentioned that he did not like it there. Just as I was feeling at home, though, the lights went out. I went to the dining room and was greeted by the owner, a real Dasho. He was once an advisor to K4, and he looked just like a person straight out of a Michael Aris book; he had a real presence about him.

There was a kaleidoscope of characters staying there, including a rather cocky, young guide from the Snowman trek, who coincidentally came from Trashi Yangste. I felt that he had designs on a female member of his party. I think she was staying in the room next to mine as she had accidentally walked into it earlier, or perhaps she was trying to escape the attentions of her guide! A friend of the inebriated Swiss doctor was also there, altogether a far more sober man in all respects. He was enjoying one of his long sojourns in Bhutan, which he invariably spent taking very long walks in the Bumthang area. He commented that he was surprised to 'zee me again zo soon'. Since I was very tired after the long day of travel, I declined further conversation in favour of an early night.

It was a cloudy start the following morning, but the clouds quickly burned away as we continued our journey. Before departing the Rinchenling however, I was told by the Dasho that the visiting Rinpoche, a religious man who gave blessings to the places where he stayed, was apparently the reincarnation of the Tibetan Bridge builder, Thangtong Gyalpo. It was he who had built the one hundred and eight spectacular cantilever bridges throughout Tibet and Bhutan during the fifteenth century. Pema said that he did not believe that story, but I did not think it was worth mentioning that to the highly religious Dasho though. The previous night all of his staff had received Rinpoche's blessing whilst I had been at dinner. Leki had joined them for that, so I felt quite disappointed that I had missed an opportunity there.

As I was finishing breakfast the next morning my new found Swiss acquaintance, Fritz, rather touchingly asked: 'may I av a five-minute meeting vis you, if you are not in too much of a hurry?' We talked and, as it turned out, he had a sad, but fascinating, story to tell. Many years previously, when he first visited Bhutan, he heard about a local boy who had been very badly mauled by a bear. He had helped sponsor his transfer to Switzerland for reconstructive surgery. The boy returned to Jakar, and when he grew up, and started a wood-turning business in Chamkhar Bazaar (even though he had been blinded by his injuries). Unfortunately, his workshop had been destroyed by the second fire in the bazaar in 2010, which had destroyed most of the retail outlets there.

He had been awarded a nominal sum from the king's fund (the equivalent of about £700) which was not nearly enough to rebuild his workshop. Fritz was going to try to raise funds to loan to him and, in the meantime, was planning to go to London to see if he could find a Braille computer. He wanted assistance locating the Royal National Institute for the Blind. I said that I could meet him in London and do what I could to try and help. I then asked after his friend, the Swiss doctor who had been working at the local hospital. He was no friend, I soon learned, as Fritz did not respect anyone who was 'too drunk to work.' Upon reflection, I was indeed relieved that none of my party needed to attend hospital there. Fortunately the doctor had only been there for six months, and had since returned home. Fritz, on the other hand, appeared to be a genuinely nice man, regularly returning to the country he clearly loves, and doing what he can for his sponsored child, who clearly needed a lot of support.

As we left the valley outside the Rinchenling, I noted that the white lining and runway numbers had been marked up on the new airstrip, and it seemed likely that the first flights would be permitted soon.

There was still no area for offloading passengers, as apparently no contract had been let for that work yet, so offloading passengers on the active runway seemed to be the only alternative. I wondered whether the even Bhutanese Civil Aviation Authority would allow such a thing though.

As we left the Bumthang Valley system behind and crossed Yotong La Pass (3,425 m), the weather got better and better. There were clouds, but they were high and generally off the peaks. Somehow, their presence provided an added dimension to the views. We passed quickly through Trongsa and hung out at the viewing point in search of a chai, but sadly the cafe there was closed. There was a short wait for the road blockage to clear, but soon traffic was coming the other way, which indicated that the road was open again. We stopped shortly in the next village, at what appeared to be a private house, for that overdue chai. It never ceased to amaze me that Pema's entreaties to people throughout Bhutan to provide sustenance to passing travellers was always provided with such grace and without hesitation.

We then headed back up into the beautiful Black Mountain valley, which even seemed to impress Pema, who I am sure had seen it all before many times. I recalled how Tina had been so moved here on our outward journey. We drove towards Pele La Pass (3,420 m) and tried to stop at the same cafe we had visited on the outward journey. Unfortunately, it was full with a coach party, so we went onto the next village of Longle which turned out to be much nicer, and the noodles and chai there were simply top-notch. On the way there we passed a troupe of monkeys sitting on either side of, and actually on, the road. They apparently were not going to be moved by anyone!

We then went over the pass and arrived at the Gantey road turning. Driving down into the Pobjikha Valley we soon found ourselves on a very rough road, which lasted for about forty minutes. Again I thought of Tina, who I was sure would not have liked this section much. Soon, we arrived at the Dewachen Hotel, which was a first for me. The sun was shining, and the valley showed its true colours.

We spotted at distance some of the fifty or so black-necked cranes reported to be in the valley.

The sky was beginning to cloud over, the precursor wisps being rather aptly called by the locals: the 'Dragon's Head'. Perhaps it was a sign to prove Leki's point that he did not like the place, and apparently the staff accommodation was very poor and dirty. In fact, the hotel was full, as was the staff accommodation, but Pema found space for them both at his friend's hotel next door. Pema was never one to finalise such details before arrival, and I was beginning to see what Leki meant as the place was not living up to my expectations.

I had observed previously on Leki's fast, then slow, driving habits. The slow driving had been particularly exasperating, particularly when he had continually given way to oncoming traffic and never pushed on through himself. Although this was probably my western mind still not fully grasping Bhutanese karma! As we had approached the Dewachen though, he had put his foot down on the pedal as if to prove his displeasure. Anyway, he kindly came to my room later to light the temperamental stove and went outside to find some more combustible sticks to get it going because the very long logs provided were not lighting that easily.

Meanwhile, I had a meeting with Pema to discuss my suggestion that he be dropped off at his home when we passed through Thimphu, whilst on the way back to Paro. I explained that I would not need his guiding services for my final two days there. Leki could drive me back there, and stay locally in the town, before taking me to the airport on departure day. Pema had also just learned that one of his uncles had recently passed away, and he would have a lot of family arrangements to attend to, so being in Thimphu would be much easier for him.

Back in my room, I settled down to feed the stove; it was not that easy with those overly long logs. I then sorted out my bags but suddenly felt that whilst the hotel had all the trappings of modern life I had left behind for the past three weeks, I did not feel comfortable being there. Later, in the dining room, I settled into my cocoon and started to read a book about the Australian outback on my Kindle. I became conscious of a very loud American man making conversation with an equally loud Australian girl, which to my mind, in my relaxed karma state, I rather self-righteously thought bordered on obnoxious interference!

A sole traveller at an adjacent table passed the time seemingly reading the label on her bottle of water and swinging her ankles awkwardly. Yes, I know that I should have made conversation, but I was unsettled by the place, and I liked my cocoon and simply wanted to return to my room where I could reflect upon my journey, and prepare myself for the return to so-called normality. Clinging onto the experience of my journey was far too important for trivial conversation with a fellow traveller who was leaving for Paro the following day anyway. I asked that my lord Buddha bless her travels. I could now see why Leki did not like it here, but I felt it would do as a stepping stone before Paro, Delhi, and the return home.

The hot water bottle placed in my bed during dinner by the turn-down staff was most welcome. I got the stove going pretty quickly too, which was nice because it was pretty cold in the room. Sadly however, the fire went out just as fast. I definitely did not have Leki's knack, even though I used the sticks he had kindly collected for me, but a sound sleep soon beckoned. It was quite cloudy the next morning, though I hoped it would burn off soon. Certainly, the overall forecast for Bhutan was for sun, and plenty of it. Anyway, the morning shower was gloriously hot, and I soon felt much better.

Bob, it just *had* to be Bob, who with 'Melbourne Jennifer' were still hard at their seemingly never-ending conversation over breakfast. They were so loud and Bob never seemed to stop talking, and Jennifer was stumbling with somewhat inconsequential responses. Chris would have rather cynically observed that it probably was a case of: 'diarrhoea of speech, and constipation of thought.' I found again that I was missing the simplicity, genuineness and peace of central and east Bhutan even more.

After breakfast, we headed for Gantey goemba where Leki and I did the 'rounds' before we managed to get into the tiny temple at the top of the very old building, and where very few guests are allowed, in order to take the holy water. Even more special was being invited into the private temple where only the most important members of the Goemba and Buddhist faith are normally permitted, but then again, I *was* the dasho. I duly lit a candle which I felt was a very suitable way to finally sign off on the spiritual side of my journey.

We then walked round the Goemba courtyard and saw the monks larking about and washing their clothes in their rather rudimentary quarters. Earthquake damage was clear on the main building. Pema then joined us and we walked past some very young, novice monks who were preparing lunch, stirring huge vats of rice and vegetables. Leki spotted some boys playing an improvised *kuru* match, and he naturally joined in. Pema and I then walked a section of the Gantey nature trail. We went through the pine forest, which was really lovely and peaceful, but I found that I was struggling a bit in the thin air.

At the start of the walk, we had seen some kids sledging on the worn grass on planks of wood with dangerous-looking nails at the front. They seemed oblivious to the possible consequences, which was true, I supposed, for most kids around the world in similar situations. We met up with Leki and continued the walk, past the school, and into a house belonging to a friend of a friend of Pema called Sonam. His family was gathering to hold a house blessing, post-harvest. The monks were there already, intoning prayers with much incense and horn blowing. Tradition has it that, at such times, a new flag is hoisted to the high point of the roof to show that the deed had been done. The gathering is great for family bonding, much like Christmas or Thanksgiving.

The dasho was invited to join in and take food and ara, the locally distilled and somewhat lethal liquor, which just kept flowing, thanks mainly to the host's brother, who was obviously 'getting there'. The dasho taught them how to toast each other and their guest, which seemed to cause much amusement. The food was delicious, especially

225

the noodles, and Sonam's specially prepared potatoes, which suitably pleased my western palate.

After convivial chat, we adjourned and made a short visit to the campfire, where the ladies and kids had gathered for singing and dancing. We made an early retreat to the hotel because I did not want to arrive too late at the Uma Paro the next day. We also had the added diversion of dropping Pema off in Thimphu, and I wanted plenty of time to say my goodbyes to Leki at Paro, because doing so on Friday morning at the airport would be too much of a rush.

So I returned to my room to sort out my kit. Leki came and started the stove again, this time with twigs and oil. Unlike the cylindrical Swiss stoves in Bumthang, these Indian stoves were devils to light and keep lit. Though he filled the room with smoke, he did manage to get it going and I did not do too bad a job of keeping it lit. It was enough to give some heat to the cold room, anyway. I quietly hoped that the hot water bottle would appear in the bed again. I ruminated to myself that it seemed that day-to-day affairs at the Dewachen hotel were left to the staff, with no sign of the owner or senior management. And though they are hard-working people, they did not offer that personal touch as proffered by the owner at the Rinchenling. I felt sure that Leki would agree. The Dewachen was a mistake; it was not really suitable for a two-day stay, and it was pretty rough for the drivers and guides. It was a long way down that bumpy road for not a lot. The rooms were cold, the stoves were inefficient, and there was no perceptible lighting regime, poor food, and non-existent management, so all-in-all it was not ideal. Anyway I felt that I had to get those feelings off my chest!

It was another cloudy morning, and this time the faint wisps of blue soon disappeared. I was glad to be leaving, but the prospect of another long drive held little appeal. There was some dispute between Pema and Leki about the distance, but it was probably around 178 km. The sky was gloomy all the way to Wangdue, though there was the odd blue-patch appearing, which gave me hope. We stopped briefly at a wayside village, it was either: Gumina, Potula or Nyatoke, in order to watch an archery match where crossbows were being used.

A chai stop en route proved impossible, so we stopped for a comfort break at the Tashling Hotel in Wangdue, where we had stayed on my 2007 trip. However because the town had since been relocated, it had become very run down and somewhat depressing. We then sped towards the Dochu La Pass and soon stopped at a roadside village for some very welcome chai and biscuits. I was amazed by the amount of traffic, especially trucks, using the road. Pema said it was in connection with the hydro project at Wangdue. The narrow roads were simply *not* up to sustaining that amount of traffic. There was no point in stopping at the summit, when we arrived there, as there was too much cloud cover, but I later learned that my returning party had stopped as the visibility was stunningly clear for them.

As we arrived back, Funky Leki announced rather grandly, 'welcome back to Thimphu Town!' We drove straight to the Swiss bakery where I said my goodbyes to Pema, though of course he knew that I would be coming back sometime. I thanked him for all his efforts with both my groups. I commented that we had been blessed with glorious weather and that I would not have missed the trip to the east for anything, even though the road journeys had been very long and tiring. Leki then drove Pema home, while I spent a slightly unnerving forty minutes in the bakery awaiting his return. And then we were off, and I noted with some amazement the amount of construction work that was going on in Thimphu.

Maybe it was because we were coming to the end of the journey, but Leki adopted his snail's pace driving technique again. He was more relaxed because he was away from Pema's gaze, and he wanted to talk about Buddhist philosophy with the dasho. For my part, I was exhausted from the four very long days of travel and, rather selfishly, I was looking forward to some western-style comforts and peace at the Uma Paro. In fact the entire return journey by road to the east had been just over a thousand miles. (See appendix 8)

When we arrived at the hotel there was the usual, slightly overbearing, welcome. All I wanted to do was have a private farewell chat with Leki. There were tears of happiness and love for the dasho shed by Leki, and that gesture was very much reciprocated. We had a mutual respect for each other, and he had helped me understand Bhutan and Buddhism so much better. The journey would certainly not have been the same without him. *Tashi Delek!* Though I knew I would be seeing him again, very early in the morning two days later, when he would be taking me to the airport.

I went to my room, not one of their best, and certainly not like the villa I was fortunate to have had here in 2009. It would certainly do though, and I planned a relaxed 'at leisure' time for the next day, my final day, as I knew that it would pass by really quickly. The comfy bed in a warm room was a joy, the clouds were again noticeably higher, and the daily *Kuensel* newspaper was forecasting yet more sun.

On the way to the Uma, we had passed the airport and saw the Drukair (ex-Air France) ATR being towed into the hangar. 'Perhaps it had been out on a proving flight today to the centre or east of Bhutan' I mused. At the end of the runway, some kids were playing with an old bicycle wheel, just rolling it along the tarmac without a care in the world; I kid you not, surely only in Bhutan!

That evening the Druk11000 and meal were pleasant enough. All the staff members politely introduced themselves to 'Mr Christopher' until they were firmly corrected: 'it is of course, dasho!' I discovered that the bar boy, Sanjay, was a Chelsea fan, but I did not hold that against him. I went to bed early, recalling Leki telling me that Pema Two had thoughtfully called him to ask after the dasho and to wish him a safe journey.

After a pretty restless night, there was indeed quite a lot of blue sky out there the next morning. I heard airport hooter sounding for the early Drukair departure. The sounding of the hooter for both arrivals and departures was somehow very exciting. The noise of the aircraft departing into the valley was truly amazing. After breakfast, I had a meeting with the hotel's general manager, Jorge, to make early plans for my sixty-fifth birthday which I hoped to have in Bhutan. I rather grandly thought: 'if Leonardo DiCaprio had a party here, then so should I!' I then adjourned to the courtyard outside by the swimming pool for some personal work where I heard, and saw, the Drukair fleet depart in different directions into the clear blue sky. It really had become quite hot, so I moved inside to the library before taking lunch in the coolness of the upstairs courtyard.

In the meantime, I had begun thinking that, whilst I had not quite sussed what karma actually was, I felt that I knew what it could do. I was, as ever, in heaven in this Land, and I felt so fortunate and privileged to actually *be* in the country. I could not say it enough: 'thank you God; thank you my lord Buddha, thank you Druk Yul, the Land of the Thunder Dragon!'

An Indian-style head massage had done the trick after the long travel days and when I returned to my room, it was nearly dark. A star was out in the clear night sky, Paro dzong was lit up creating an almost mystical sight. I then went to the bar for my final Druk11000 of the trip and I wondered why we could not get such tasty nectar in the United Kingdom. Perhaps it was the altitude that made it taste so good! I teased Sanjay about our respective football clubs, Chelsea and Liverpool, before having my final, rather rushed, meal there. Passing the upper courtyard on the way to my room, I saw a group of cyclists having a party around a bonfire that had been specially set up for them. It all looked so magical. As ever, I would miss everything about Bhutan, but I especially knew that the easy, winning smiles in the east, would linger in my memory for a very long time.

So after yet another restless night, I awoke early in order to be ready for collection by Leki. It was a gloriously clear morning, but it very cold. In fact I learned that Leki had trouble starting his vehicle because the diesel fuel had frozen. He had gone knocking on doors in Paro town in order to find some matches. On the way down to the airport Leki said some further very nice and caring words and after another big hug, he was all too quickly gone. We shall miss each other very much; Leki, 'Funky Leki', and his invariable response: 'yes my dasho'. As it happened, there was plenty, perhaps too much, time before departure, but some of it was taken up watching the ATR depart to Kolkata. There appeared to be someone important, perhaps from ATR, on the ramp to make sure all was well. The aircraft seemed to need all of the runway's length to lift off, and I wondered how it would fare on the shorter regional airstrips.

And then it was all aboard flight KB204 for the ride of a lifetime. 'Is there any better flight than this?' I wondered, though seats on the right-hand side of the aircraft are best. Twisting up and out of the Paro Valley, Gangkhar Puensum came into view and then, as ever and even more impressively, Jhomolhari appeared. What a very special mountain it is. It was a little bit shaky as the A319 hit the Himalayan winds, and the wings certainly flexed. We travelled down the line of the Himalayas and past Kanchenjunga, Everest, Lhotse, Makelu, Annapurna, and many more peaks. Plenty of photos were taken, but they cannot tell the full story, the vistas have to be seen to be believed.

We descended into a very foggy Delhi area. Actually, I felt more concerned about the interminable circling there and the descent into the fog than I was during that aborted approach in the clouds when heading into Paro airport at the start of our trip, well that is Bhutanese karma for you! I was met by Ashish, who took me back to the Uppal hotel where I checked in online for my BA flight later that night and got some rupees that I was told I would need for a new departure tax (perhaps to pay for their new terminal building, I thought). The first texts in three weeks starting appearing on my phone, but I could not retrieve my voicemails. I felt that I had not quite re-entered the so-called 'real world' just yet. As Ashish was going to pick me up very early in the morning, I was going to have another quiet afternoon, which was just fine because I needed to reflect yet further on the past three weeks. There had been tears welling up in my eyes as we departed Paro, just as there had been when my party split ways in Bumthang. I thought: 'leaving this land is going to be such a wrench and it will hurt so much, but I shall return 'ere long and until then it is *Lazimbe jon* (goodbye)

Spice Market Old Delhi

Drukair shows the way into PBH

*one happy Cameron from here
on I knew it would work*

that's what I mean

Nigel gasping atop Chelala

Chelala summit

heavenly Haa

sisters!

meet the locals

join the line

tears of joy

Class of 2011

Dochla Offering

Tenzin + Tenzin

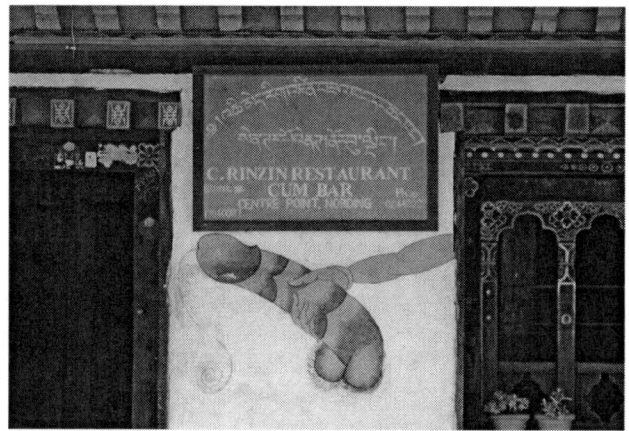

Bar at Nobding!

unmissable!

new friends

tour group at Wangdicholing

always Karma

monsoon damage on NH1

blue and green

Thrumsingla

picture picture!

great exhortation

Trashigang Dzong

Duksum pitstop

Duksum Boys

Trashi Yangste Dzong

main street Trashi Yangste

pillar box red

Chorten Kora

shop on the edge of town.

en route to market

Bomdeling massive

Black necked crane landing ground

in the Dzong

contemplation

stupa + faces

school uniform wash

surreal

beyond festoon

Gantey turn

monks kitchen

Gangkhar Puensum

the blockage at Trongsa

Uma view

Bhutan and its sacred guardian

lucky lucky flight crew

Everest approach from the East of Bhutan

EPILOGUE

I have already broken what, for many, is the golden rule of travel: *never go back.* Folk do of course, perhaps by putting down roots by buying property in their favourite place. The sentiment has some relevance though, as return visits quite often do not have the magic of the first. The golden rule has been broken five times by me now and I am shortly to return again.

I wonder what I shall find there when I do so after a three year absence. There is bound to have been significant change, but could I accept that? My previous return visits have all been different somehow, made more so by the varying itineraries and by the differing groups of people accompanying me. So I had somehow I had managed to get away with it!

My imminent return does hold some concerns though. There is no doubt that the profile of Bhutan has increased massively all over the world; there now are not so many glazed eyes of bemusement when the country's name is mentioned. As a result of regularly appearing in travel reports, tourist numbers have been boosted to an extent I could not possibly have imagined at the time of my first visit, which was only eight years ago. Virtually all such travel reports speak of it being a *must see* destination, so tourists, and not just the more discerning and adventurous, will naturally follow.

There is now a new government, the second of the nascent democratic years, and apparently they are not so sworn to the concept of GNH and the mighty economic buttress of neighbouring India. I saw from my last visit in 2011 that despite being very much poorer in the east, mobile phones and the use of social media was ubiquitous, even in the dzongs. Knowledge, and perhaps more importantly awareness, naturally follows. So would the sanctity and secrecy of the hidden away last Shangri-la be gone too?

On a personal level I have detected from Samdrup that it may be time for me to move on from Dobji, though there will be many other deserving and needy causes to support, particularly in the east. However I know that will be a painful process even though it will always remain in my heart.

I can still vividly recall my first visit and those feelings I had when our group stopped at Kamji. Those precise feelings can never be replicated, nor should they be, as it was a life changing moment. I know that I have somehow been different since that time, spiritually stronger, and blessed with just a little of that very special *karma* that oozes from every pore of the land. I know that I have passed that on to others who have not, so far, been able to go there themselves. Somehow they can detect that difference in me and are fascinated by it.

As I hope has been adequately explained in these pages, that deeper connection is deeply felt by me, both on Lewis and in Bhutan. Both are not a little daunting to travel to, and both have very dramatic landscapes and strong spiritual values. However, in the case of both, it goes much deeper than that. One cannot help but feel a different interpretation of the world somehow, brought on by the sense of a long and troubled history on Lewis, and a riven past history but utter peace and contentment prevailing in Bhutan now.

They are 'Promised Lands' indeed.

APPENDIX 1

THE WANGCHUCK DYNASTY

K1	Ugyen	1907–1926
K2	Jigme	1926–1952
K3	Jigme Dorji	1952–1972
K4	Jigme Singye	1972–2008
K5	Jigme Khesar Namgyel	2008–

APPENDIX 2

LEKI

'On the peak of the white snow mountain in the East
A white cloud seems to be rising towards the sky
At the instance of beholding it, I remember my teacher
And, pondering over his kindness, faith stirs in me.'

Song of the Eastern Snow Mountain (Tibet)

He is such a devout and spiritual man.

He confided in me that, when he has finished his children's education, he wants to become a Buddhist monk. This would likely be in the east, near Trashigang, where he had purchased a parcel of land and planted some lemon trees. He said that, by becoming even more devout, he would be better placed to rid the world of its ills and inequities. He had not yet told his wife, but seemed confident that he could convince her of the correctness of his decision. She must, of course, already have had an inkling of his plans.

However, for the time being, he is a driver. Sometimes he drives trucks; other times he drives taxis. He also drives the various bus routes that radiate from the capital, Thimphu. He often does the run to Trashi Yangste, which takes, in his words, 'only two days.' This is for a distance of just over 600 km. There is a night stop in the Bumthang area. It is an incredible strain on one driver who only has one companion, a boy who helps with the baggage and passenger needs. The current fare is equal to £8.50; and that is only after a recent price increase! There is a surcharge for heavy baggage such as corn. Each bus carries nineteen passengers in addition to the driver and the boy. 'What a strong-willed man to carry that burden' I thought. 'It is just my job, my dasho', Leki would have replied.

I first met him on my trip in 2009, when he was the driver for my brother, Robin, and me. After my trip in 2011, he immediately returned to the Trashigang area with his family for a month's stay. He needed some rest and time to tend to his trees, and anyway his wife's family lives in a neighbouring village.

He ran away from school in the Radi Valley after school beatings and bad karma got the better of him. He became a truck driver and self-taught mechanic. He is versatile, speaks decent English, and is a good man. He wants the best for his kids (his son is fourteen, and his daughter is eight). They are currently being educated in Thimphu, though Leki may move his son to a school on the border of India, at Gelephu. His heart is in the east though, where he finds a simpler, more complete life. It seems many senior figures in Bhutan come from there, including the last prime minister, the Je Kempo, and various police and army chiefs.

May the lord Buddha bless you and your family, Leki!

ROADS IN BHUTAN

'You wouldn't want to look down, seriously!'

The author (and many other travellers)

Precipitous geography means *very* precipitous roads! Apart from the pretty rough ones connecting Phuentsoling, on the border with India, with the capital Thimphu, and Wangdue, no roads really existed until the east–west National Highway 1 (NH1) was constructed in the early 1970s.

I actually met, by coincidence, one of the route surveyors/engineers of that road at Delhi Airport in 2009. I recall that he was going to the Uma Paro in Bhutan to celebrate a significant birthday. Much of the road system built since was carried out by the Indian firm Dantak, which still engineers and maintains the roads to all the border crossings. The others are maintained by the Bhutan Department of Roads (DoR). Currently, both Dantak and the DoR are going through a process of widespread road widening – and in the case of Dantak, significant realignments, many in very remote mountainous areas.

Both operations involve huge engineering and logistical challenges. There is no room for detours, so travel around (and particularly across) Bhutan is often interrupted by such works. Sometimes, there are rolling road blockages that move while blasting and rock clearance is carried out. These procedures can take several hours, and tour guides are given schedules so that their charges' journeys are minimally disrupted. These works are often carried out in very dangerous locations with no apparent safety precautions for workers or travellers. Hence the exhortation to avoid looking down! Sometimes, one passes recovered vehicles that failed to take heed and have fallen over the edge.

Now, though, there are some very good, very smooth sections despite the ubiquitous hairpins. The situation has been further helped by the programme, started in 2011, to re-blacktop most roads and improve the final road surfaces. All this work has to be carried out outside the monsoon season, when avalanches regularly destroy the most exposed mountain sections. However, teams of migrant workers are posted near the most exposed spots so that repairs can commence quickly. Despite the extent of some landslips, mainly caused during the monsoon season, roads are not normally blocked for more than two or three days, which quite frankly, is an incredible feat. Similarly, in winter, when the high passes get blocked with snow, those teams keep the roads open as best they can and here again blockages usually last no more than a few days.

All the hard work is mainly carried out by migrant workers from India, Nepal, and Bangladesh. They mostly live in what can only be described as hovels, usually at great heights and in all seasons. Many have their families with them, and quite often, one will see very young kids doing their bit of work, too. Despite the abject poverty, the people *always* smile and return waves from the passing tourists. It is life enhancing and humbling in equal measure.

These workers contribute to the miracle that is the effective (albeit a little slow) Bhutanese road system. I have not even mentioned the farm road system here, which is another miracle in its own right. Doubtless, all will change with the opening of the regional airstrips in Bumthang and Trashigang.

APPENDIX 4

HOUSES IN BHUTAN

Virtually all housing – indeed, most buildings – are based on the traditional farmhouse-style as decreed by K4. It was an integral part of his concept of GNH, namely to maintain, as far as was possible, the history and heritage of this land. The outstanding buildings in Bhutan are the twenty massive dzongs, mainly built but by the Shabdrung in the seventeenth century as combined forts and temples. The enormous walls contain inner structures made from huge timbers where no nails have been used at all. Their primary colours of white and deep red make for an extraordinarily impressive sight, enhanced by the precipitous locations in which most have been built. The architectural themes found in these very impressive buildings find their way into all forms of Bhutanese architecture.

Construction of private housing now seems to follow a pre-ordained pattern. First, all the materials (mainly wood) are delivered to the site. The house is then erected in stages: ground floor, upper floor, and finally the attic. Wooden scaffolding is used as temporary propping and for access to the upper floors. The scaffolding is made from bamboo, and is very strong, thus is used all over south-east Asia and the Indian sub-continent for this purpose despite its precarious appearance.

In earlier times, animals would share the living space on the ground floor, but no longer. It is now used as the main living area as in most western countries. Sleeping takes place upstairs. The attic is used for storing and drying crops. Toilet facilities used to be located in a separate privy hut outside but more and more new houses now have bathrooms and toilets inside.

Roofs are constructed of wooden tiles weighed down with stones and straps. All wooden cornices and window frames are painted decoratively. Sliding latches and padlocks are fixed to front doors. To ward off bad karma, graphic depictions of male genitalia are painted near the front door or wooden phalluses are hung from the four corners of the roof.

By decree of the government and K5, all houses will have electricity by 2014, which effectively means that all houses will be linked to their nearest communities, in many instances by means of 'farm roads', many of which are simply roughly hewn out of the hillsides. Maintaining these can be very problematical, particularly after the monsoon.

Following the earthquake in the east in December 2009, and the two serious fires in Chamkhar Bazaar in 2010, many new roofs are now constructed with tin, which is more practical, but not as aesthetically pleasing to look at.Incidentally, there was some suggestion that although the first Chamkhar fire in Bumthang was probably caused by an electrical problem, the second was likely the result of arson, apparently fuelled by jealousy after others in the town saw the quality of the government sponsored rebuild following the first fire. In view of the largely wooden construction of houses generally, and particularly the dzongs, fire is an ever present risk, and once started are very difficult to extinguish.

APPENDIX 5

POPULAR DEITIES IN BHUTAN

Gondo Ludrup (The Serpent Saint)	2nd–3rd Century
Guru Rinpoche	8th
Marpa Lotsawa	11th
Jetsun Milarepa	11th
Terton Pema Lingpa	15th
Drukpa Kunley	15th
Thangtong Gyelpo (The Bridge Builder)	14th
Shabdrung Nawang Namgyel	16th

LUNGHAR – WIND HORSES
FLAG COLOURS

Blue	Space/Ether
Green	Water
Red	Fire
Yellow	Earth
White	Air

RELIC POT CONTENTS

(FROM GOM KORA)

Long-life Buddha
Long-life relic
Wealth relic
Healthy relic
Peaceful life relic
Good dealings relic
Eight lucky symbols
Eight grains blessed in the temple
Seven items from holy places
Small pieces of lucky rock
All good fortune
Blessed spring water
Blessed herbs and minerals
Long life, health, and happiness
Small piece of my lord Buddha's hair
Six different cereals
Pieces of sandalwood
Nine different pieces of cloth

Six pieces of good luck charms
Saffron and camphor
Three pieces of body, speech, and mind from my lord Buddha
One item for which there is no translation

(Translation from dzongkha: thanks to Leki Dorje)

Bhutan Rediscovery & Explore (2011) – road

DISTANCES

Paro – Haa	68 km
Haa – Thimphu	121
Thimphu – Wangdue	59
Wangdue – Punakha (Return)	46
Wangdue – Trongsa	129
Trongsa – Jakar	68
Jakar – Mongar	193
Mongar – Rangjung	113
Rangjung – Trashi Yangste	75
Trashi Yangste – Mongar	145
Mongar – Jakar	193
Jakar – Gantey	118
Gantey – Paro	178
Total	1506 km (1004 miles)

ACKNOWLEDGMENTS

There are so many to make, it would be impossible to mention them all.

I must however thank and acknowledge those who are mentioned herein by name, but especially those who I have not told that they would be: though always in love and karma, and I hope no offence is taken, as none was given or intended. I mention variously throughout this book that I am very fortunate to have a very large, diverse and dare I say eclectic group of Family and friends. Their friendship and love are my ultimate inspiration, and although as we all pass through life, those connections can sometimes become diluted from time to time their love and inspiration always remains with me. I am truly grateful to them all, and privileged beyond measure. Equally, for those not mentioned, the omission should in no way be construed that they do not fall into the category of cherished friends as nothing could be further from the truth. To you all, and dare I say you know who you are, thank you from the bottom of my heart for making my life so rich, full and rewarding.

To those many that have encouraged me, with just a little goading to get this done, despite any reaction at the time, I am forever grateful.

Thanks particularly to Jason for being so right with the revised book title, Georgie for the anthropological supplements, and Steve and Holly for the Coronation humour!

To my friends at Author House, this has been a sharp learning curve and I am sure with across the Atlantic differences in language and culture, let alone the Himalayas, this has been a steep learning curve for them too!

To those I have journeyed with through this most special and amazing of Lands, and to those I met there along the way and who helped me touch the karma, you too know who you are, and I am forever indebted to you.

Many book acknowledgments make mention of those who have tirelessly helped the author with proof reading. In my case I am truly indebted to dear Simon, who carried this burden entirely himself. As in so many matters, his advice, support and guidance has been priceless. This is the first book I have attempted to write, and many an experienced publisher and writer will no doubt spot the 'freshman' nature of it, its naivety and doubtless the myriad of mistakes. These are my responsibility alone.

This approach is not borne out of a self-righteous belief that I know better than the experts, or out of a natural wish to maintain total control, though I am well aware that is one of my personal traits, which some of my friends may be surprised to hear, I am not always comfortable with. No, this approach is because of the very personal nature of this book and some, I am sure, would observe, perhaps too personal. On one occasion when seeking rare advice from friends over dinner about this project when in its early stages, I mentioned that I might enrol on a writer's course. All the rather disparate characters present strongly counselled against that, on the very premise that dilution of very personal nature of this book would likely spoil it irrevocably. So, blame that un-named quorum if you will!

To my 'Fair Coz' Ann, who knows far more about the publishing world than most, thank you for your insight and 'that shoulder to lean on'. To dear Tony, thank you for your love, support and deep interest in all matters pertaining to Bhutan. May you rest in Peace and Karma.

To My Lord Buddha, the Shabdrung, and the current king K5, who have and are making this country what it is.

To the People of Bhutan, for their modest but ever inspirational lifestyle, their smiles, their magnificent dzongs, Dobji in particular, the mountains of the Himalaya, their selfless prayer flags forever blowing peace and karma to the world, that we so desperately need now, and doubtless always will.

Ka drinche la, thank you, for I, and dare I say the world, are the better for Bhutan being there.

Tashi Delek! Good Luck and may fortune be with you!

Lightning Source UK Ltd.
Milton Keynes UK
UKOW05f0128160115

244527UK00003B/113/P